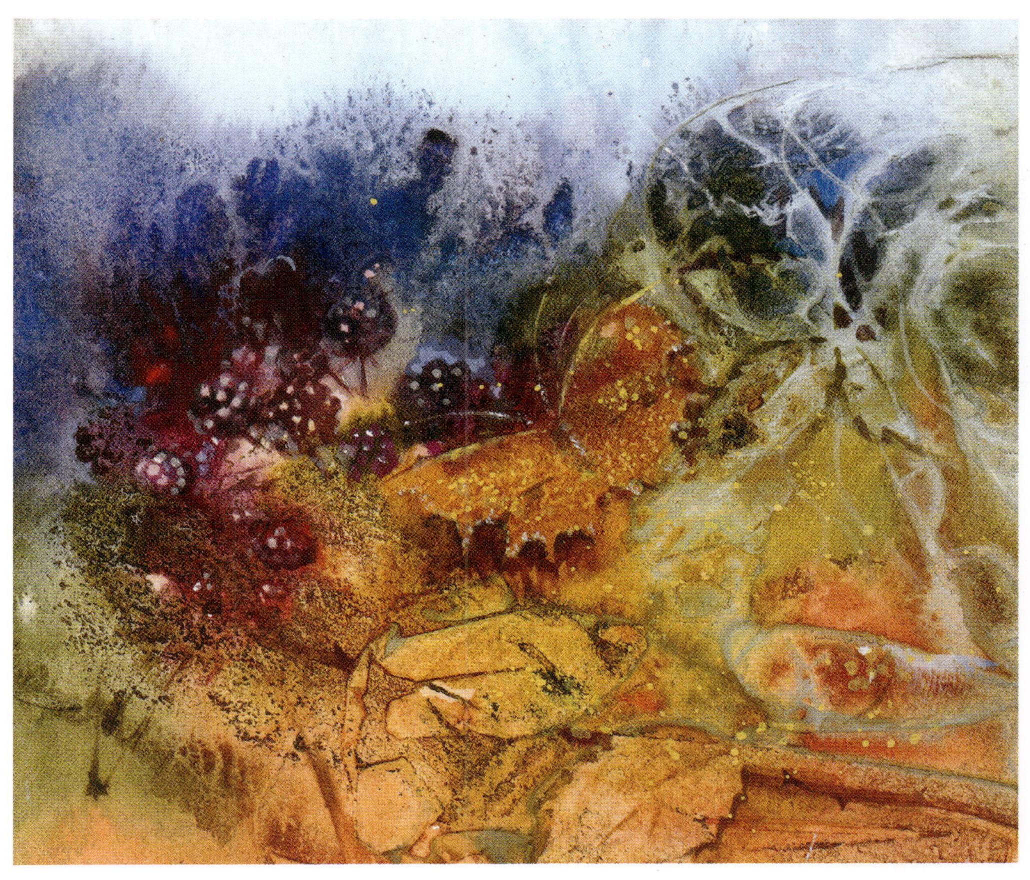

Ann Blockley's
WATERCOLOUR WORKSHOP

PROJECTS AND INTERPRETATIONS

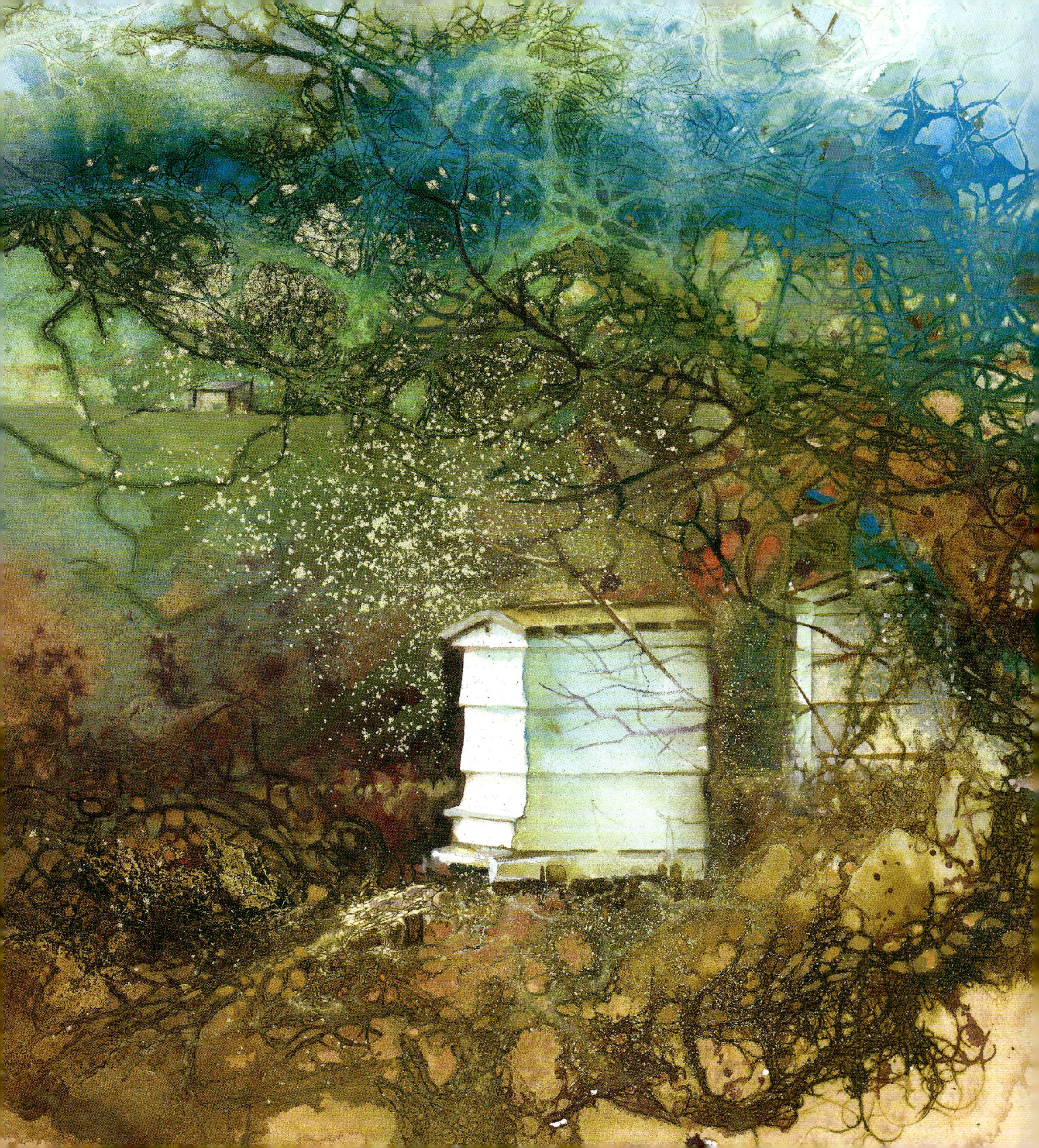

Ann Blockley's
WATERCOLOUR WORKSHOP

PROJECTS AND INTERPRETATIONS

BATSFORD

Dedication

To imagination, integrity, and interpretation; to being true to yourself.

First published in the United Kingdom in 2018 by
Batsford
43 Great Ormond Street
London WC1N 3HZ
An imprint of B.T. Batsford Holdings Limited

ISBN: 9781849944625

A CIP catalogue record for this book is available from the British Library.

30 29 28 27 26
12 11 10 9

Reproduction by Tag, UK
Printed and bound by Toppan Leefung Printing Ltd, China

This book can be ordered direct from the publisher at
www.batsfordbooks.com, or try your local bookshop

Distributed throughout the UK and Europe by Abrams & Chronicle
Books, 1st Floor, 22–24 Ely Place, London EC1N 6TE and
57 rue Gaston Tessier, 75166 Paris, France

www.abramsandchronicle.co.uk
info@abramsandchronicle.co.uk

FSC MIX Paper | Supporting responsible forestry — FSC® C104723

page 1 *Butterfly Camouflage*
page 2 *The Secret Life of Bees*
below *Norwegian Fishing Hut*

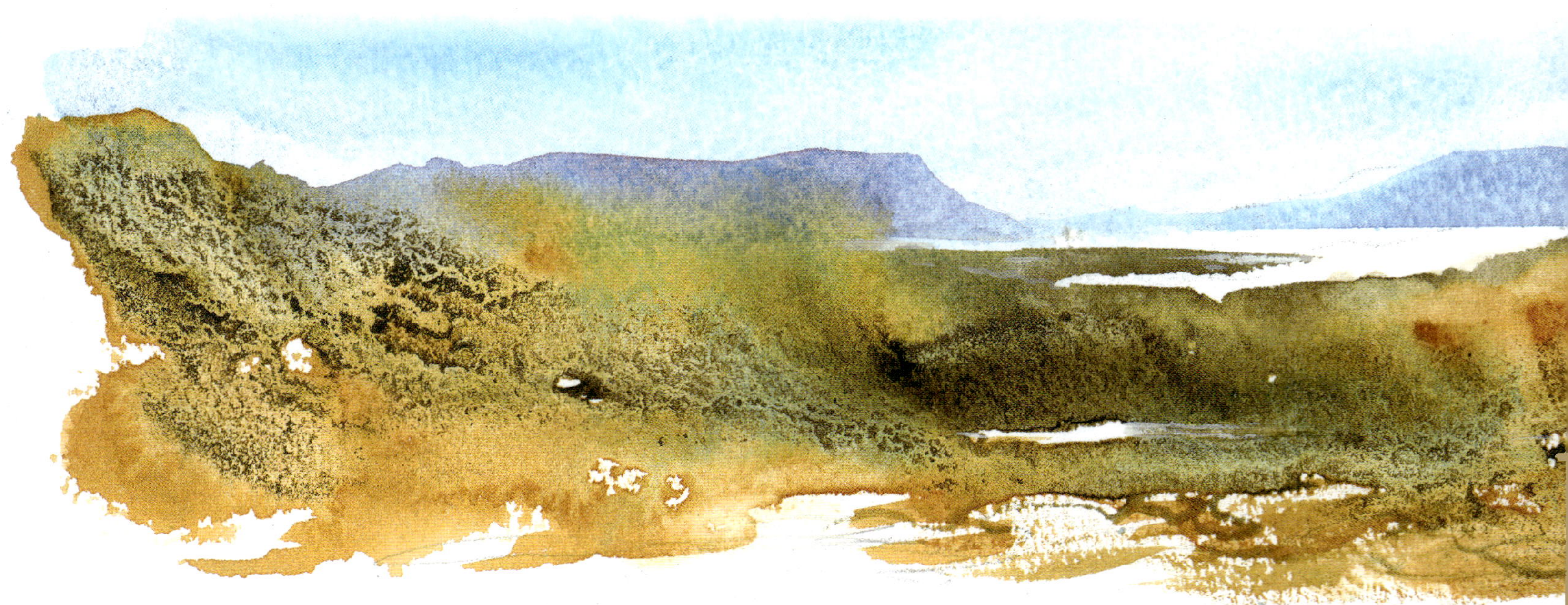

Contents

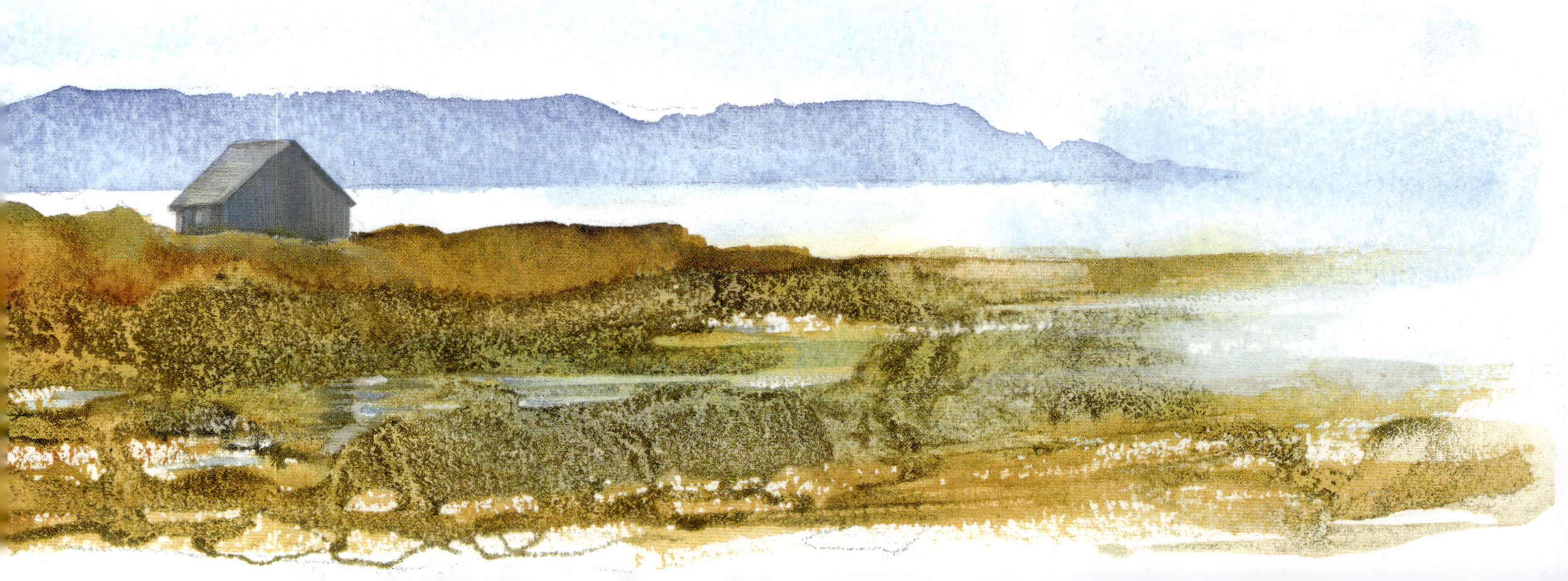

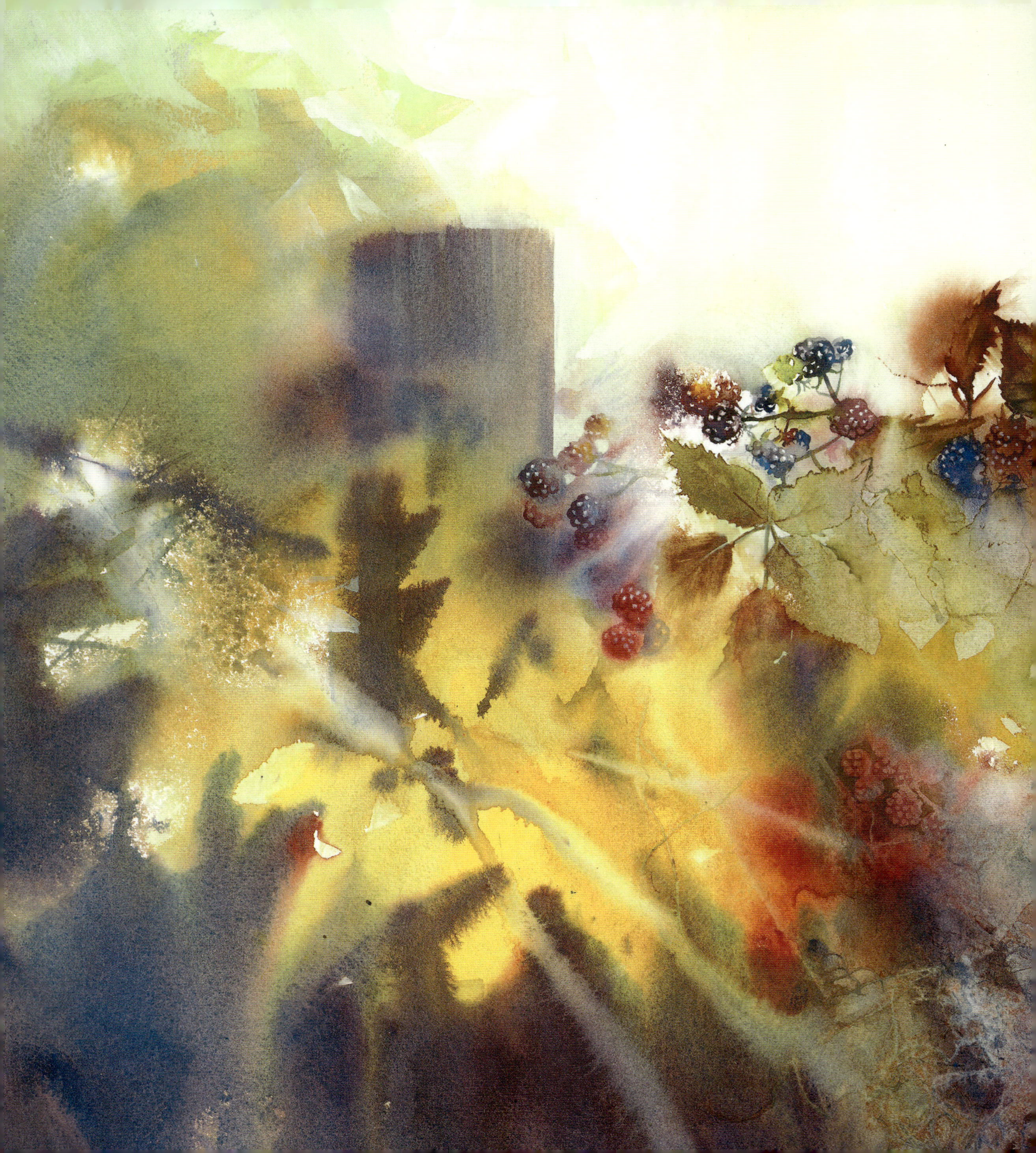

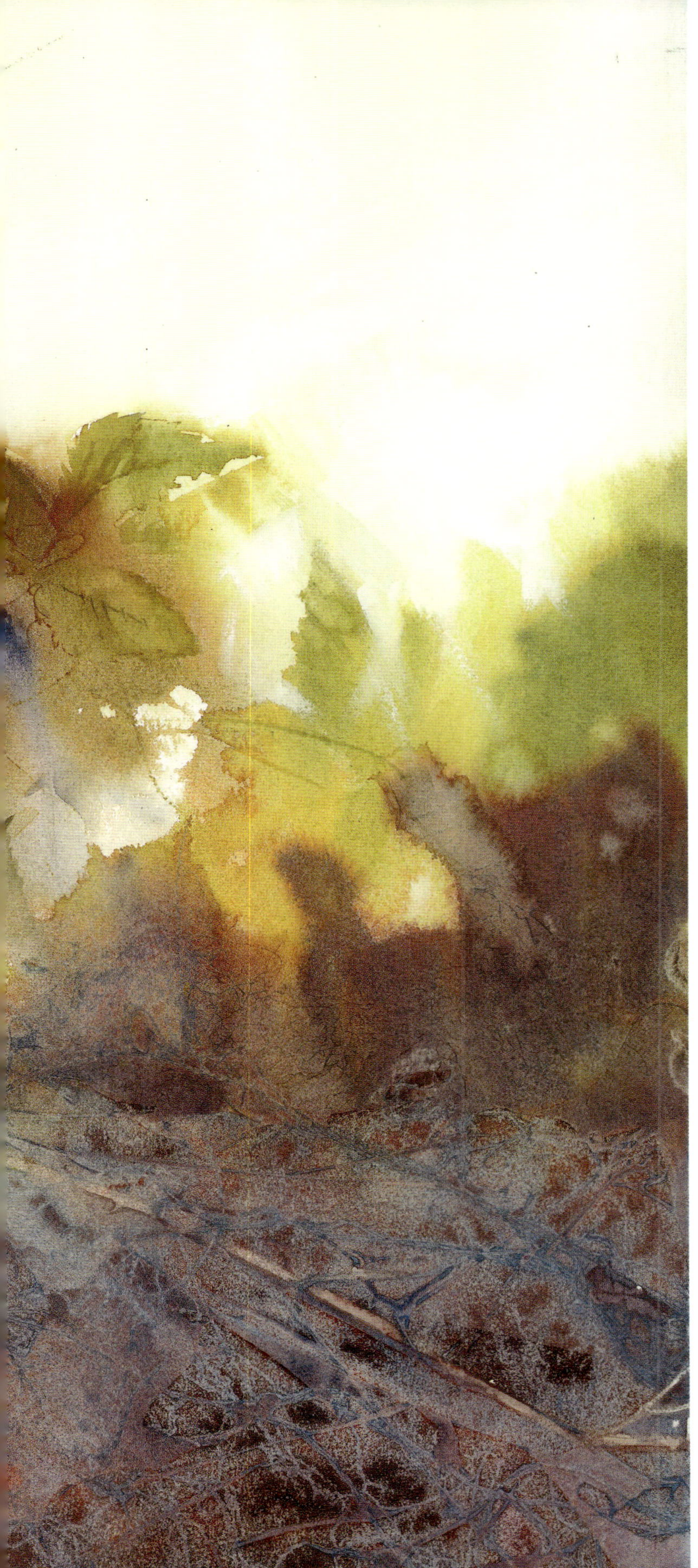

Getting started

This book is about YOU. It is designed to help you create your own personal workshop and make unique interpretations. I am passionate about the idea that artists at every level should create work that reflects something of themselves, expressing an individual viewpoint. The following pages are about ways of seeing as well as ways of doing. I cannot see through your eyes but I can act as facilitator while giving you a practical helping hand to encourage you as you play with paint, develop your own voice and interpret your world.

"AS PRACTICE MAKES PERFECT, I CANNOT BUT MAKE PROGRESS; EACH DRAWING ONE MAKES, EACH STUDY ONE PAINTS, IS A STEP FORWARD."

VINCENT VAN GOGH

◁ *Blackberry Hedge* (detail)

About this book

I have called this book *Watercolour Workshop* because it is packed with practical advice about water-based mediums. However, its main aim is to be a springboard to inspire your creative development. I have divided the book into flexible projects, including demonstrations with optional alternative techniques to be used as starting points for your own adventures. I have deliberately not shown every minor stage in order to encourage an adaptable approach. Traditional 'step by steps' can give the idea that there is a set formula to painting, when of course there are an infinite number of possibilities. The purpose of the demonstrations and interpretations that follow is to stimulate inventive thinking.

The projects do not need to be followed in order; you can pick and mix between them, as the content is interchangeable between chapters. For example, the wildflower meadow on pages 26-29 can be painted simply or made more complex by following ideas from the later abstract section. You might like to swap experimental methods for traditional ones according to your level of experience. If you are a fledgling painter you will probably stay close to my ideas, but take courage as you begin to fly and explore further. Banish the pressure to perform by planning to repeat the exercises, each time varying the colours, tones, composition, brushwork and marks or altering

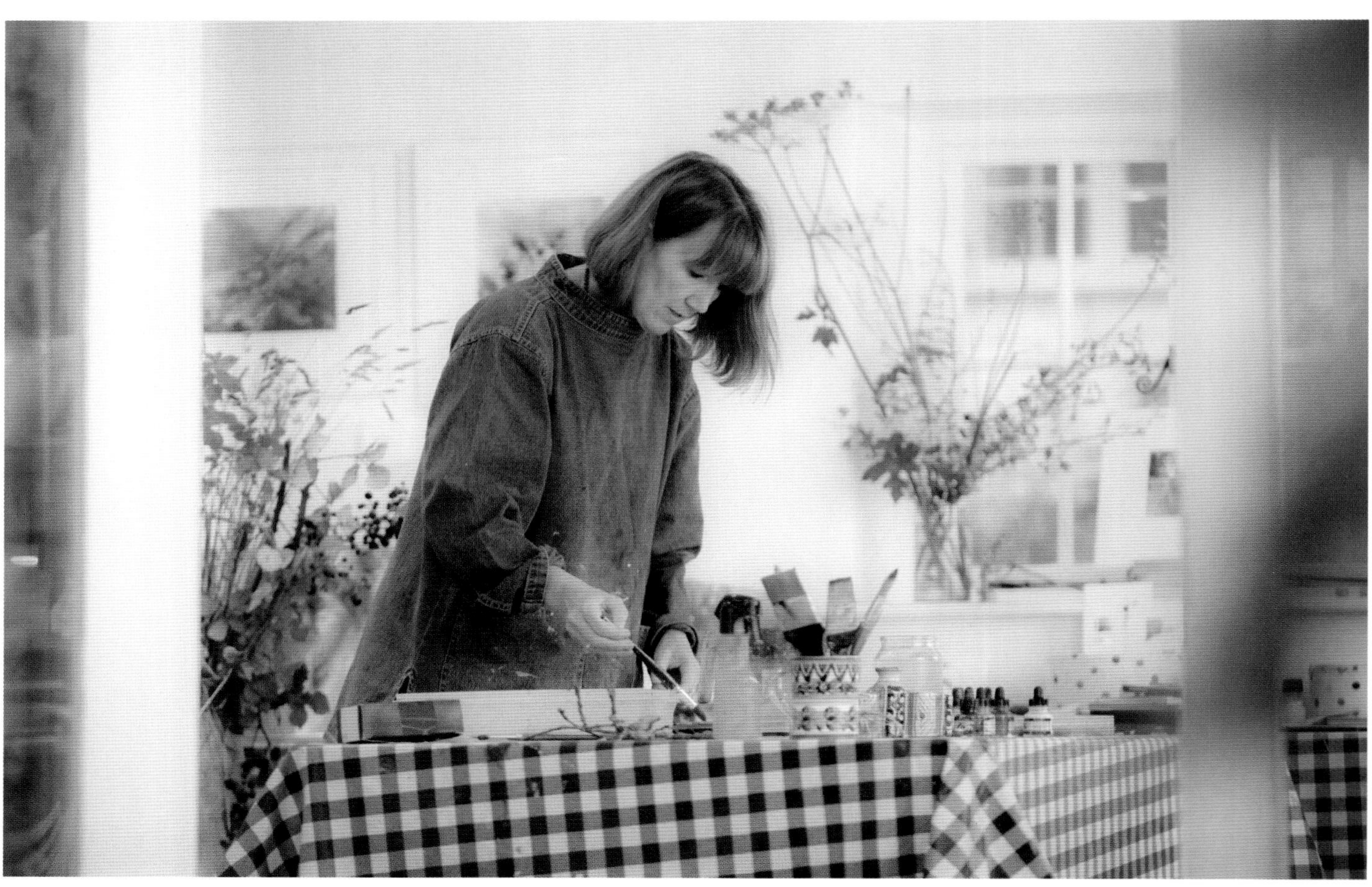

the focal point. There are also suggestions for taking things further and for adapting the subjects using your own reference material.

In the demonstrations I have sometimes included a sketch, photograph or still-life material to show what inspired the painting. This is the vital backbone to artwork. Ideas flow from a whole feast of personal experience and my advice is to prioritize the gathering of your own library of explorations. It is this personal selection that will ultimately give your paintings authenticity. Techniques are just a small part of being an artist, so please don't skip through the sections about exploring and looking in order to get to the tasty technical tips!

Each chapter has been organized into subjects to give cohesion to the book. However, the subject is secondary to the painterly choices that help to make a unique interpretation. Thinking in abstract terms helps us to loosen up and steer away from pedantic detail. I have called the final section of the book 'Towards Abstraction' as it takes these thoughts a stage further.

The watercolour aspect of the workshop is simply that all the images were painted using water-based mediums and a basic knowledge of traditional methods is assumed. However, there is plenty of advice to help you use watercolour in different loose and expressive ways. When you practise the exercises, remember that watercolour varies according to many factors such as consistency, paint, colour mixing, temperature and humidity. Your own interpretations are likely to vary from those shown here. Remember that there is no right or wrong way to do it – this workshop is about enjoying watercolour and using it in your own way.

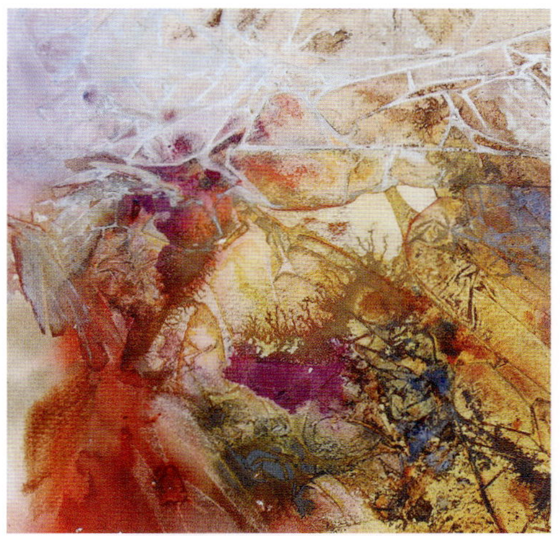

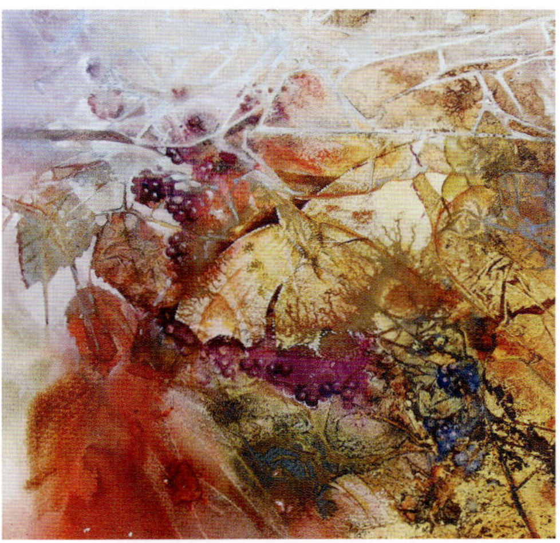

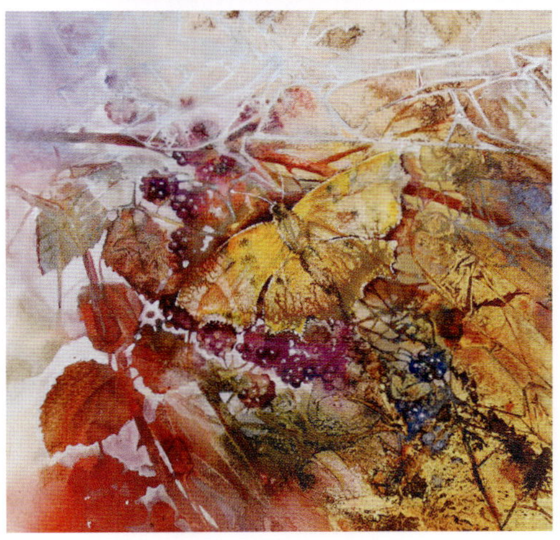

△ *Metamorphosis*
Paintings metamorphose like a butterfly unfolding from its cocoon. I hope this book will help your creativity unfurl.

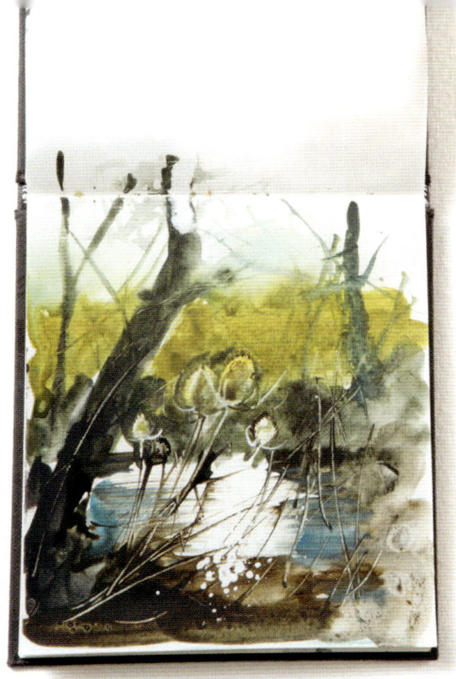

Watercolour interpretations

One of the main lessons of this book is about interpreting your subject. One definition of interpretation is to 'bring out the meaning' and as artists what we find meaningful helps to define our individual voice. Sometimes interpretation can mean the point when we depart from reality and use imagination rather than simply representing our subject. It may also mean exaggerating or emphasizing particular aspects of what we see in order to make a point. More subtly, it may be the relative emphasis we give each element of design to determine the overall mood.

Another way of looking at this is that when you explore a subject you are weaving a uniquely descriptive visual story around it. You may want to whisper, shout or sing your tale depending on your mood or personality and you need to decide what is and is not relevant to the plot. Your storytelling or how you interpret a subject is what makes it original. In painting we use mark-making instead of words with adjectives and nouns. However, thinking of a subject in terms of the adjectives that describe it can help to clarify your selection of appropriate methods and marks. This also seems to encourage movement to a looser, more impressionistic approach.

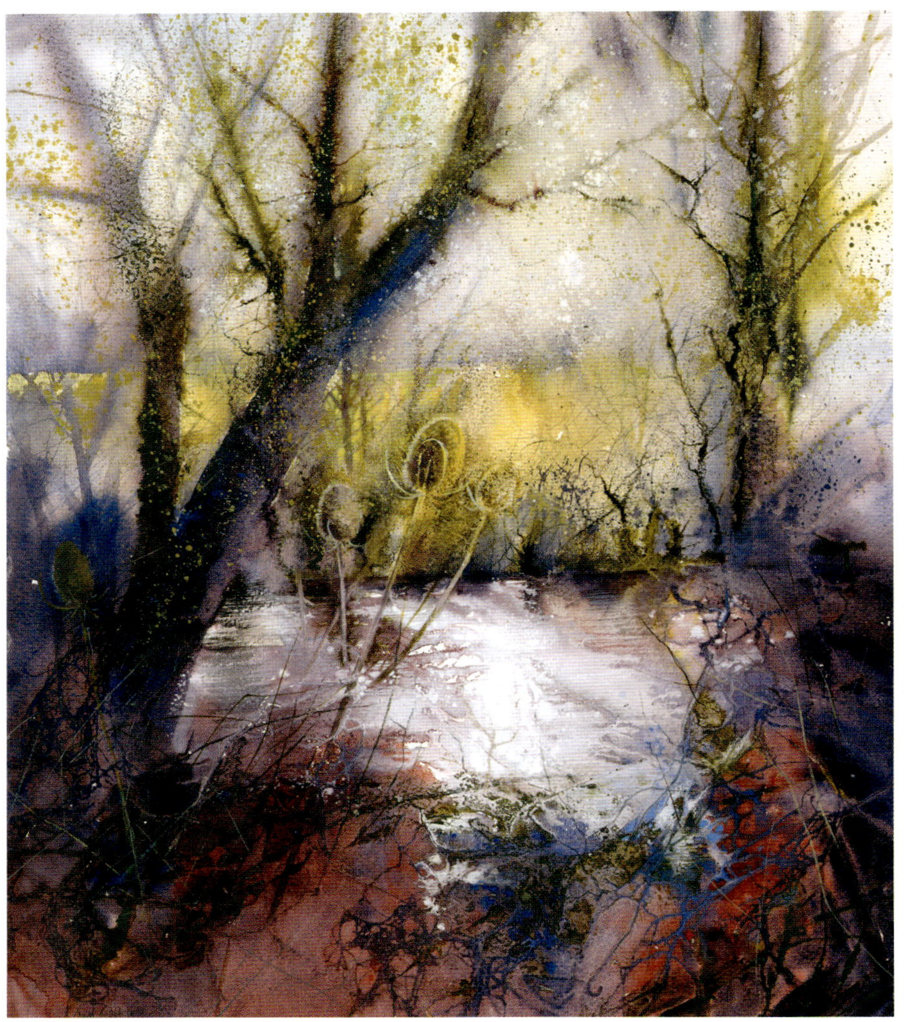

◁ *Winter Teasels by the Pond*
In this version I have changed the colours to a more wintry palette of blues and purples. Even the colours of the tree trunks share this colour scheme.

Throughout the book, after each project, I have extended the theme with other interpretations of similar subjects. These show varied moods, colours or textures, depict different seasons or times of day and use alternative methods or levels of detail or realism. They are not included to showcase my paintings but to ignite your excitement about creating your own images. Try to get into the habit of thinking in series so that your paintings are part of an ongoing project. The changes between each version may be dramatic or subtle. Working on a series can help to take the pressure to perform away and leads to a deeper involvement with the paint and the subject.

My late father, John Blockley, wrote a book called *Watercolour Interpretations* many years ago. In it, he wrote: 'The process of extending one's imagination to produce interpretations of similar subjects is exciting in itself, but it is also self-perpetuating, with one discovery leading to another and resulting in changes of direction.' I have always found this an inspiring idea and have unashamedly borrowed it as a fundamental concept of this book.

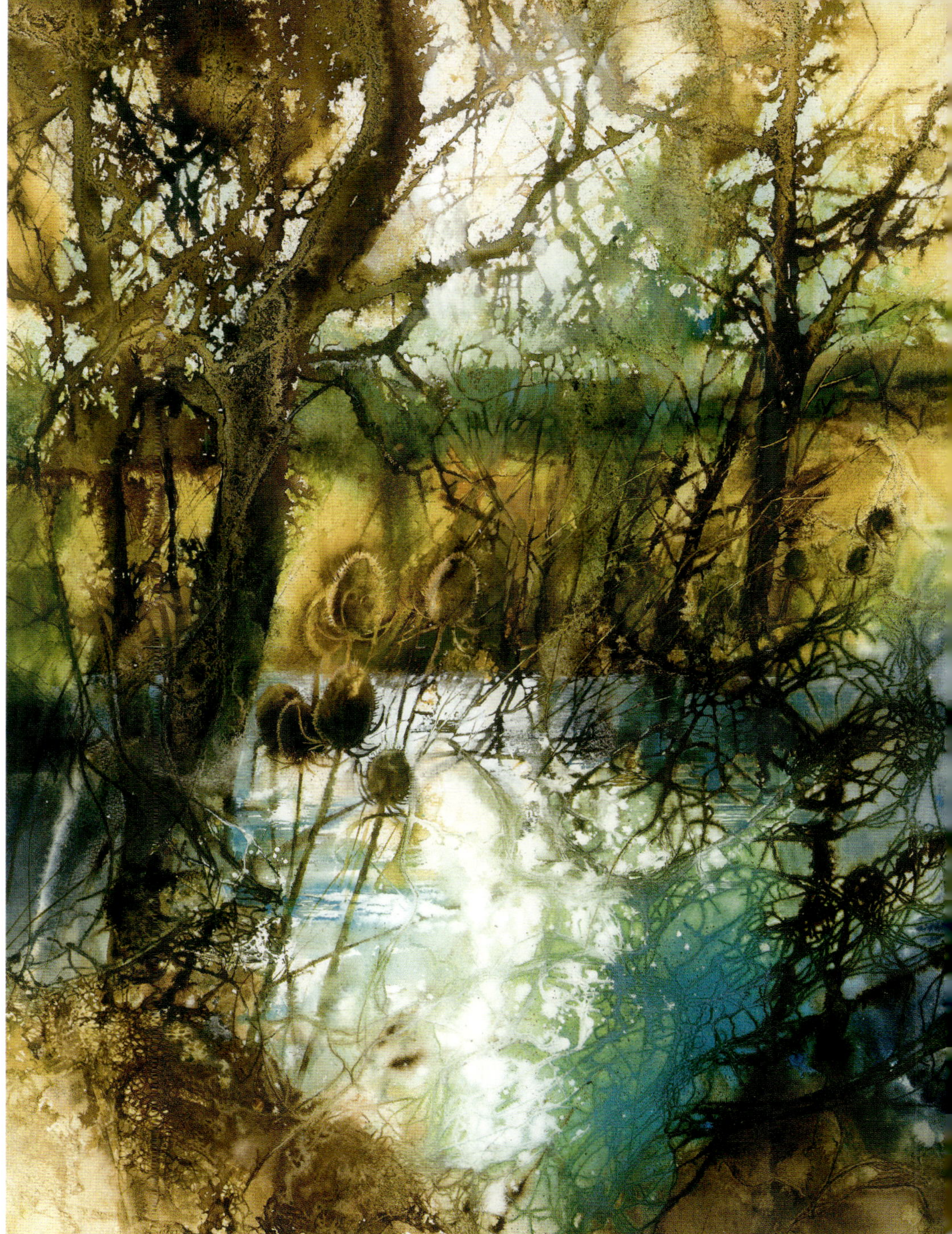

△ Teasels by the Pond

I see this clump of teasels by a local pond on an almost daily basis and enjoy painting different versions of it. Some of the interpretations vary considerably, while others contain only subtle variations. In this interpretation I illustrated my mental description of 'sparkles' and 'tangles'. Thinking about the tapestry of undergrowth and light on the water as adjectives helped me to see them in a more decorative way.

Ways of seeing

Interpreting is not simply about using a different colour or technique; it is to do with your individual way of looking at things. The way to develop this artistic facility is to spend just as much, if not more, time on looking and recording before you paint as you do on your finished pieces. To get away from the habit of seeing a scene in its potentially boring reality you need to use 'artist's eyes' and the more you practise that creative selection through sketching the quicker new habits will develop.

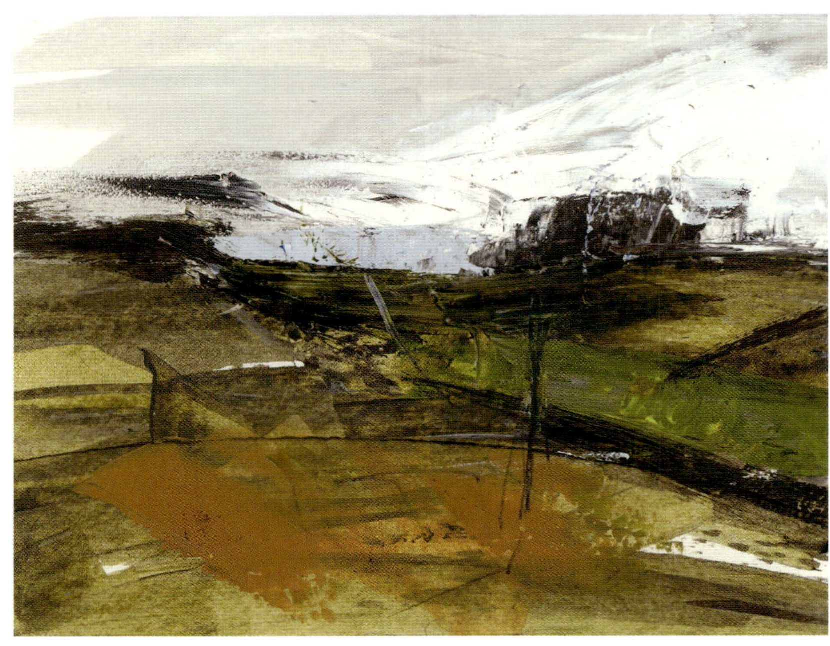

▽ The photo below and the quick paint sketches (shown right) were all made at the same location. The process of sketching helps you clarify which features are most important to you and can help raise your subconscious thoughts to the fore.

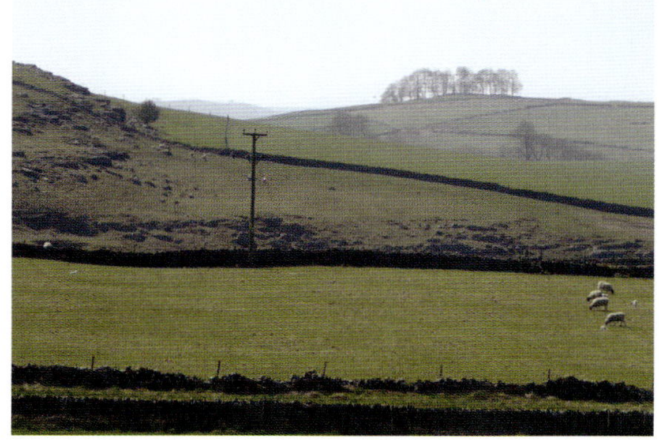

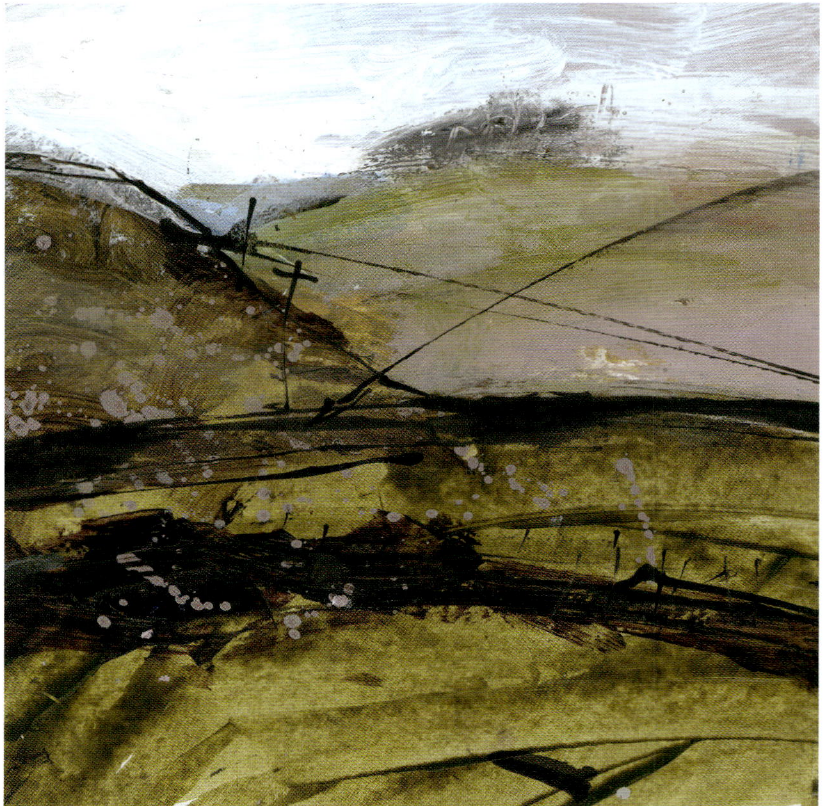

Sketching and photography both
have a role to play in the gathering of
information for paintings. Photography
has the advantage of being convenient
and quick. The benefit of sketching
from life is that it also teaches you how
to look in a different, more interesting
way. You have to be ruthless when you
select and make choices.

The *plein air* landscape sketches here
were all made in a few minutes each.
They were done in acrylic but the
medium or method you use is of less
importance than the activity itself.
When you compare the sketches
with the snapshot taken at the same
time it is astonishing how the colours
of the landscape on a fairly drab day
have been transformed in the painted
versions. I simply would not have
thought to include these pigments in a
finished painting of the scene without
having gone through this process. This
is because the information-gathering
was not just through a restricted
rectangle in a viewfinder but grew out
of being immersed in a 360-degree
experience using all senses. What is also
clear is how the unromantic telegraph
poles and other mundane shapes that
you may normally banish from your
painting have been recorded with marks
that convert them into the eloquent
abstract shapes that they actually are.

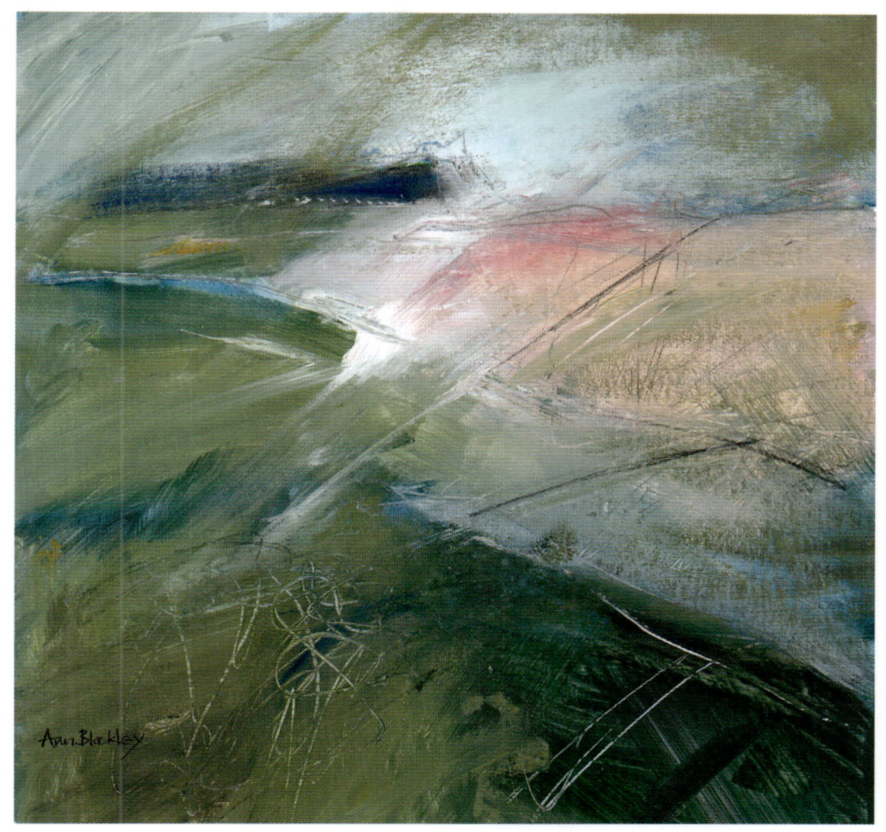

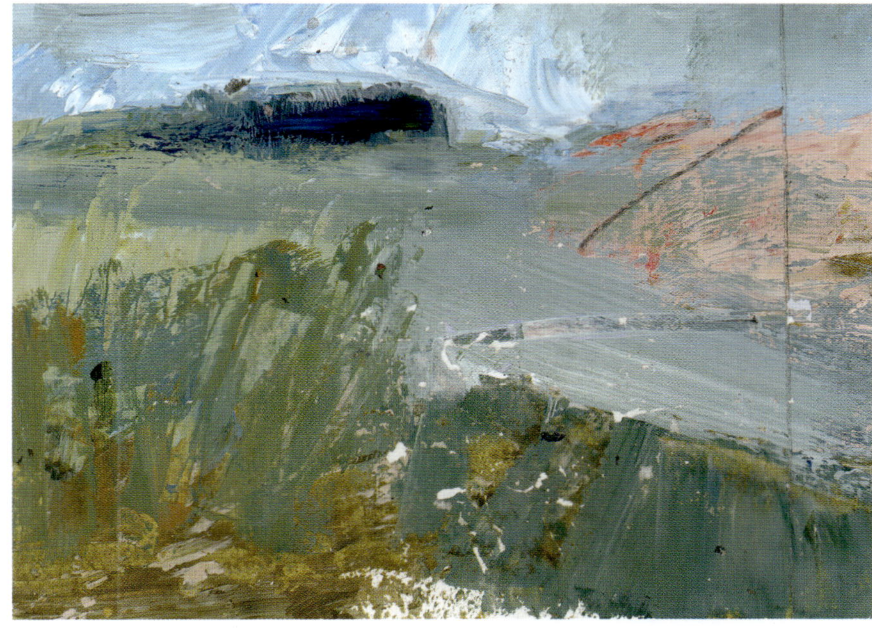

Drawing and exploring

We have looked at how sketching from life enriches your paintings, but I also want to highlight how the more you draw and explore a particular subject the more familiar you will be with its different characteristics. As your knowledge grows you will find that certain elements interest you more than others and this will inevitably feed into your paintings. When you are confident about the correctness and reality of something it can free you up to be more imaginative and let go of some of that information. The more selective you are the stronger your voice.

Your explorations can be made in the traditional way with pencils or ink or be more experimental. One of these sketches has been made by painting on top of a torn piece of photograph. You can do anything you want. The important thing is to have fun with your observations, immersing yourself in a theme and becoming thoroughly obsessed with it. When you dig deep, you can discover treasure!

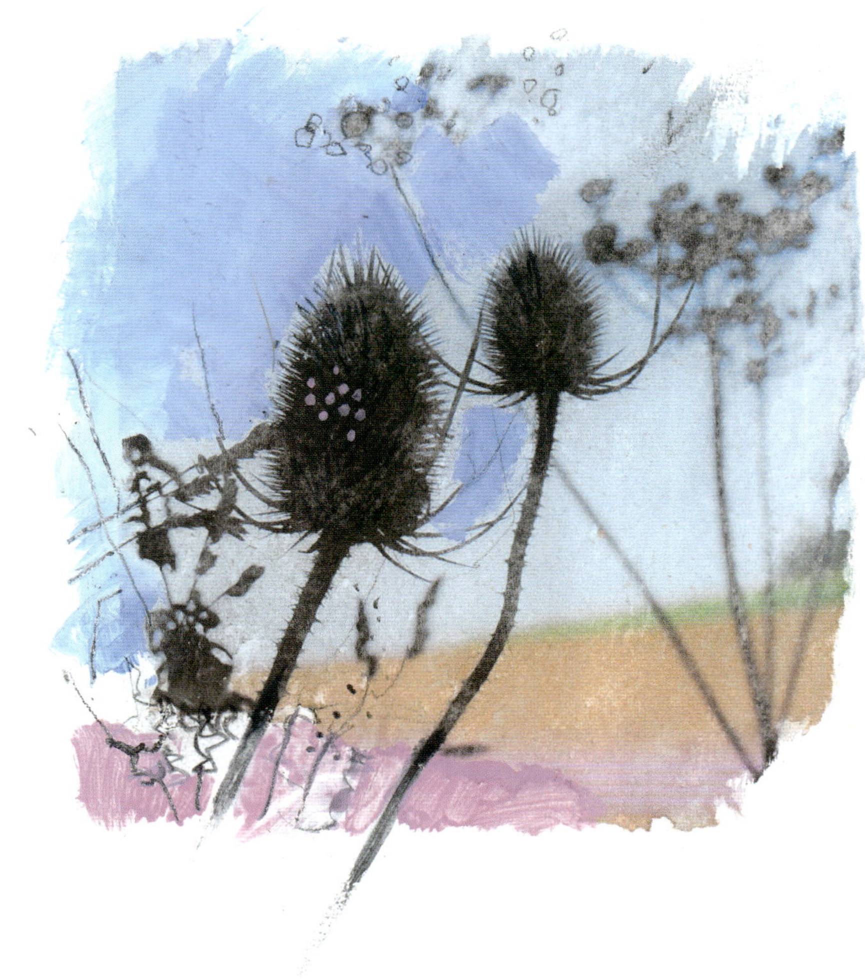

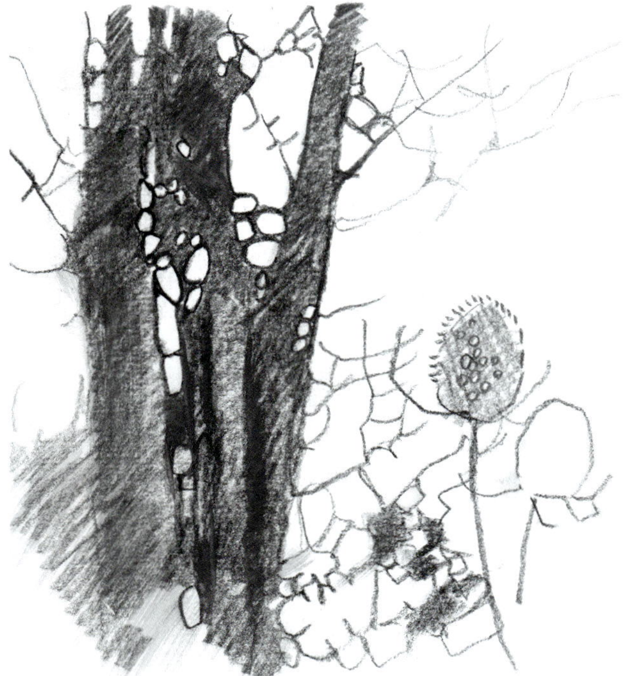

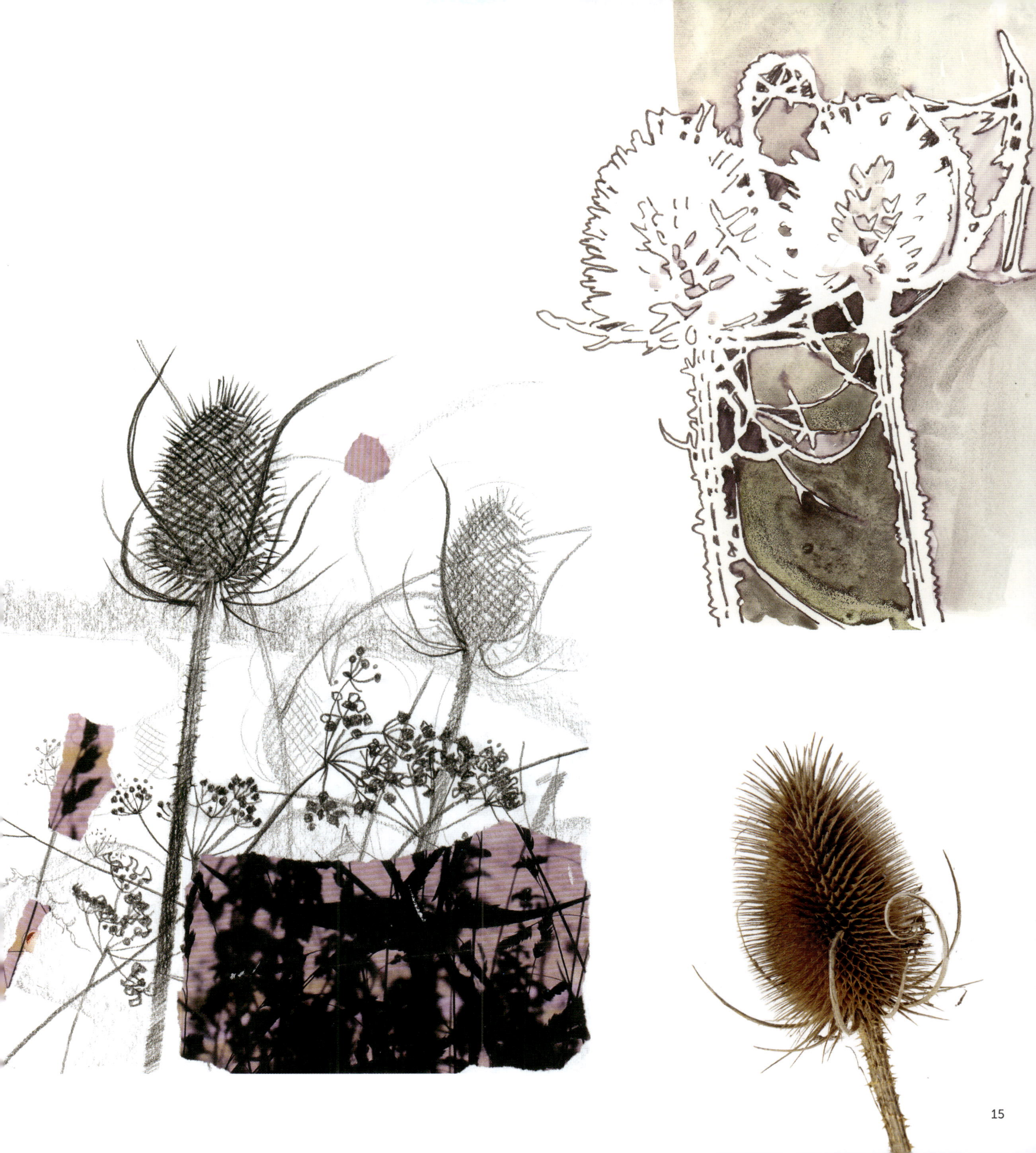

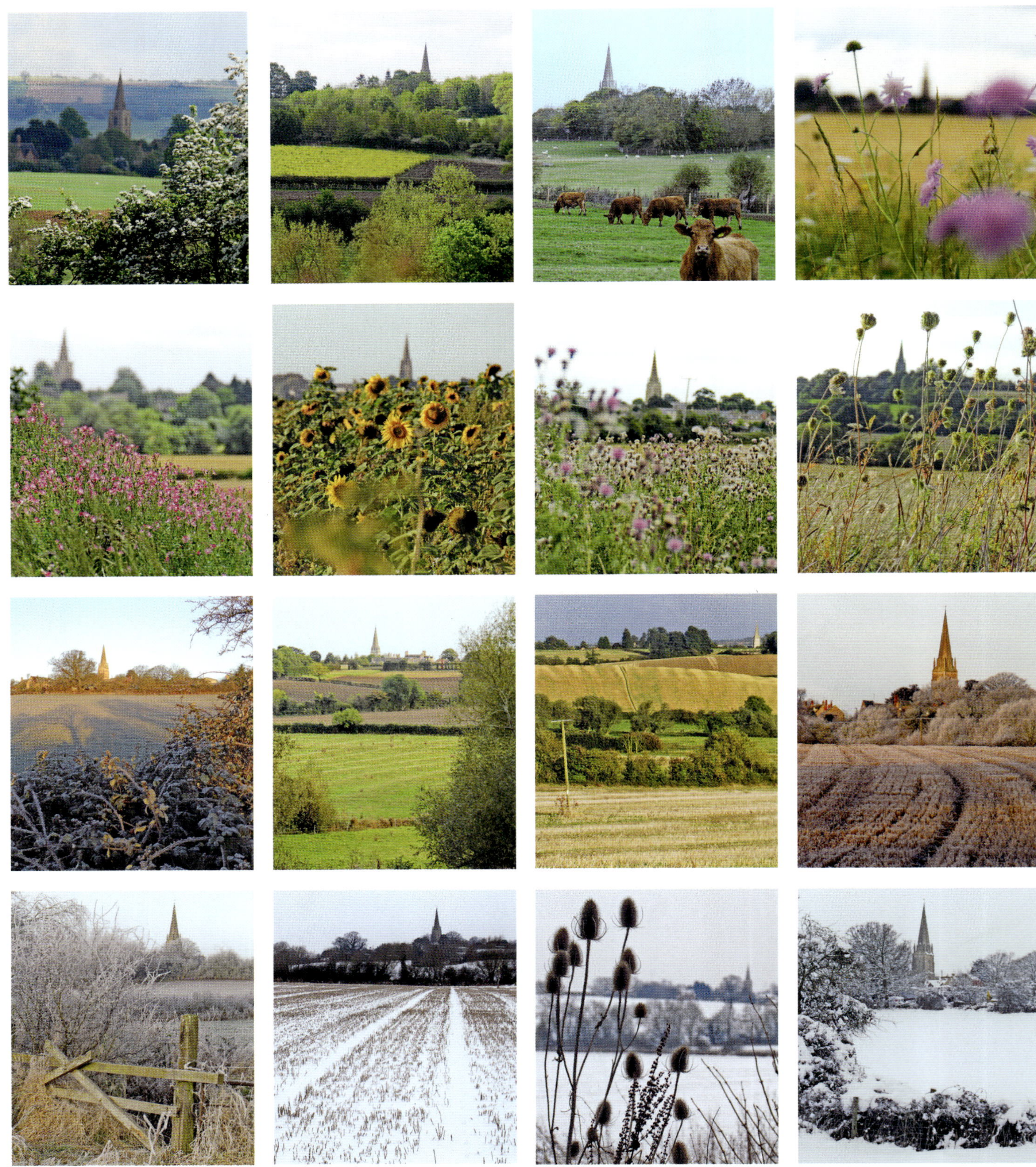

Photography

It is very important to draw and sketch, but photographs definitely play their part. I love my camera and am as passionate about taking large quantities of photographs as I am about the idea of using sketches. A collection of images has an exciting cumulative effect that single snapshots do not achieve. This energy will nourish your subsequent paintings alongside the other information you have gathered. When there are technical issues in an isolated photograph such as the colour being distorted or a tone too contrasting you have the rest of the crowd to support you with the missing information.

If you too use photographs for reference, try to be selective and avoid including every detail as this can easily lure you into a tight style. Having several photographs in front of you alongside sketches or still-life objects will help you to avoid the pitfall of simply copying. If you want to paint freely, try to view photographs as basic information that you can select from or change. If you find this difficult, one way to help your imagination is to play with the photographs digitally before you begin. For example you could change the shape, contrast or colour and enlarge, reduce or crop into small areas. Remember there are no rules and if using technology works for you then go for it.

◁ I love photographing a subject from different angles through the seasons.

▷ It is also fun to manipulate your images in different ways – like this altered view through the sunflowers.

Decision-making

Drawing, exploring and photography all help towards identifying your interest and what you want to say. The next step is making choices about how to communicate these observations in a painting without getting side-tracked by other extraneous detail. Decisions will include choosing which marks, methods or colours best emphasize your chosen theme. This may involve considering not just how to represent something accurately but how to change it to suit your key interests. In the paintings on this page the halo of light is the main subject, rather than the sheep, and the challenge was to work out how to re-create this on paper. The decision-making becomes simpler when you have isolated special aspects like this to concentrate on.

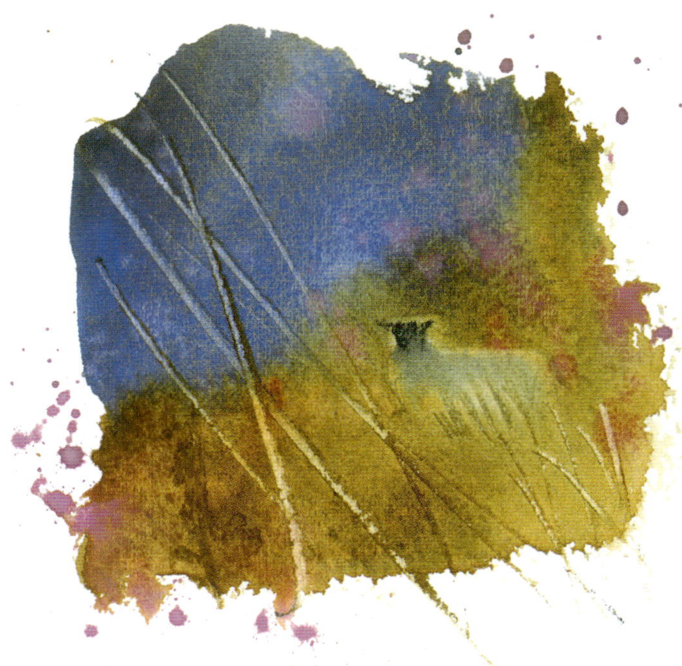

△ I tried a few colours out in this little sketch, including Cobalt Blue, Cobalt Violet and Quinacridone Gold. The halo around the sheep was lifted out of the damp wash.

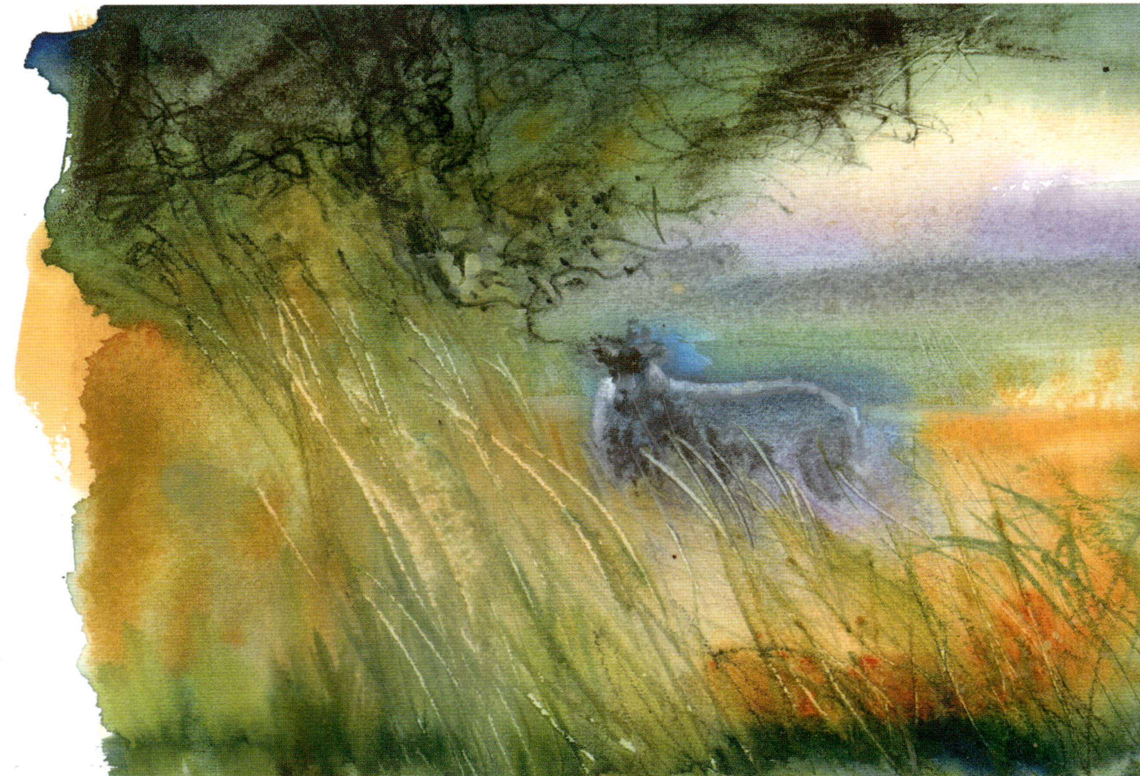

▷ This sketchy experiment was done on watercolour paper and I used a little white gouache for the halo of light around the sheep. The shadow colour of the sheep was painted in the slightly shimmery blue-grey Daniel Smith Kyanite Genuine.

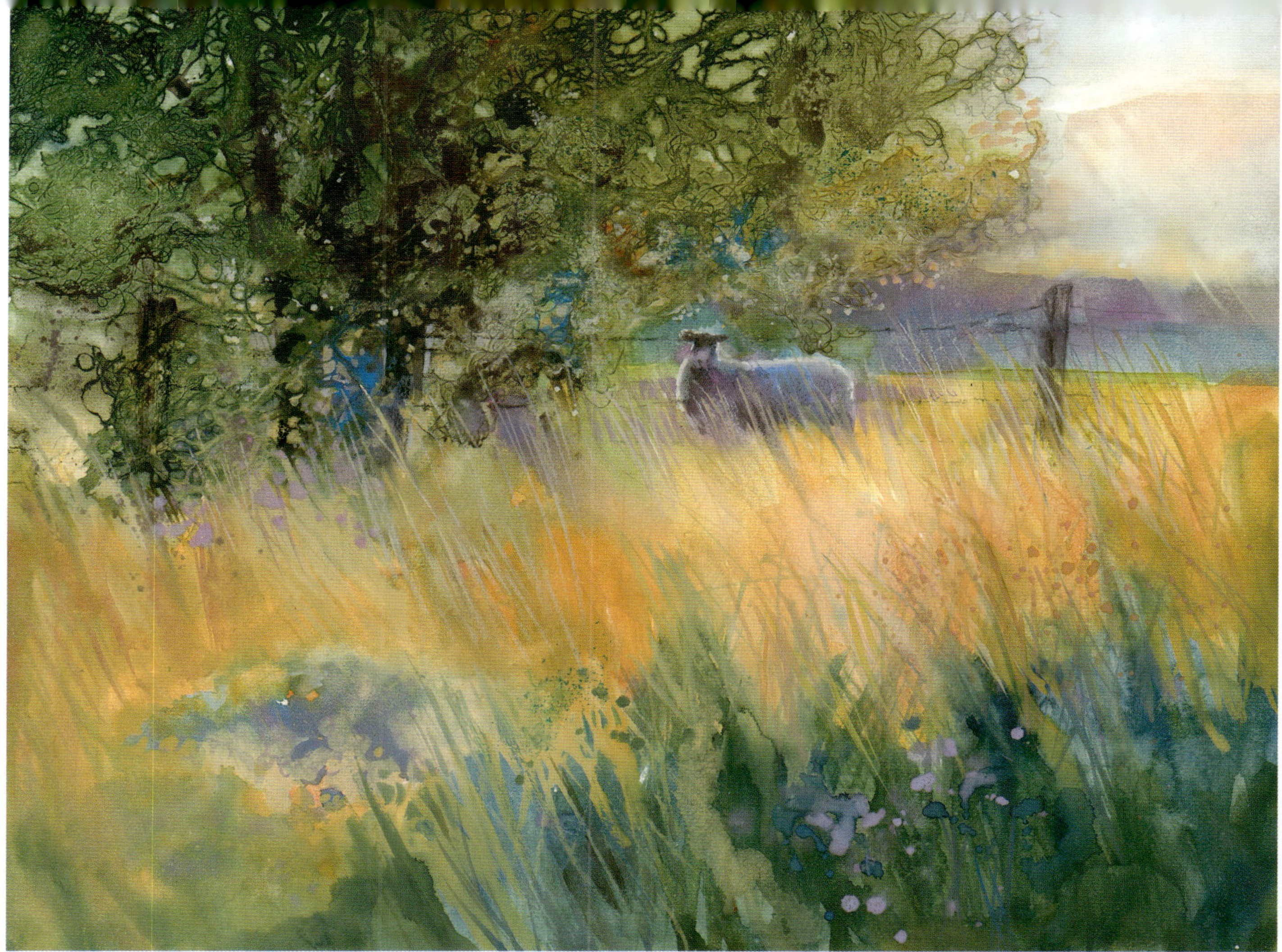

At this decision-making stage I strongly recommend you make some preparatory paint sketches rather than leaping straight into finished-painting mode. This will help you to make choices such as planning your colour palette or the kinds of mark-making or medium you will use. Not only will this sharpen your focus on the important points that you want to highlight, it will also help you to loosen up both physically and mentally before you begin. I feel that it is particularly important for a watercolour artist looking for a painterly style to make these paint sketches before reaching a final decision.

Use the same materials you intend to work with in the 'real' version. There is no point trying out techniques and ideas on scraps of thin cartridge paper as it will not look the same when you move onto the next stage. One of the goals is to iron out some of the potential problems in the preliminary exercises as well as identifying what works. Sometimes the process becomes an ongoing theme in itself. It is not unusual for one of my preparatory pieces to become the one I choose to frame, although that is a bonus and not the aim.

△ *Sheep in the Meadow*
This finished interpretation retained most of the colours I had explored in the preparatory paint sketch but I changed the sheep tones to the more colourful mauves and blues of the colour sketch. I also used a different surface called Ampersand Aquabord. The halo of light proved particularly easy to lift off this smooth surface.

Materials

The choice of art materials available is so wide that it can be mind-boggling. By all means enjoy the fun of experimenting with different products to avoid getting stale, but you will find that it makes life a lot easier if you simplify your basic kit. The paintings shown in this book have all been created using the following materials.

Watercolours You will achieve the most vibrant, rich results using **artist**-quality watercolour from tubes rather than pans. It is vital to be generous with paint in order to complete washes in a flowing, juicy way and this is difficult to achieve using small pans.

Gouache I have used mainly white gouache in the projects but there are many colour options available. You can also choose to mix white gouache with watercolour for paler opaque versions of a particular pigment.

Ink Always check that inks are lightfast. The bottles with pipettes in the lid are useful. Opaque inks granulate best; Indian ink is another option for making granulating textures, but black can be a bit dominant on a small scale.

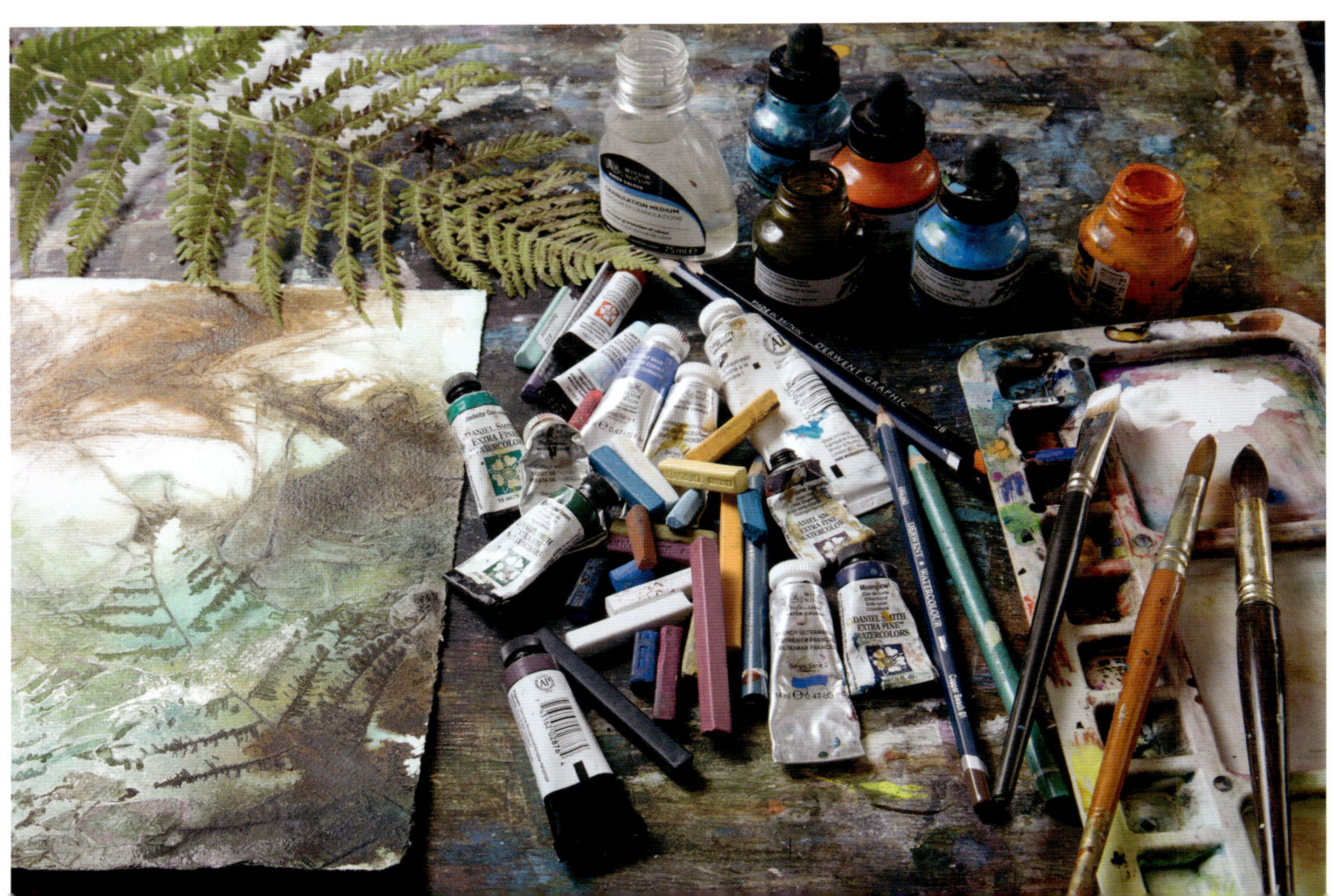

Winsor & Newton Granulation Medium I find this medium usually works better with inks than watercolour. An alternative is to use the very granulating Daniel Smith watercolours.

Pencils and crayons I mainly use Derwent Inktense blocks (sticks) and watercolour pencils that can be used either dry or wet. However, there are many types to play with.

You will also need white gesso, tissue paper and flat collage materials if you want to try a more mixed-media approach; cling film (plastic wrap) and table salt for textures; a very large waterpot so that you always work with clean water; and a large palette with compartments. You can dilute individual colours and let these mix themselves on the paper or mix pigments within the palette.

Colours

Colour is a very personal choice and a key component of your creative voice, so it is vital to develop your own palette over time. The following watercolours are some of my favourites: French Ultramarine, Cobalt Blue, Cerulean Blue, Cobalt Turquoise, Lemon Yellow, Indian Yellow, Cobalt Violet, Quinacridone Magenta, Quinacridone Gold, Brown Madder, Cadmium Red, Perylene Maroon, Raw Umber, Green Gold, Burnt Sienna, Indigo, Phthalo Blue, Perylene Maroon; Daniel Smith's Moonglow, Cascade Green, Lunar Black and Bloodstone Genuine; Winsor & Newton's Winsor Red.

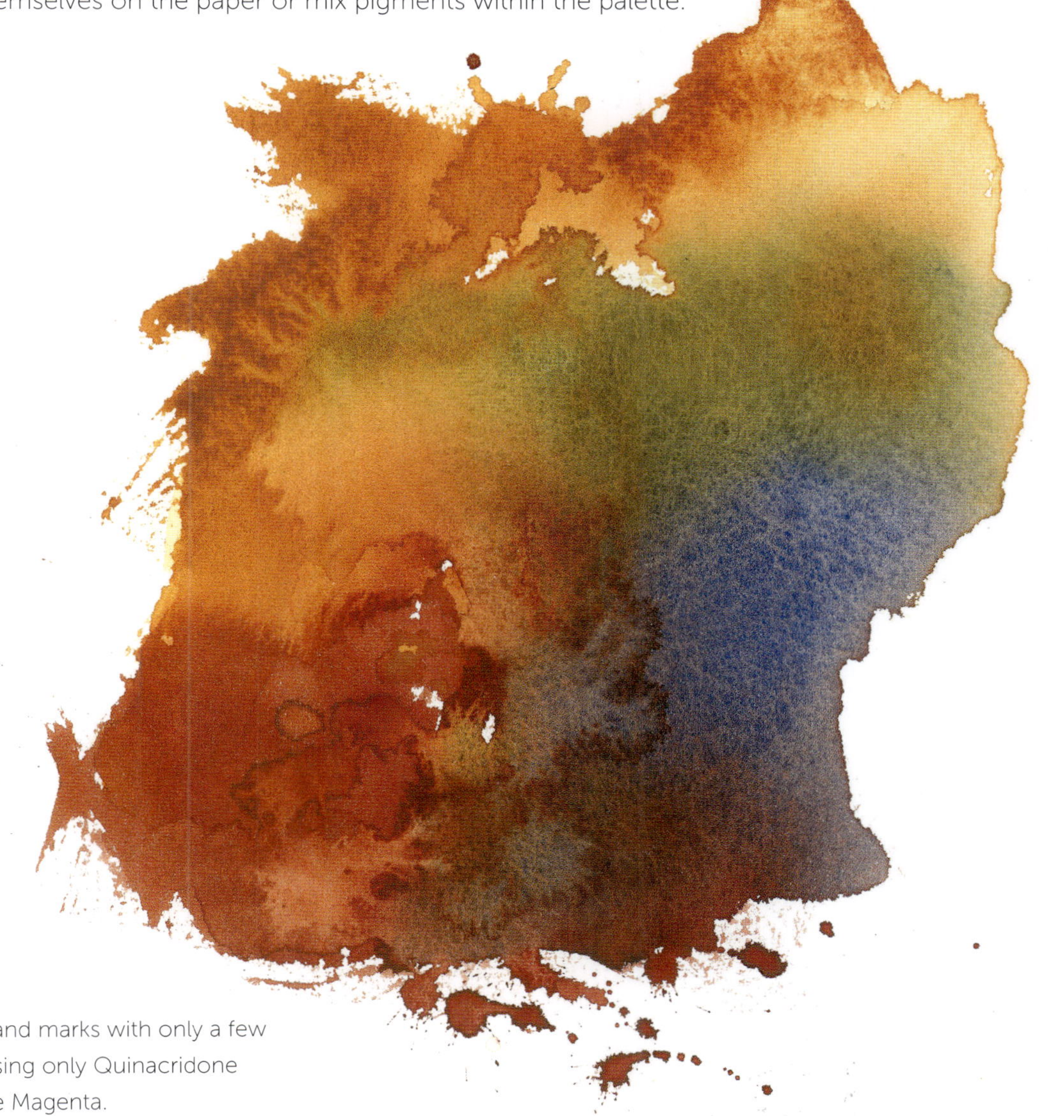

▷ You can create a huge range of colours and marks with only a few pigments. This splashy swatch was made using only Quinacridone Gold, French Ultramarine and Quinacridone Magenta.

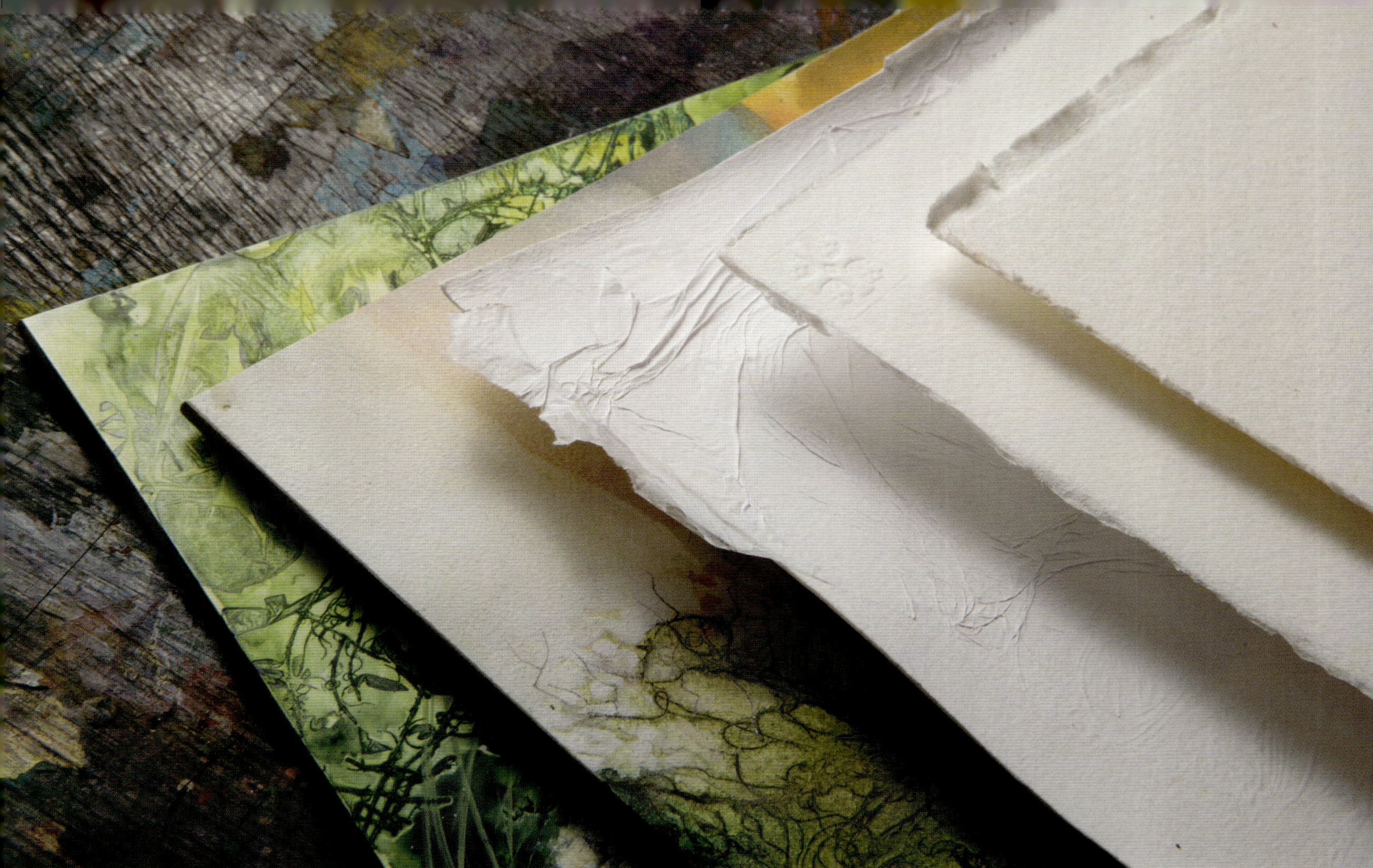

surfaces

The majority of the paintings in this book have been painted on Saunders Waterford watercolour paper. I prefer to cut up loose sheets of paper rather than using glued pads as it is useful to be able to move and manipulate the paper for certain methods. For this reason I never stretch the paper onto board but use heavy 425gsm (200lb) or 638gsm (300lb) paper when working large so that it does not cockle. If on rare occasions it does, I simply wet the paper on the back when the work is dry, put clean paper and a board over it then weigh it all down with something heavy such as a pile of books. When the painting is dry it will be flat again. I use lighter weight 300gsm (140lb) paper to paint small watercolours.

Use a solid board underneath the loose, flexible paper when you are painting so that it can be angled to a tilt to help washes flow while keeping the paper rigid. Experiment with different surfaces to find out what suits you best. I like Rough for highly textured work and CP (Not), for a combination of flow, texture and detail. I have also been experimenting with Ampersand boards which come in a variety of surface choice. Aquabord and Claybord have unique characteristics that lend themselves to different kinds of texture (see pages 48–49).

Brushes and other tools

Buy brushes that are reasonably good quality so they hold their shape. I use a range of flat brushes from 10mm to 50mm (½–2in) and sometimes angled ones to get into corners. The firmness of a synthetic flat brush can be useful, but buy sable round brushes if possible. You can probably get by with only one medium-sized round brush, such as a size 8, but it is useful to have several bigger sizes – about 16 to 18. Although this is an added expense it allows you to load brushes with different colours when painting large areas without having to rinse and waste paint every time you change pigment. Small, flexible sable riggers are useful for fine lines and details and have recently become a favourite with me.

A sharp scalpel is invaluable for scraping crayon, sharpening pencils and scratching lines. A small palette knife can be used to splatter water and paint and to draw with, using the edge. A pen and nib is also useful for drawing detail and linework – and signing your masterpieces!

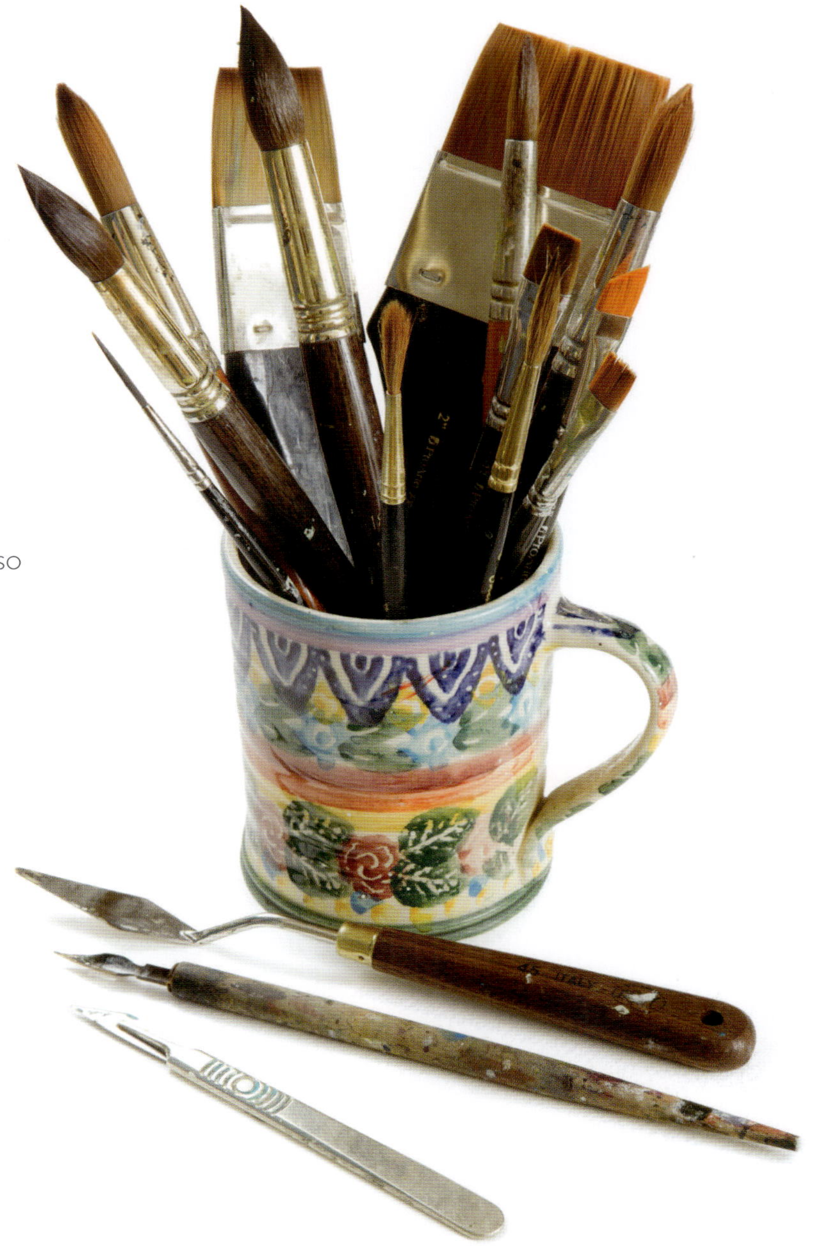

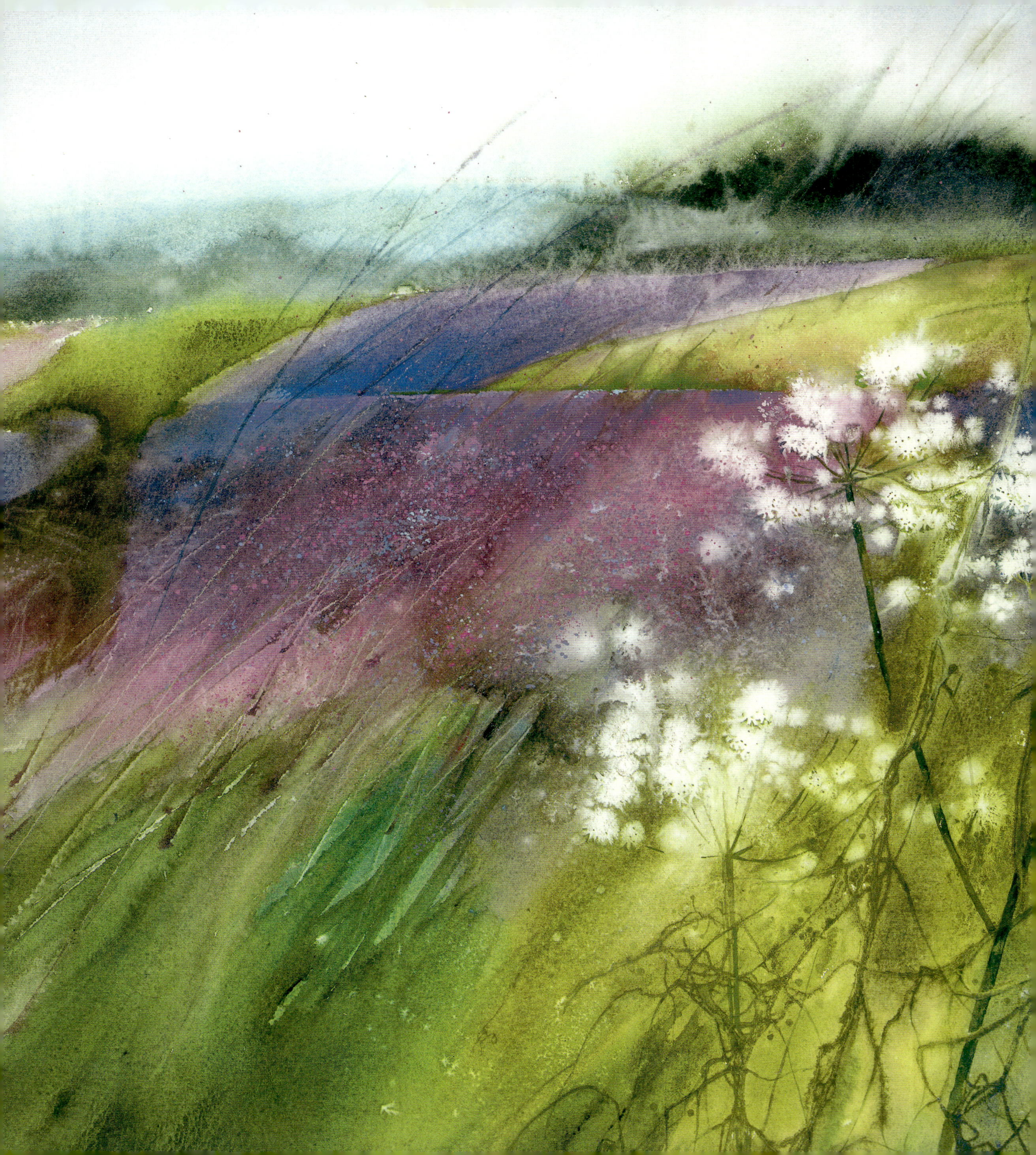

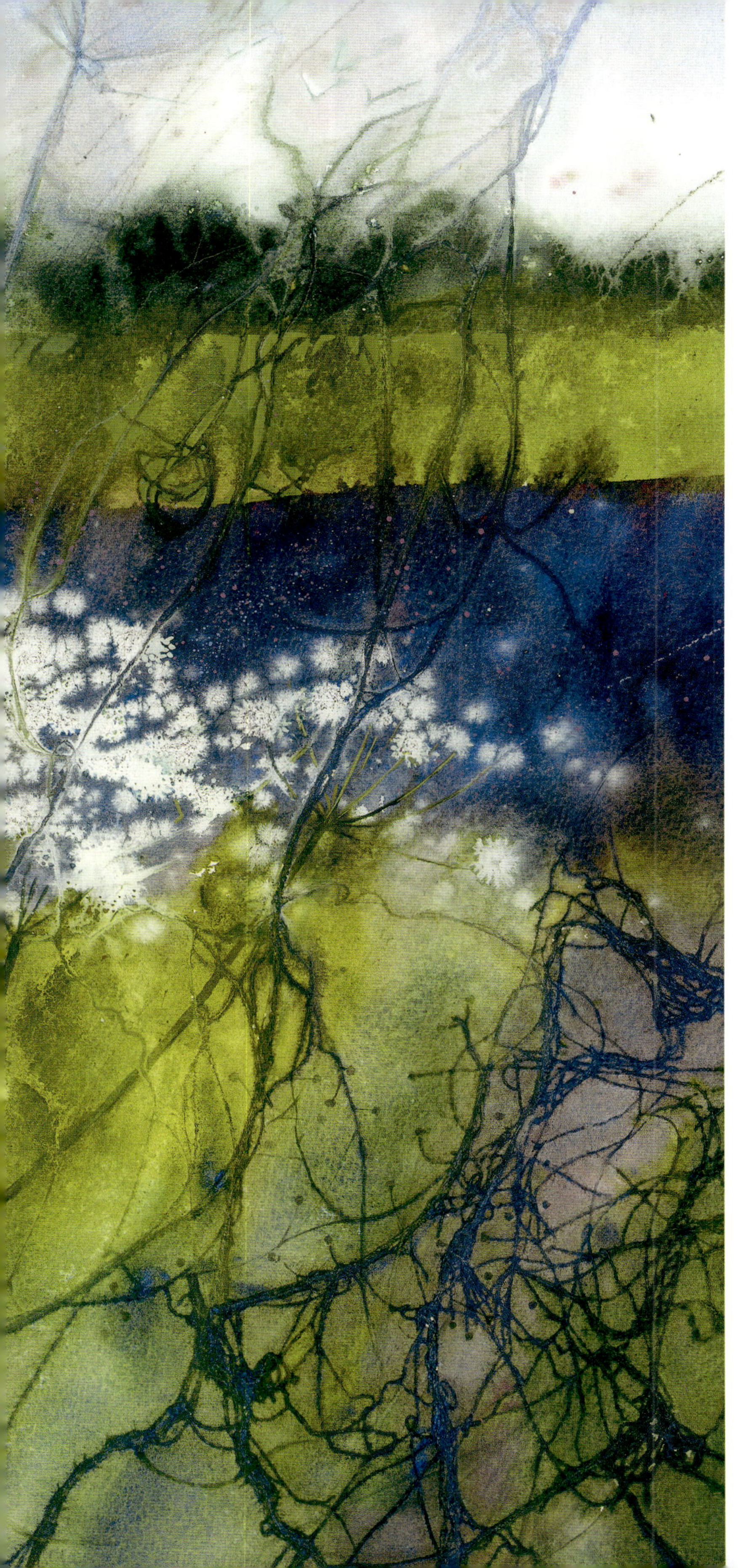

Flower and field

It is time to take out that scary piece of white paper and make a start – and where better to begin than with the kaleidoscope of colour, texture, shape and pattern found in nature? The flowers and plants within the landscape or in close up offer perfect opportunities to play with watercolour in an unrestricted manner.

The best way to learn how to create loose watercolours is simply to start painting and see what happens. Learn from the way the pigment reacts in different circumstances. Watch and take note of the flow and unexpected 'accidents' in a mindful way, learning and growing stronger from each adventure. Develop your relationship with watercolour by responding to it instead of trying to control it.

"GREAT ART PICKS UP WHERE NATURE ENDS."

MARC CHAGALL

◁ Cow Parsley and Lavender Fields

Project: WILDFLOWER MEADOW

This project is based on fields of mixed wildflowers. It is about playing with loose watercolour rather than painting individual flowers, though you can do that if you wish to. However, when flowers grow in abundance in a field and are viewed from a distance the details tend to disappear and the overall effect is their colour and texture.

The emphasis in these interpretations is the effect of the flowers as splodges and dots of colour and the linear marks of the grasses. I have used aspects from two photographs as starting points for my explorations. You are welcome to work from these but your interpretations will ultimately become more meaningful when you use your own reference material that records your personal experiences and environment.

The photographs are taken from similar low viewpoints but they contain different challenges. One is a mouse-eye view looking through grasses, whereas in the other the grass is part of the overall texture. Both lend themselves to loose explorations of the qualities of watercolour: juicy washes, watermarks, splashing and splattering to create the organic textures and patterns of the flowery field. You can put these abstract marks into context by including some sky or distant hedges and add as much or as little detail as you like in the foreground or background.

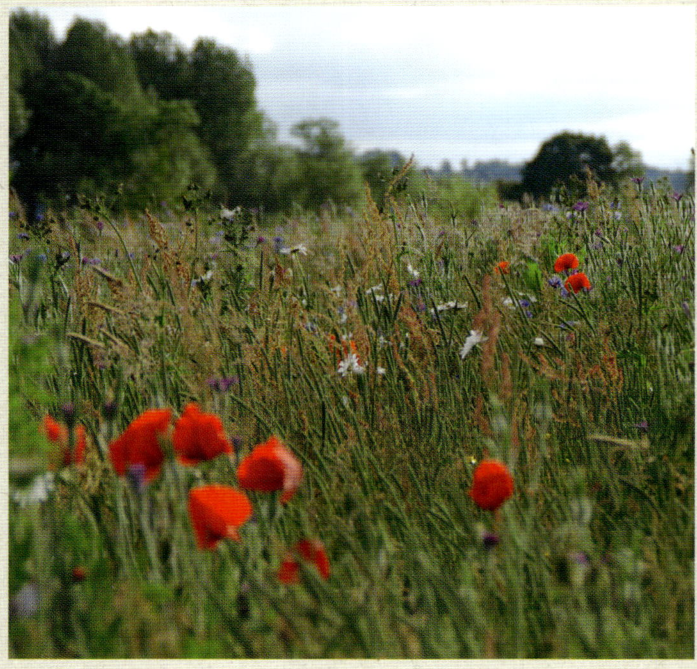 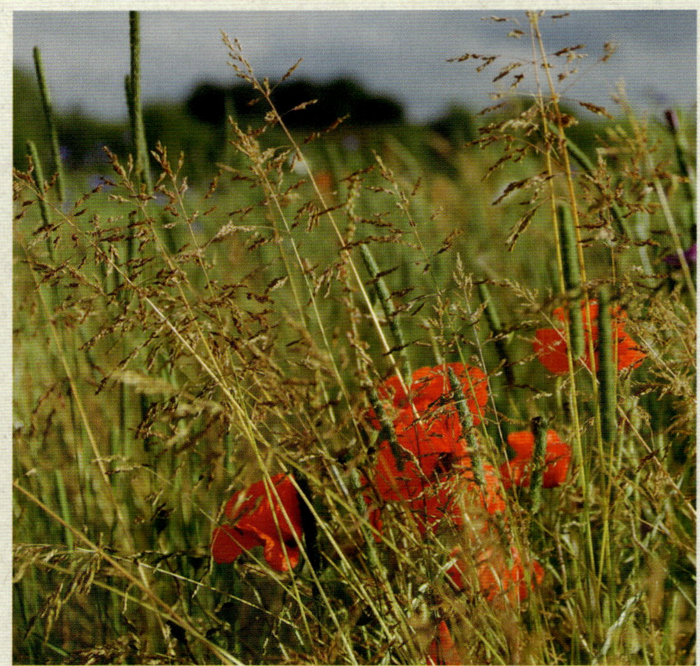

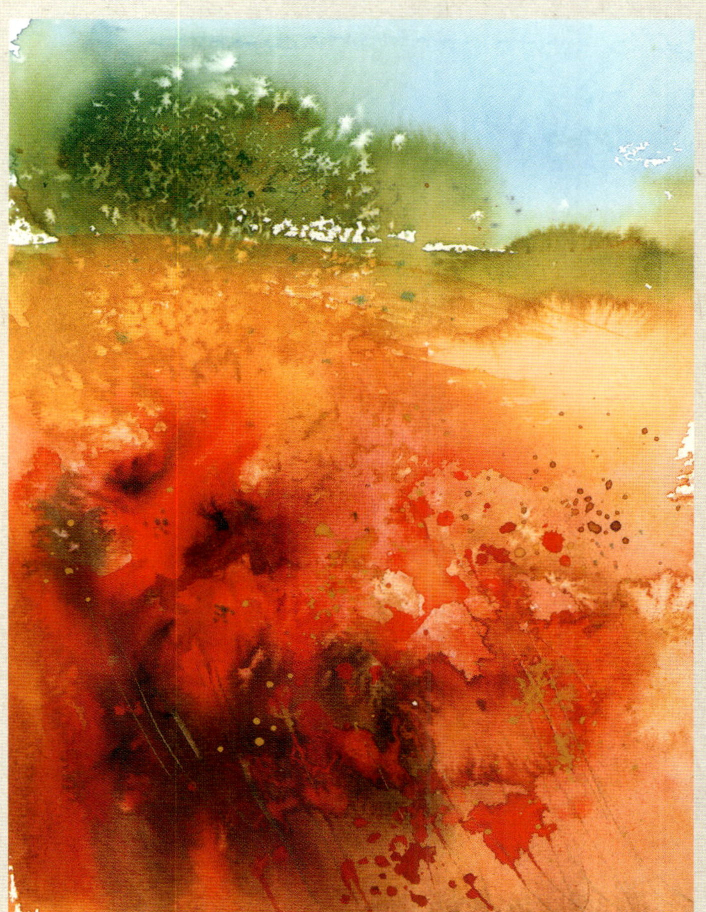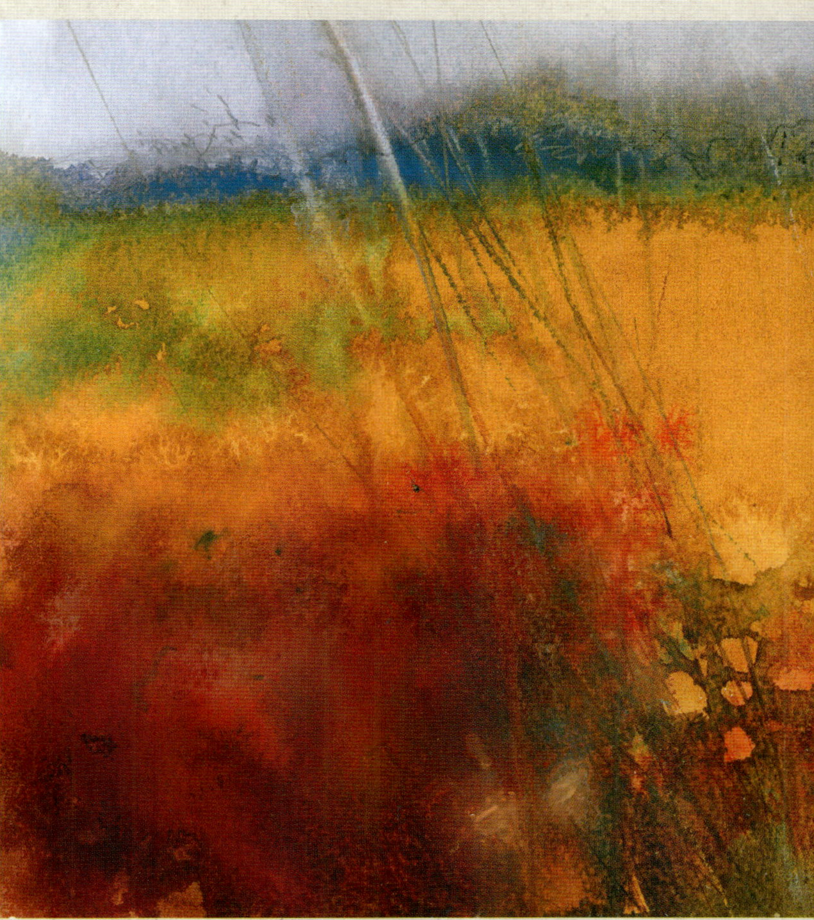

In both loosening-up sketches I played with combinations of yellows, reds and blues to see which combinations I liked. These included Indian Red Deep, Winsor Red, Yellow Titanate, Quinacridone Gold, Cobalt Blue, Cobalt Turquoise, Phthalo Blue and Prussian Blue. In the sketch shown above left I sprinkled salt into the damp wash as a trial idea for suggesting the speckles of flowers and background foliage as seen in the reference photograph (opposite, left). The pale salty textures in the distant tree need toning down. In my second colour sketch (above right) I drew rapid lines through the damp washes with different kinds of pencil. This had the effect of both scraping out and adding lines as an idea for interpreting the foreground grasses of the other photograph (right).

If you are at the beginning of your journey into watercolour this is your chance to explore the possibilities of this medium. More experienced painters can push the limits of the subject using some of the alternative ideas shown on the following pages. We have already discussed the concept of paint experiments to try out colour combinations and mark-making before you start a more planned painting and this is how we will begin here. I used CP (Not) watercolour paper. It is important to practise on the same paper you use for the next exercise. Hold onto your practise pieces as they may be useful for exploring further ideas later. You never know – your unfettered beginnings may even become your preferred interpretations. Mine often do!

1 Begin by using 'real' colours to represent sky, poppies
   and hedge. I used Cadmium Red, Cobalt Blue,
   Quinacridone Gold and Cobalt Turquoise. Later we
   will look at interpretations using imagined colour.
   Prepare all the mixes before you begin so there
   are no interruptions. Dilute the red and the blue in
   separate areas of your palette and mix green using
   blue and gold. Cover your paper with washes letting
   one colour flow into the next – do not worry about
   specific flower shapes at this stage. The area of dark
   wet colour here is where colours have mixed on
   paper to create brown. This pool of pigment is wetter
   than elsewhere which created the beginning of a
   potential 'watermark'. If this occurs just go with the
   flow as you can use this later.

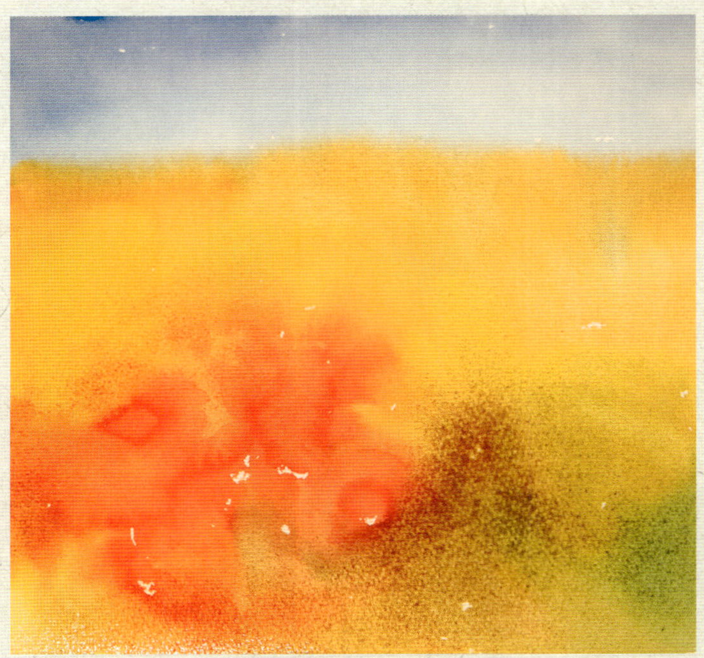

2 At this stage it is important to assess the drying of
   each wash area in order to layer and create edge
   values. I added a strip of green hedgerow when the
   sky was dry enough for most of the hedge top to stay
   crisp. However, some of the field wash was damp so
   the hedge bottom stayed soft-edged. If your wash
   is dry you can blend the hedge using a clean damp
   brush. I splashed paint or water into the now patchily
   drying field to break it up into soft organic textures.
   In my example the watermark blossomed when I
   added further moisture and I encouraged it to do so
   in order to suggest the beginnings of a petal edge
   (see page 30). If your wash is dry the splatters will
   be hard-edged and that is also fine as there is no
   'correct' way to do this.

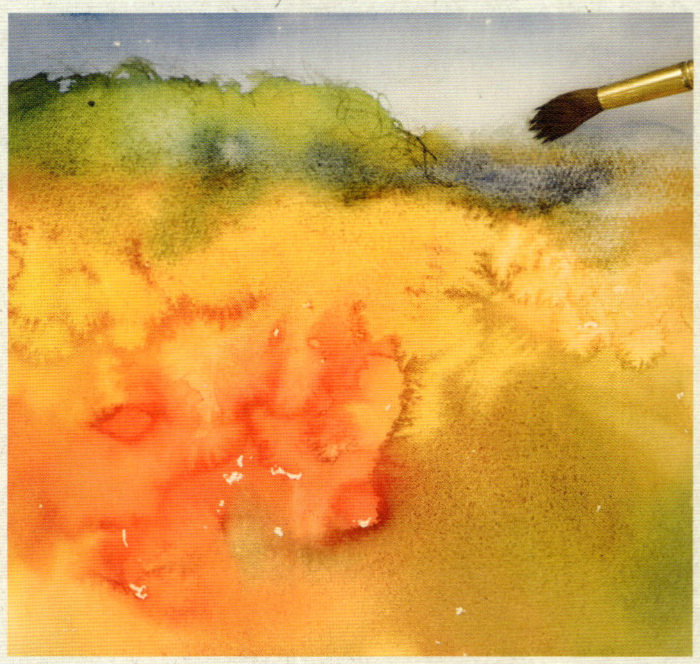

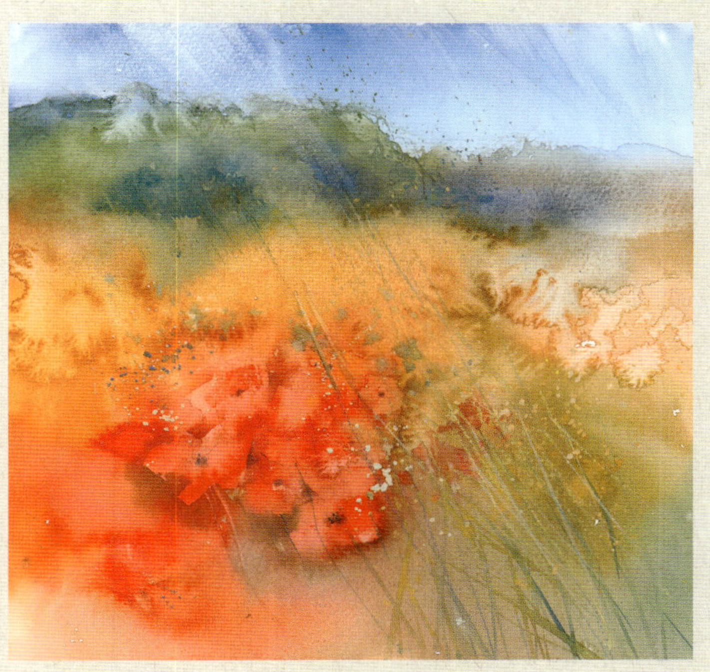

3 When you have finished playing with textures it is important to leave everything to dry before continuing in order to stay in control. Then you can hint at flowers and details. The poppies here have been created out of the wash with darker negative painting (see page 31). I added the grasses with a rigger brush, using dark watercolour on top of pale wash areas and light opaque gouache where the background is dark. You could add pale or dark flowers on top in the same way. I also dragged a hint of white gouache across the painting with a flat brush to echo the direction of the grasses, but this is optional. Another way to add grasses is to lift or scrape lines out of the background colour using a firm brush or scalpel.

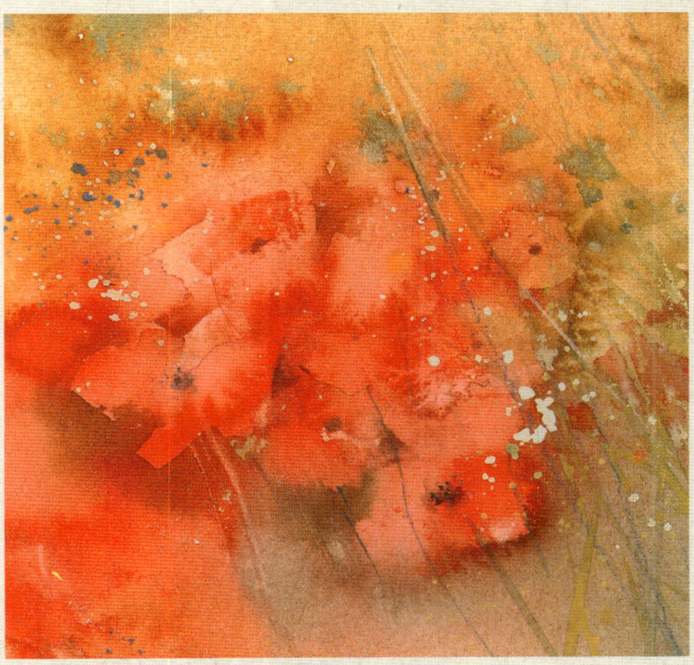

4 The detail shows the loose textures of the flowers. Note how the selective negative painting and watermark are all it takes to define them, with the addition of dots or smudges to indicate an occasional centre. Keep it simple and try not to tidy everything up. Allow the paint marks to be the star of this show. Your subject is the watercolour – the actual flowers are secondary to that. Leave your painting at an almost finished stage, as by that time it probably *is* finished! Now you can start again with another interpretation, using some of the ideas on the following pages.

Techniques

Creating juicy washes

Mix your paint to the consistency of milk. There should be enough pigment to keep the colour rich and enough water for the paint to flow and gather at the bottom of the wash on a tilted surface. Think 'juicy washes'. Your mouth should be watering as you paint! Use as few brushstrokes as possible, preferably only touching each section of paper once without going back over it. Slightly overlap each stroke, letting the paint blend itself.

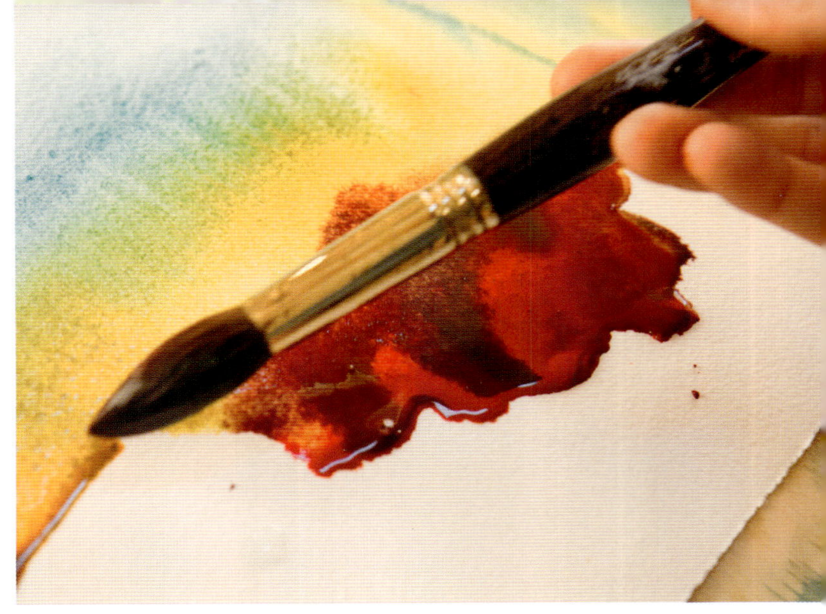

Enjoy your watercolour

The joy of watercolour is the quality of the paint itself. Do not be afraid to let it do its own thing and enjoy the marks that happen. Try painting on damp paper for a really soft wet-into-wet look. For more control, work on dry paper as illustrated. This will enable you to paint washes around shapes, leaving areas of white paper. If the paint is uncontrollable it may be too diluted. Think of watercolour as a friendly pet. It is not your enemy and if you lead it but also give it some freedom, it will be your friend for life.

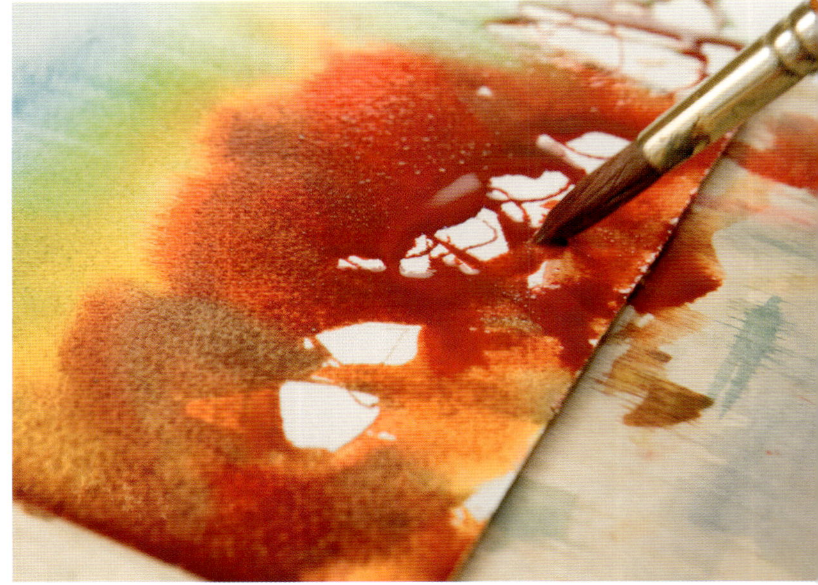

Watermarks

The ragged marks known as watermarks can occur when a drying wash is disturbed by adding wetter paint or where adjacent wash areas are unequal in their moisture content. They can be encouraged as a means of creating texture. By curling the paper the pool of paint that gathered in the demonstration was persuaded to flow back to meet the dryer red area and form a rough petal edge. If you prefer not to have these marks, practise making them on purpose so that you know what to avoid.

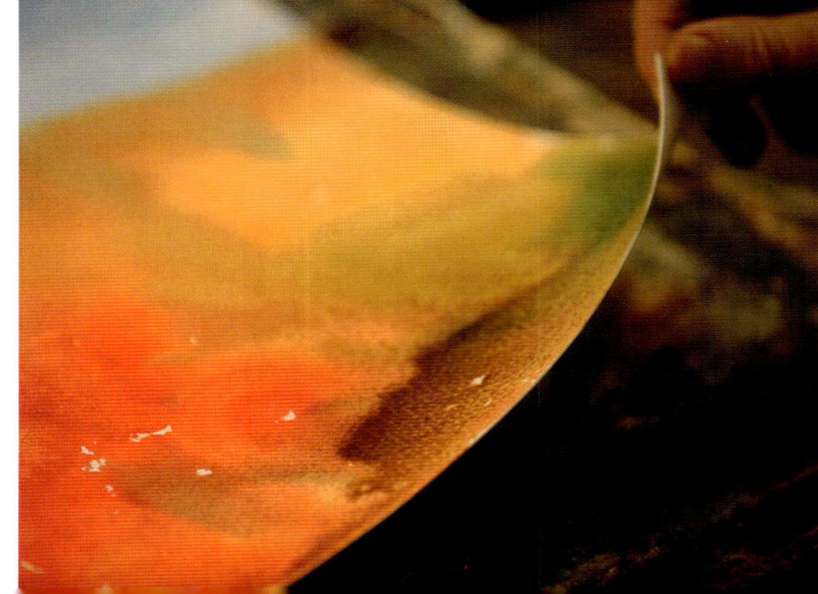

Negative painting

Painting around a shape rather than painting the shape itself is known as negative painting. This should always be done over a dry wash. Paint a halo, or area of darker colour, around parts of the outer edge of a shape and blend it back into the wash with clean water. Try to avoid painting all the way round as this results in an artificial 'cut out' shape. Instead, leave some parts undefined to create atmosphere in a 'lost and found' way.

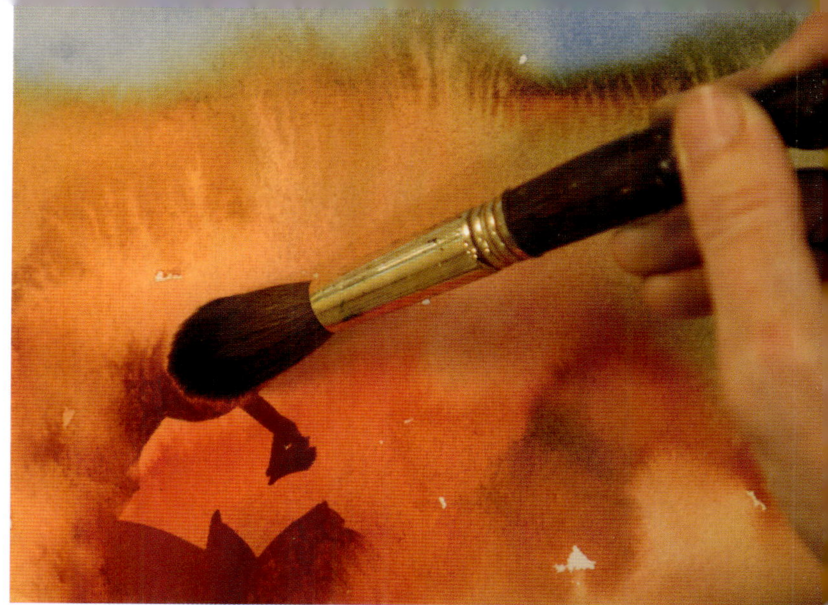

Softening edges

When you add darker shapes on top of a dry wash you will have hard edges. If you want to soften some of these, try splaying the tip of a round brush into a feathery shape and teasing some of the new colour into a softer mark while it is still wet. If the colour has dried you can still soften it with a damp brush, but be careful not to scrub and lift off too much paint.

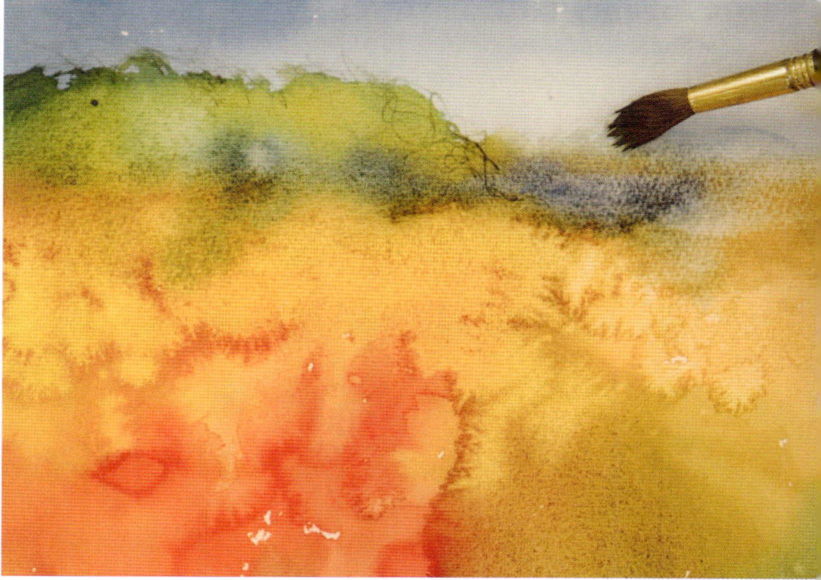

Controlled spattering

A palette knife is a great tool for spattering. Load dilute paint on the tip but turn it over to face the paper to start spattering. To control where the marks go, use a thumb and finger to hold the blade firmly and flick using another finger. The closer to the top you hold it the greater the control. If your first wash is dry you can protect areas so that dots can only go where you want them to. If the blobs are too big or in the wrong place, quickly blot them off while they are still wet.

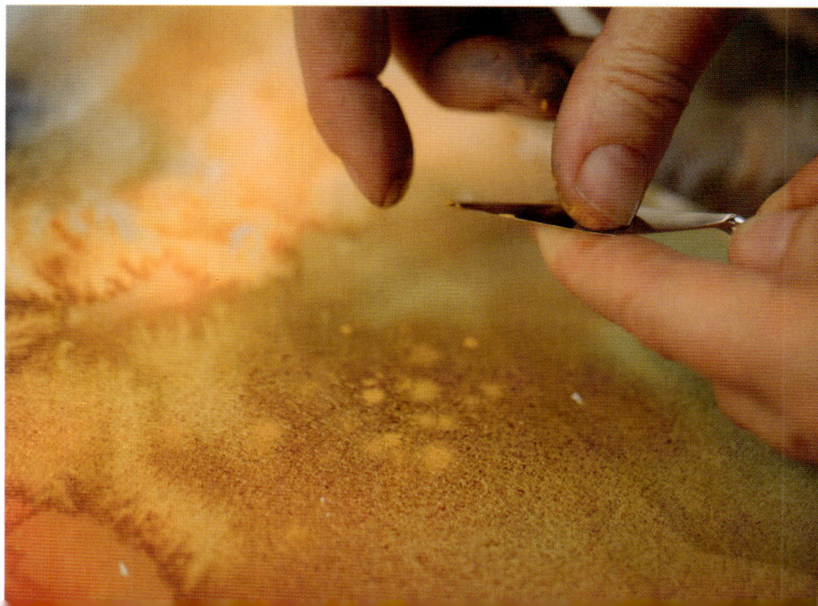

Taking it further: ADDING OTHER MEDIUMS

The first exercise explored using watercolour in a loose, unrestricted way. The opportunities for varying the look and style of your interpretation increase even further if you change your medium or combine it with others. Different kinds of water-based paints and inks are all compatible. I particularly enjoy applying opaque gouache on top of watercolour, sometimes into a wet wash but often when the watercolour is dry to cover up and change direction. The big advantage of using an opaque medium in this way is that you can be incredibly free with your initial application of watercolour and the normal rules of largely working light to dark no longer apply. You can also use gouache to paint on top of dry ink.

You could try painting over one of your initial meadow exercises (see pages 26–27) using gouache and see how you can alter or improve it. I have not used much acrylic paint in this book but that is an alternative option. You can just add details such as further pale flowers over dark washes or change a whole area such as the sky. Gouache does not have the same pure, fresh look of watercolour as it is not translucent. However, it can create a special atmosphere all of its own and you can add as much or as little as you like. It can, of course, be used as a planned medium in its own right.

A different effect could also be achieved using opaque crayons or pastels on top of your dry watercolour. Press hard to get solid marks or pass lightly over the surface for softer, broken texture. If you prefer a vibrant style to the chalky look of gouache another choice would be to use lightfast acrylic inks. These are either opaque or translucent and very bright colour can be achieved. I like the Daler Rowney ones but it is good to experiment with different brands to get a full range of colours.

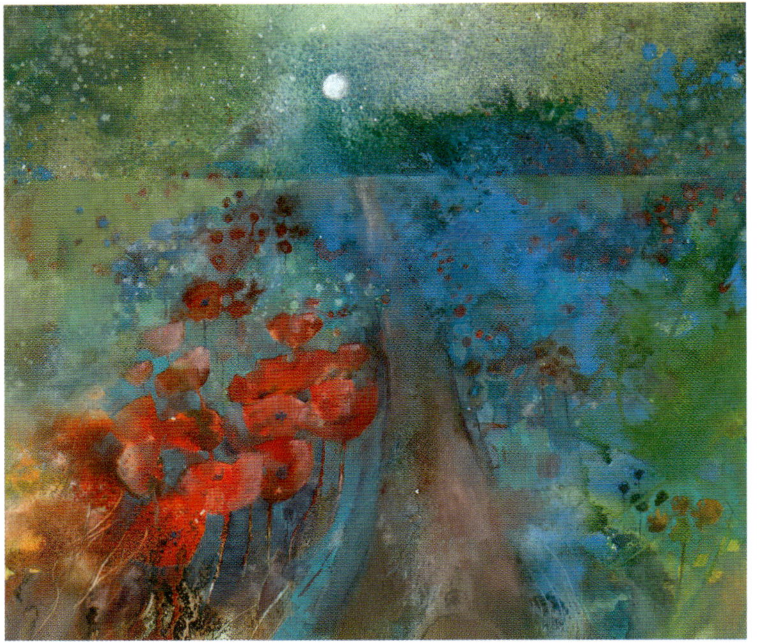

◁ But Pleasures Are Like Poppies Spread

I painted over one of my watercolour beginnings using gouache. It was very busy, with too many marks and textures in all the wrong places. If that sounds familiar, read on! The beauty of using an opaque medium is that you can cover up and change an unsatisfactory beginning. I toned down some overly bright splashes with a glaze of dilute paint and used thicker paint to add more defined flowers, a pathway, a new horizon and the moon.

▷ Of Flowers with a Scarlet Gleam

This version was painted with inks. The sky was one of those lucky but rewarding accidents that came from a frustrated last attempt to rescue a bad beginning. The brightest poppies are bits of collage on top of the first layer. They were carefully positioned to catch the light filtering out from the cloud.

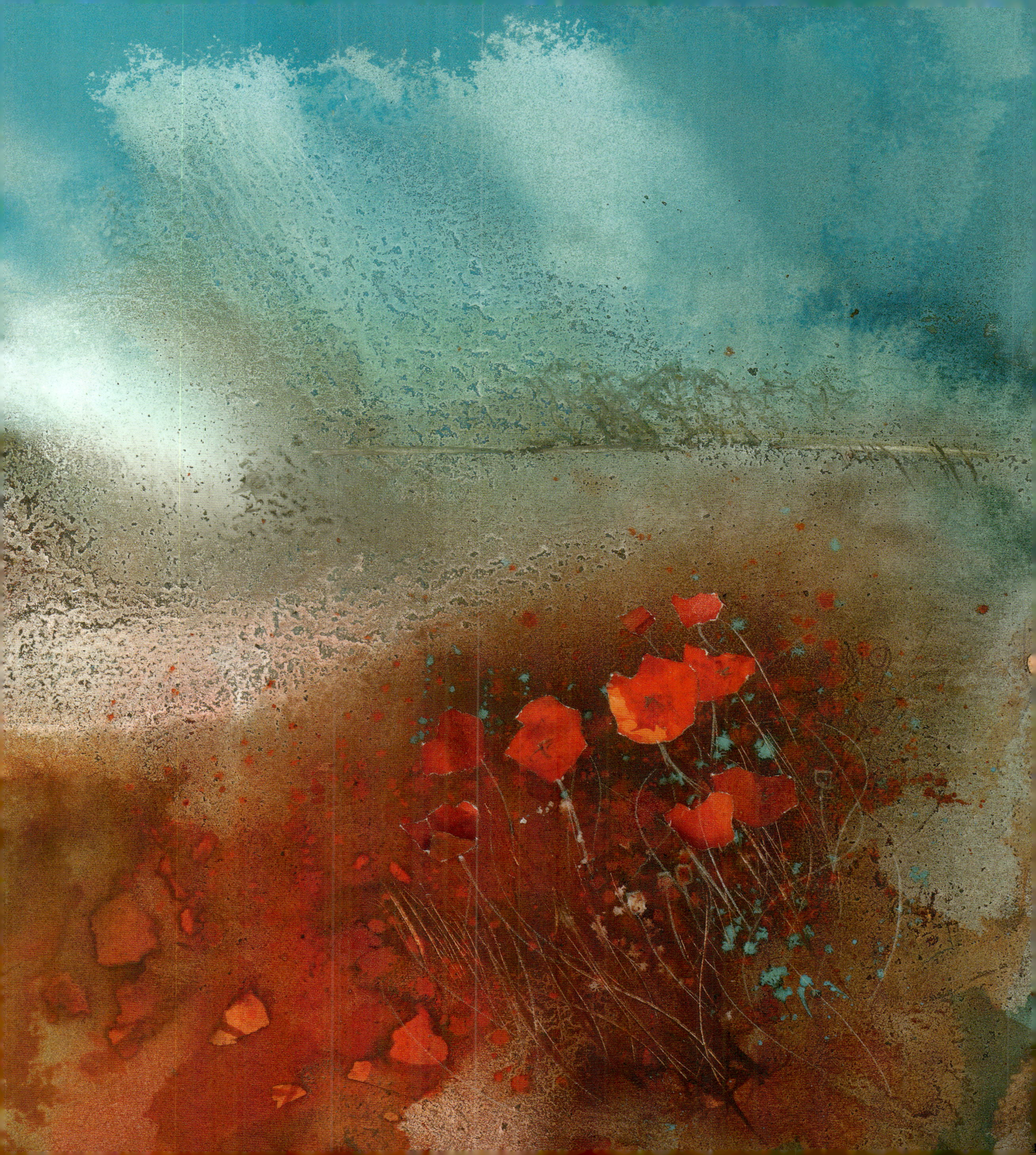

Varying your palette

In the demonstration on pages 28–29 I used colours that reflected the reality of the subject. Now see how you can make more atmospheric interpretations by changing the palette. For example, use magentas rather than reds for the flower shapes, mauve hedges in the distance and a pale pink or black sky. Make your paintings dark, hard-edged and dramatic or dreamlike, soft and whimsical. How about combining colours that clash such as orange with purple? Alternatively create more harmonious colour themes using either cool or warm hues only. The paintings shown here demonstrate quite restrained palettes but having written this I am now itching to do other versions in a more flamboyant way!

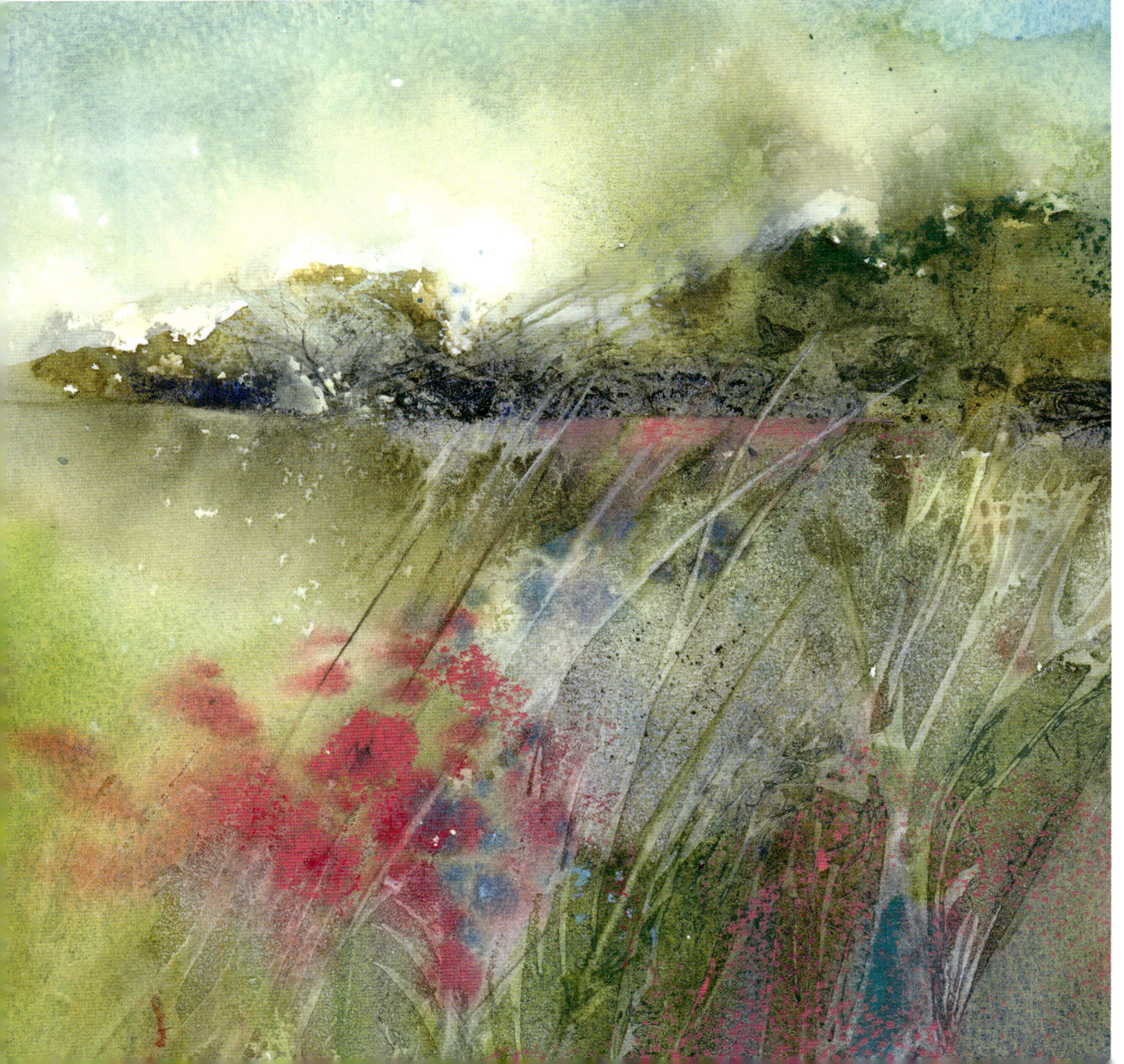

◁ Of Intermingling Hues

In this loose interpretation I wanted to investigate further ideas to describe pale grasses amid a darker wash. My demonstration largely concentrated on the organic textures of the flowers. The grasses were merely hinted at with a few fine rigger strokes, supplemented with some lines of crayon. To take this further here I used cling film on top of a first wash, stretching it into concertina lines to suggest grasses as well as adding movement (see pages 104–105). This broke up the watercolour into a more abstract design. I worked into some of the marks afterwards so that it is difficult to see which parts are cling film and which are handpainted.

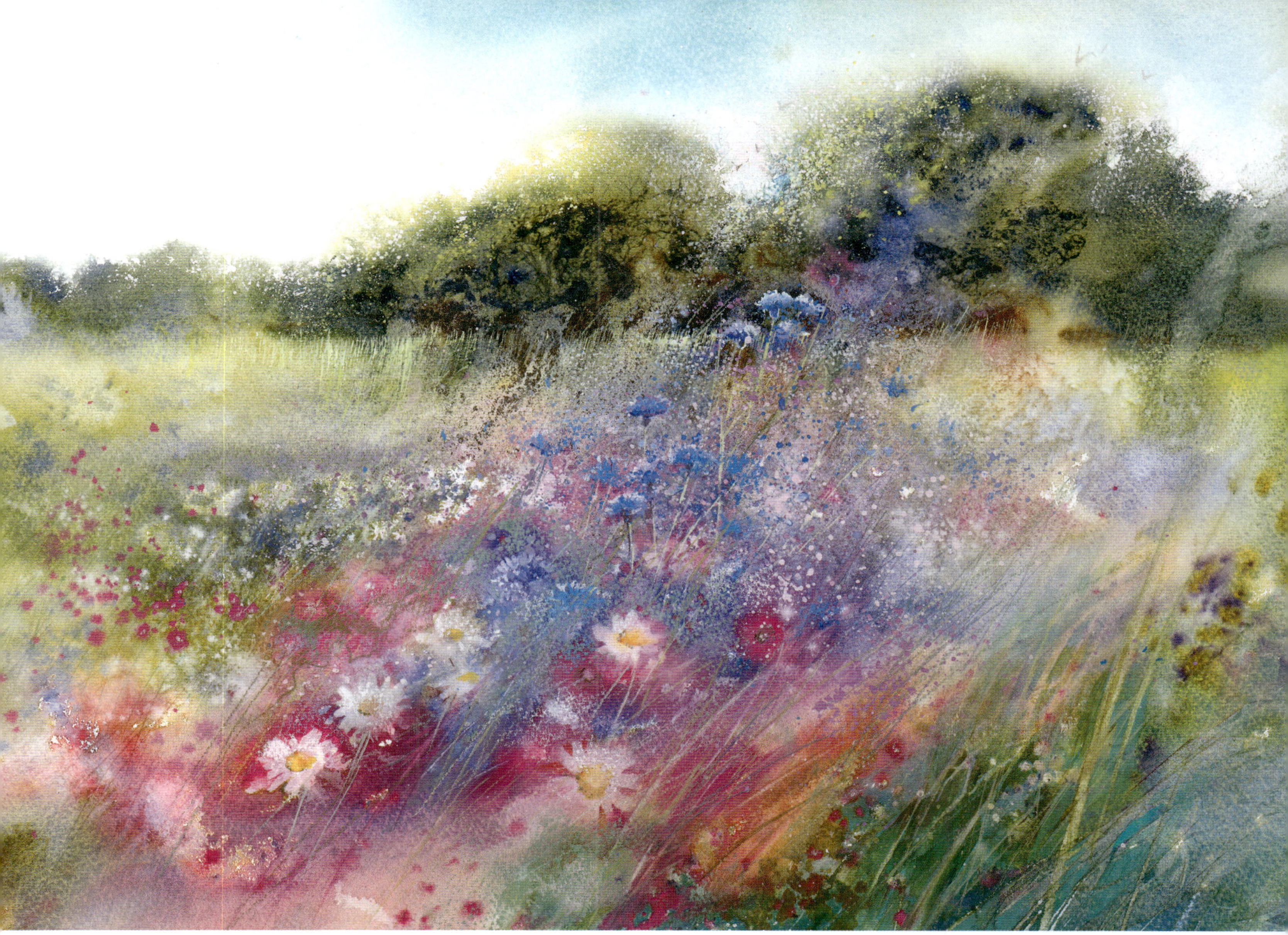

△ Spreading Herbs and Flowerets Bright

If you sit in a wildflower meadow you will see and feel the flowers and grasses sway and ripple in the breeze. There is birdsong, the buzzing of insects and the scurrying of small creatures. In other words, it is not a stage set – it is full of movement and activity. I tried to interpret this energy and life in my painting by using diagonal, directional sweeps of colour. I also used crayon on top of the watercolour washes to create a broken shimmer that gave the picture a 'buzz'.

Adding collage details

I needed a focal point for this interpretation of lavender fields and held various plant stems over some preliminary landscape exercises as a device to assist my decision-making. I chose some cow parsley for the foreground as a contrast to the stunning lavender colour. The challenge was deciding how to paint these lacy pale shapes against the coloured background. One option to create this complicated design would be to use masking fluid applied in a textural way, such as splattering it on then painting a wash over it when dry. For a softer look you could splash white gouache into a damp wash to give starry splodges, reminiscent of lacy petal clusters. I used gouache here but decided to develop it by applying collage on top of the dry paint to turn it into something a bit more unusual.

Collage can be applied either over or before your watercolour to achieve a quirky style. To continue the meadow theme you could cut or tear small circles of printed or painted paper to build up patterns of wildflowers on a background. They do not need to be realistic shapes – simply decorative. You could even use bits of photographs, cuttings or words from a garden magazine. With a bit of imagination your choices are limitless. Use PVA glue or acrylic matte medium to apply collage, taking care to avoid smearing any excess on the painted surface. Try to choose materials that are appropriate to your mental description of the subject, just as you would do when using paint marks.

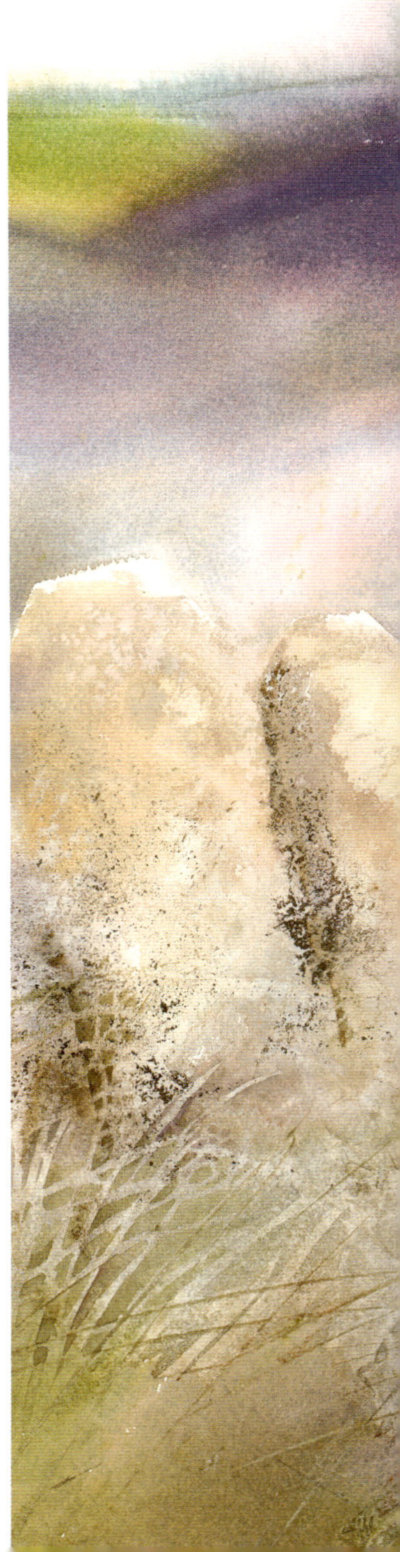

▷ **Cow Parsley and Lavender**
Bold washes describe this soft-edged patchwork of fields. I applied collage selectively on top to create quirky interest and definition, using a delicate torn paper with holes and lacy ragged edges that echoed the ethereal quality of the flower.

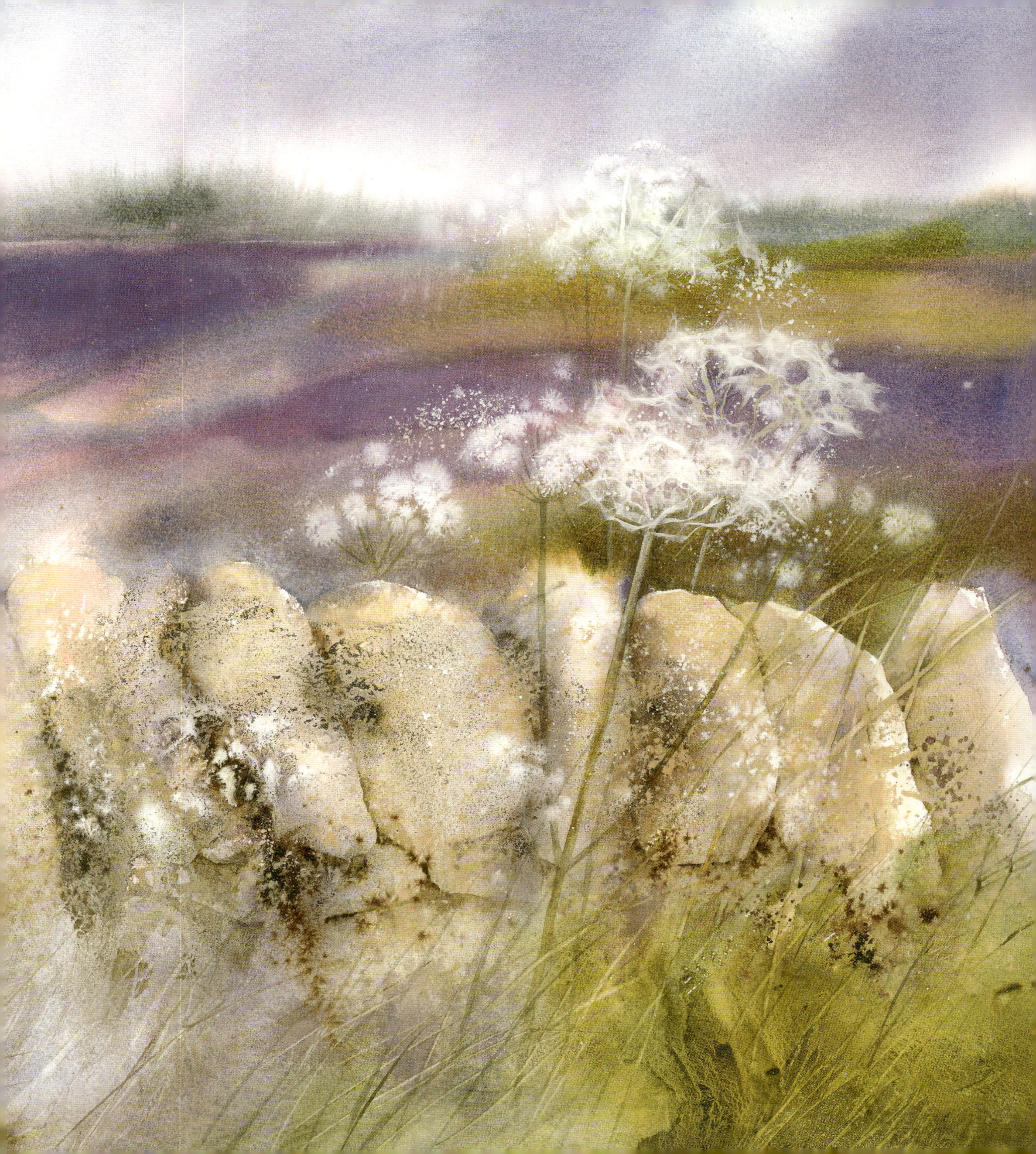

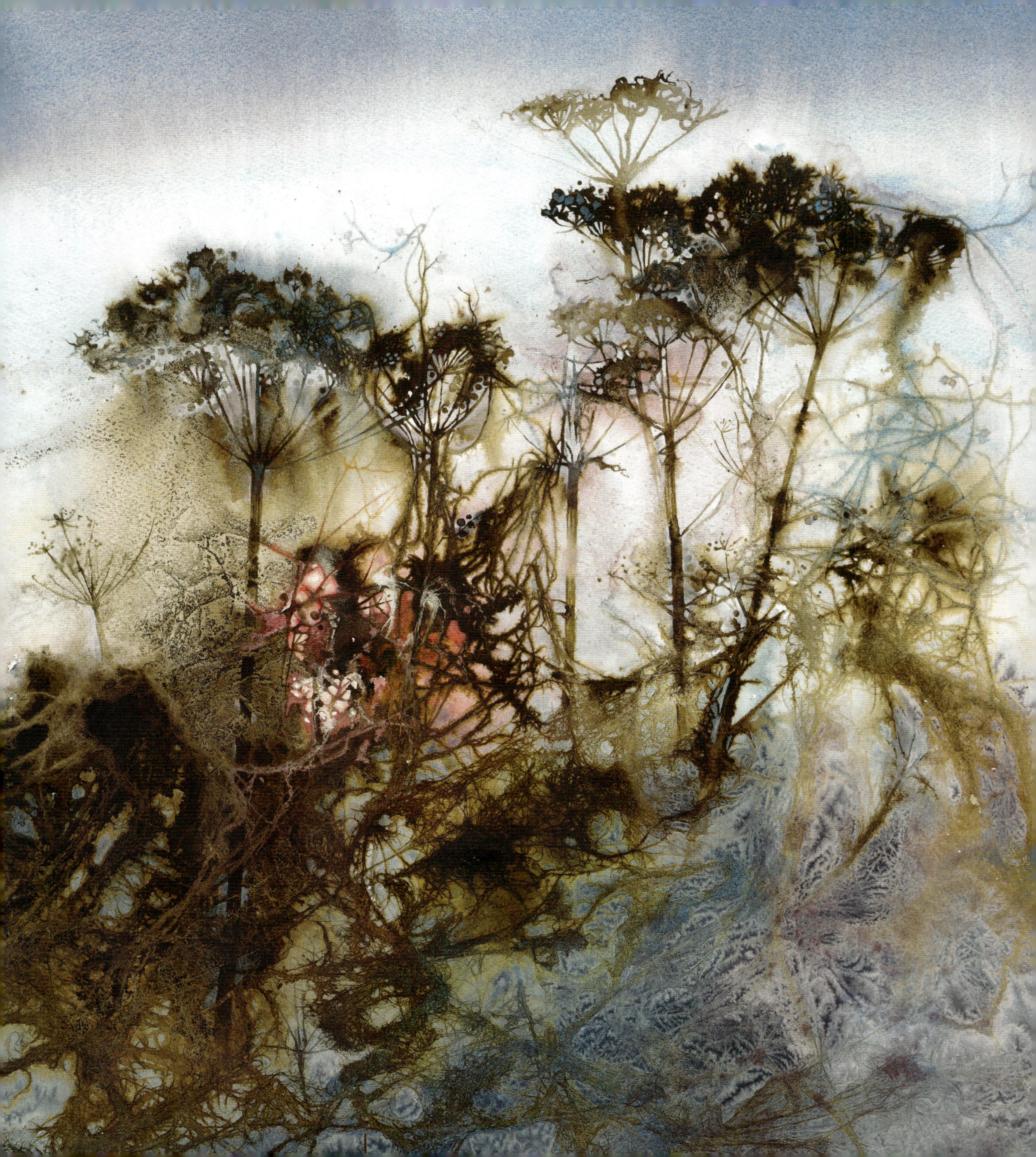

Expressive mark-making

Plants with complex forms can be confusing to paint if you try to analyse every detail. Instead, look at the overall personality of the patterns and shapes then find marks to summarize this. The essential character of a summer hogweed is, for me, the floral clouds of lacy texture. In contrast, a winter hogweed is very hard-edged, with the umbels, stalks and seeds having a graphic, tactile quality. Your visual summaries will vary according to your interests and sketches will help to clarify these. My hogweed explorations confirm my enjoyment of their linear patterns in relation to the tangles of other plants. I am more interested in the stylized holes and negative spaces than the botanical accuracy of the subject itself.

When you sketch, try to use mark-making techniques that encapsulate the subject in a shorthand stylized way such as scribbles to indicate tangles or jabbed pencil marks to represent seeds. The profile of an intricate shape like a winter seedhead might be indicated in random serrated or zigzag patterns. This could be simplified further to a silhouette punctuated by circles to represent holes and gaps. Your creative language may feel artificial at first but it will become more natural the more you practise. Then you can translate drawn marks into painted versions. This process will help you to ignore some of the overwhelming information that the factual side of your brain is grappling with and help you to look at subjects in a simpler way.

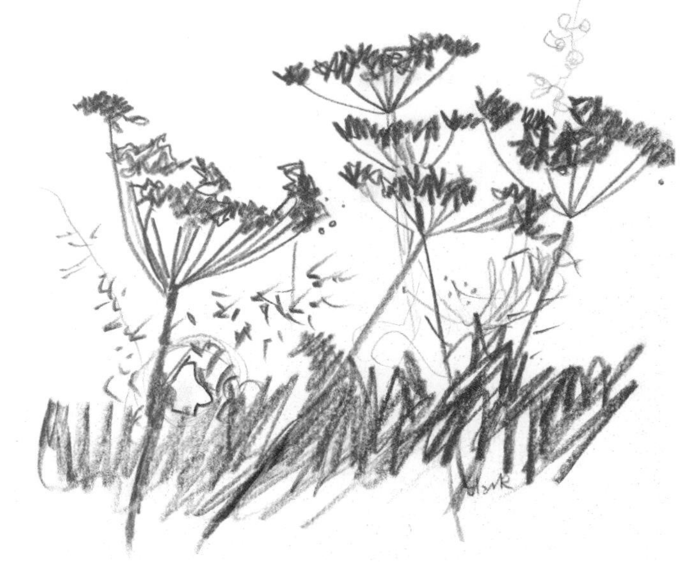

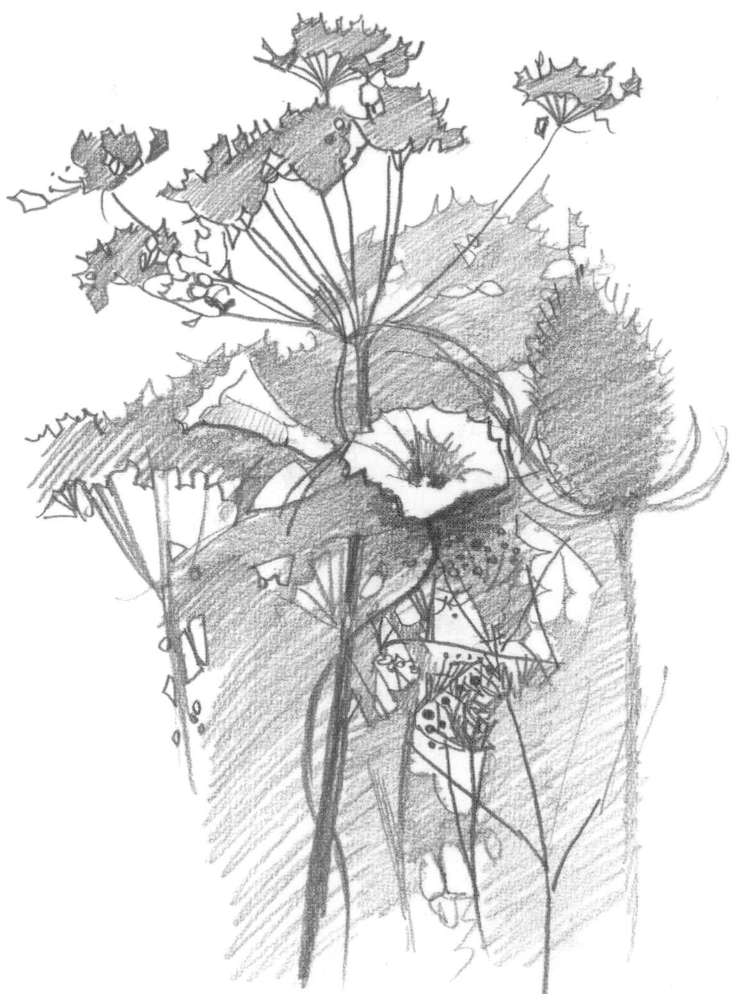

◁ Wayside Tapestry

I observed the shapes, patterns and negative spaces of winter hogweed in relationship to its habitat through a series of pencil drawings. These enabled me to paint confidently with freedom and expression in the watercolour version.

Using your imagination

The information for the hogweed interpretation on page 38 was selected from sketches. If you inject some extra imagination and depart from your reference material you can push these ideas further. In the painting shown opposite small circles describe seeds. The 'sky' is patterned and the negative shapes and marks are exaggerated or embellished. The drab greens of real life have been discarded and a new colour scheme invented.

This hogweed is pulled out of a backdrop of rusts and earthy hues with hints of mauves, pinks and greys. These are not colours seen in one particular 'view'. They are colours based on memories of chocolate-coloured ploughed fields, blackberry-studded waysides and citrus sunsets. These ideas are moving towards a more abstract approach and there is a whole section about this later. I have positioned this interpretation here for you to compare with the version on page 38. This juxtaposition highlights the fact that an abstract approach should not be seen as something separate to the other work in the book – it is merely an extension of these thoughts.

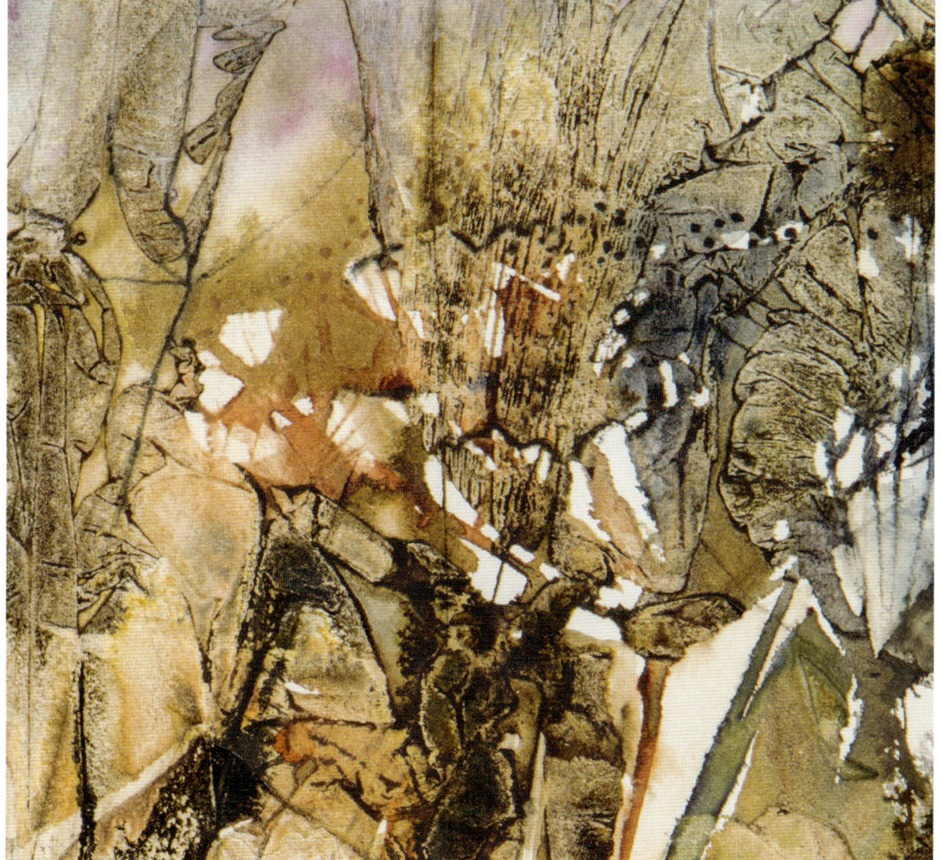

◁ **Winter Seedhead Patterns**
(detail, stage 1)
This detail shows a small area of the painting before I worked into it. I used my imagination to turn some of the shapes and patterns into designs that suggested and echoed forms rather than replicated the skeleton of a winter seed head.

▷ **Winter Seedhead Patterns**
The seedheads in this interpretation are decorative and less 'real' than those featured in *Wayside Tapestry* on page 38. This is because I concentrated even more on the abstract descriptive qualities. I developed the shapes out of a pattern created by placing cling film in a wet wash (see pages 104–105). My interest was in the network of negative and positive marks and lines that built the tangle of pattern.

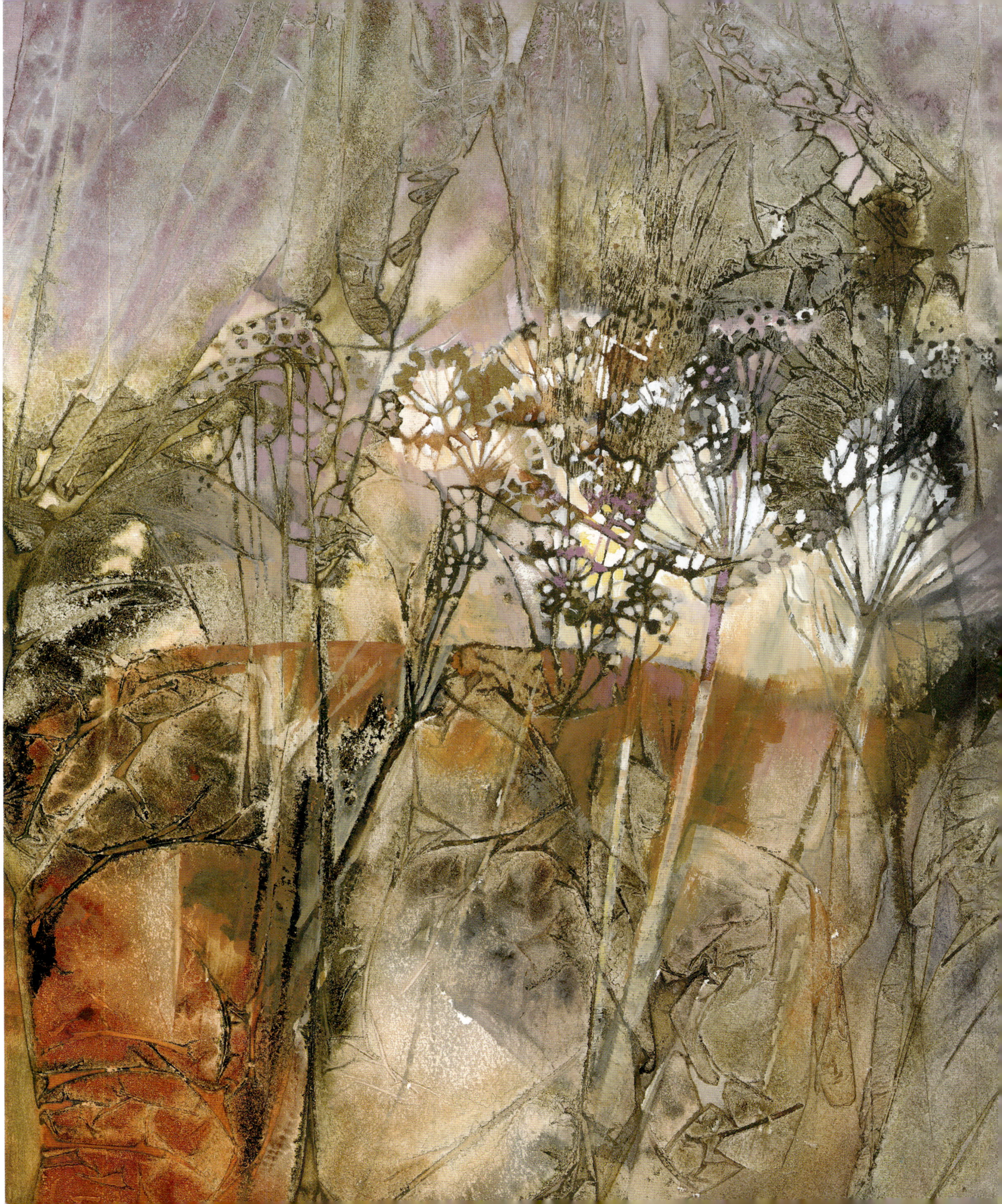

Project: WHITE FLOWER

This project is about defining a pale shape, whether a
flower or other subject, by surrounding it with loose
washes and shapes. I created vignettes, maintaining
plenty of white paper, but you can paint to the edges if
you prefer. Start with an uncomplicated form such as
this blossom to help you to concentrate on the qualities
of the paint. Loosen up before you begin with quick
exercises, like the one shown here, to do your planning.
The washing-out technique (below) works well on
Saunders Waterford CP (Not) – if you are using a
different paper practise first, as some soft papers
allow too much paint to be washed away.

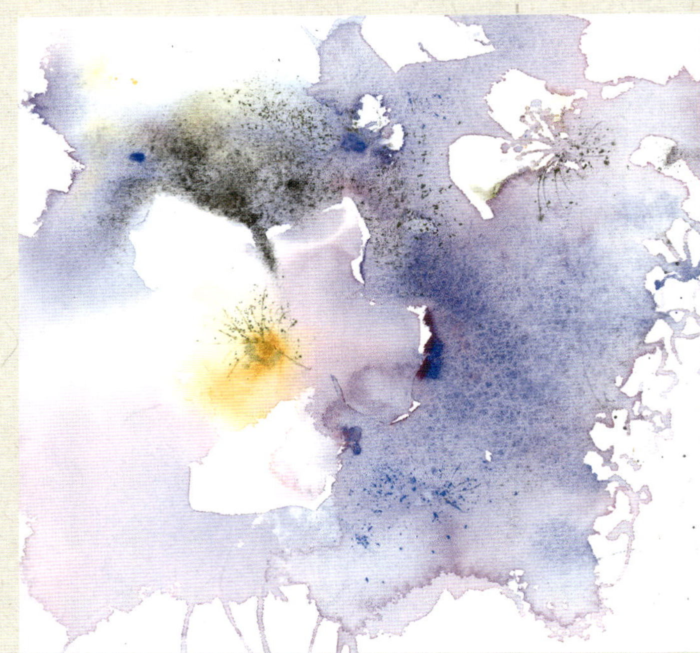

1   Begin by mixing your watercolour thicker than usual
    to a creamy consistency and painting simple solid
    leaf shapes on dry paper. I used a combination of
    French Ultramarine and Quinacridone Gold. Now
    have fun watching the paint dry! The timing is critical
    as there needs to be a combination of dry and damp
    patches within the shapes. Be guided by the fact that
    paint is shiny when wet but dries matt. Wash some
    paint away by directing a stream of water into the
    shape. Angle the paper to help the fluid run off the
    edge away from the areas you want to keep clean
    and dry. The finished leaf should have soft textures
    within crisp, dark edges.

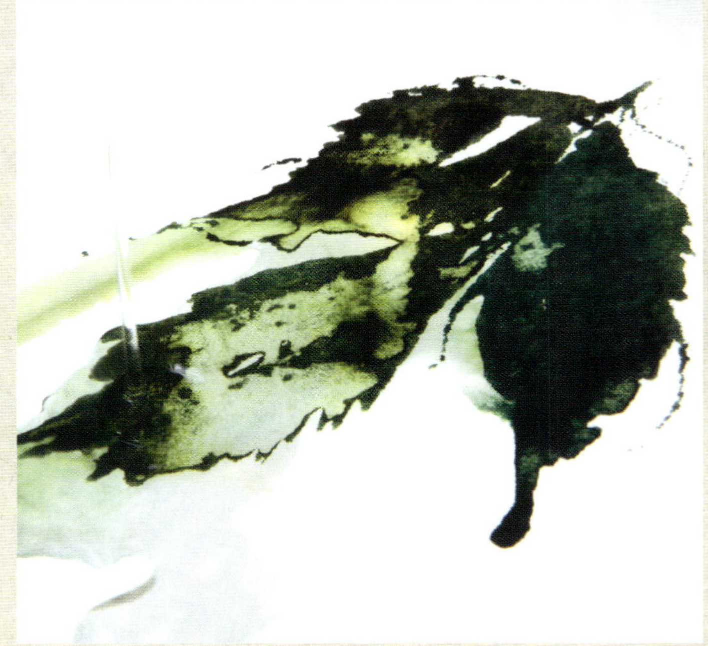

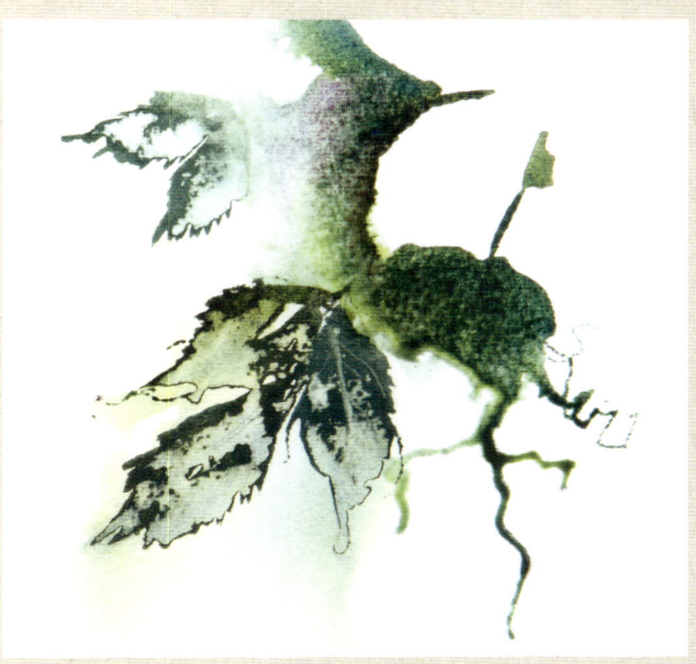

2 If you prefer a more controlled method for the leaves, you could paint them and blot out patches of colour to create a similar texture. If you take this route, try softening some of the edges to make them less graphic on the white background. While the leaves are still wet, continue to use a similar wash of colour around the contours of the petals. Lightly draw these first if it helps you. This detail shows how I also dragged excess paint into twiggy lines using the wrong end of the brush. You can paint these details later if there is not enough excess wet paint to do this.

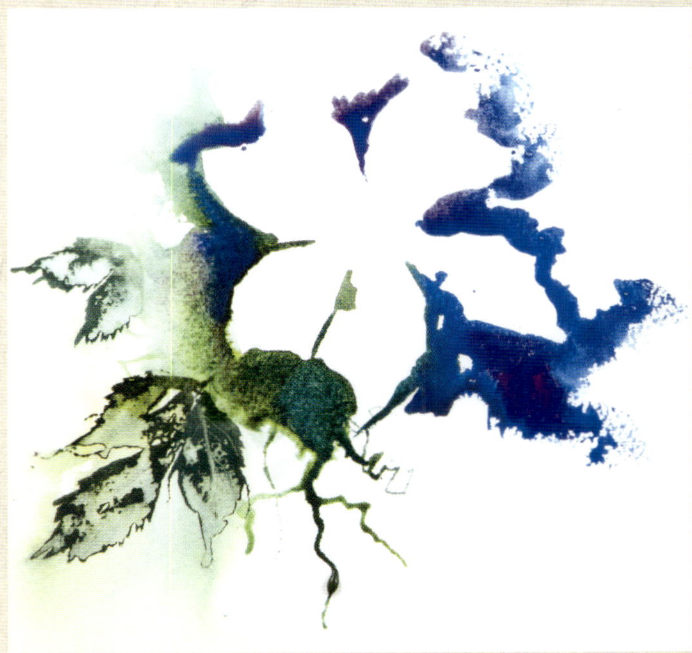

3 Change colours to blue only as you move around the blossom, keeping its edges crisp but creating rough textures at the wash perimeters. If you work slowly, consider making the areas where you stop and start into meaningful shapes that might suggest the edges of flowers or leaves. That way it will not matter if the paint dries. I have worked on dry paper for a crisp look. You could also explore dampening some of the paper if you want to create a softer, flowing atmosphere.

4 Continue the background, adding some Cobalt
   Violet and another version of the green, this time
   with a higher proportion of the gold than the blue.
   See how the edges of the wash end in frilly patterns.
   In my mind this suggests further blossom.

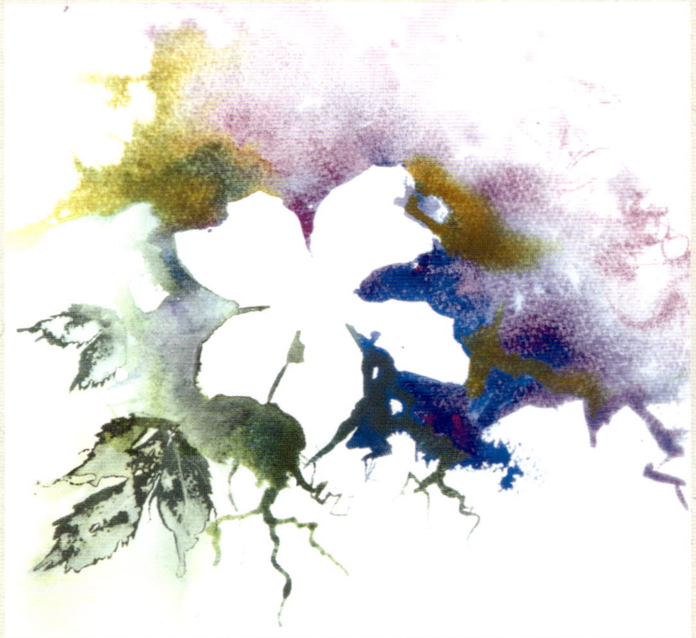

5 If you paint shadows into petals while the background
   is still wet you can carefully avoid the edge and keep
   them tidy or allow your brush to touch it and let the
   wash flood into the petal as shown here. It is a bit
   messy but that suits me! Crisp edges step forward
   to be a focal point and soft ones retire into the
   background. A balance can be achieved by letting
   the surrounding wash dry a little then using a damp
   brush to blend some of the edges.

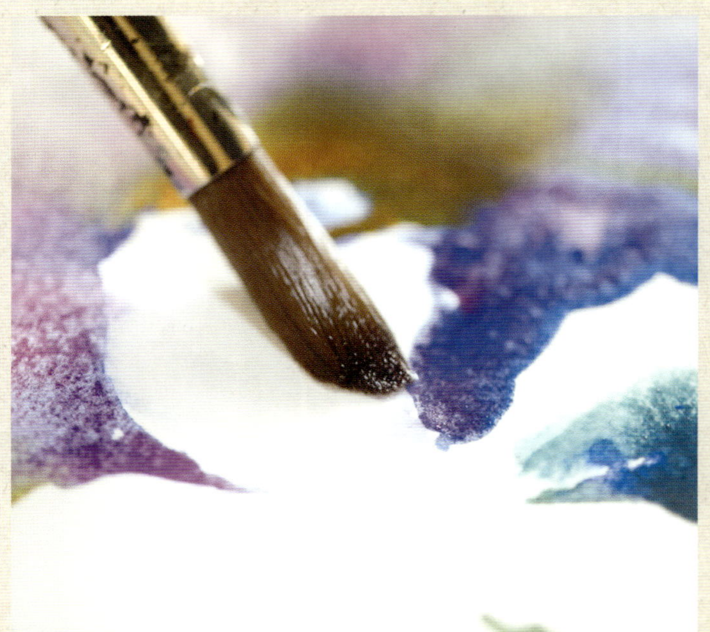

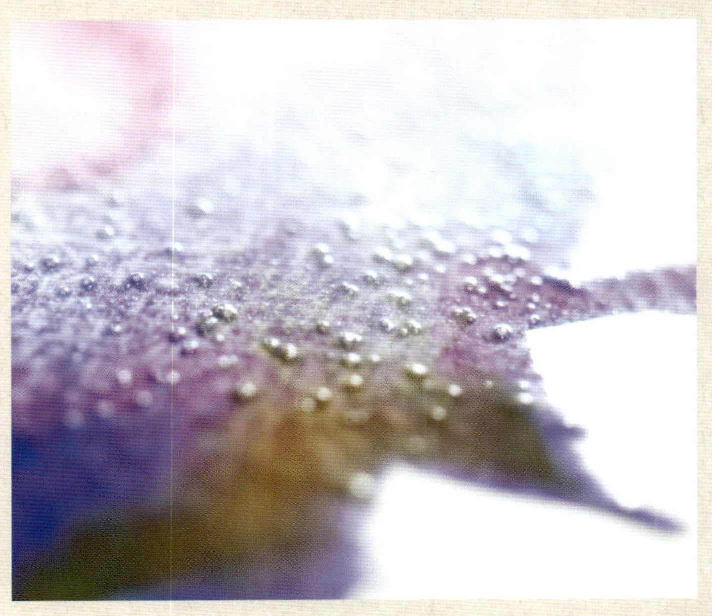

6 If you would like to add texture to your background, sprinkle coarse table salt into it, but only if the paint is still damp. The tiny florets of texture will not develop if the paint is too wet or dry. Be sparing with the amount, using only individual crystals as illustrated. Let it dry naturally then brush the salt off. The effect will vary but an example is shown in the background of *Blossom 2* on page 47. In this context the salt patterns suggest further small petal clusters.

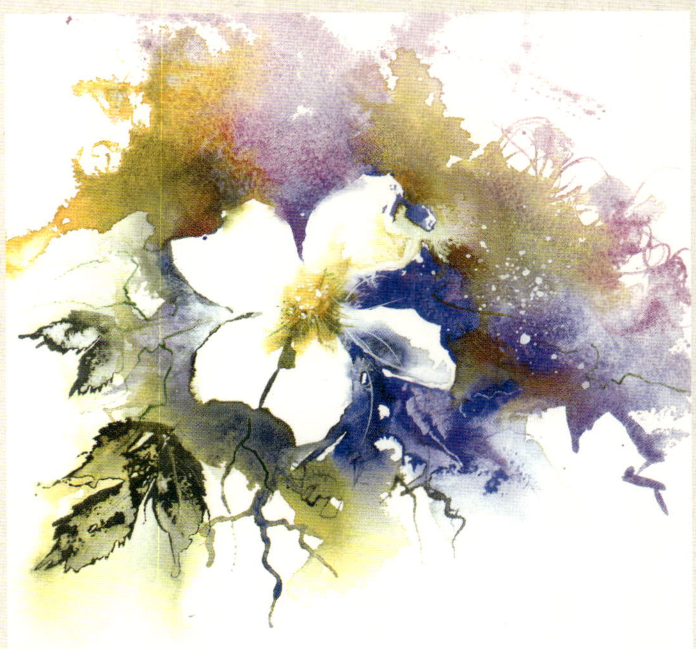

7 Work on the blossom by softening edges or adding shadows without getting too engrossed in the 'real' details. The idea is to interpret rather than replicate the subject. Dampen the middle and drift in some colour to establish the centre. Keep it soft so that it belongs to the flower and does not look stuck on. Let this dry then add dots and marks to represent stamens. See page 46 for suggestions on how to do this. Add dark watercolour or pale opaque gouache stamens to suit the painting rather than the reality of your reference or still-life arrangement.

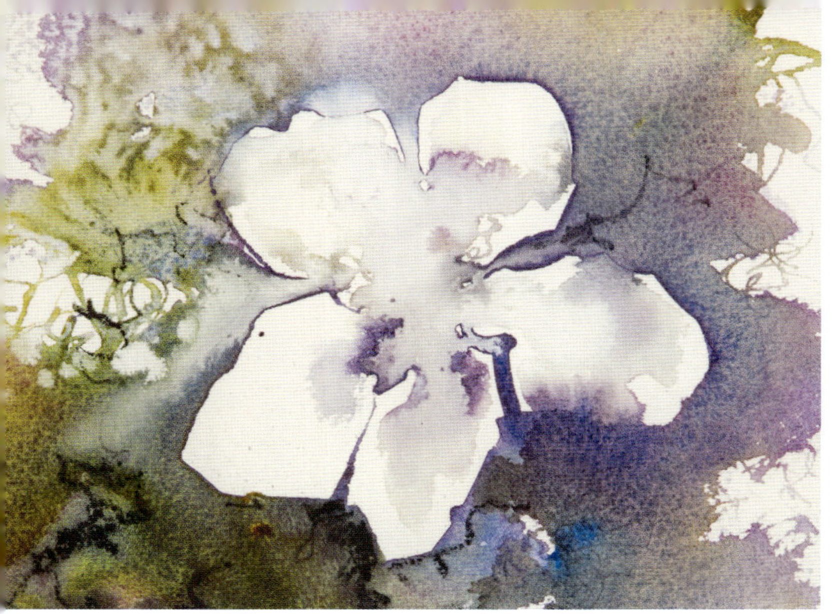

Techniques

Flower centres

This is a close-up of *Blossom 2* before the centre was added. Flowers without this final information are like faces without eyes. See what expression you can put into your flower faces using different techniques to paint centres that suit their mood or characteristics.

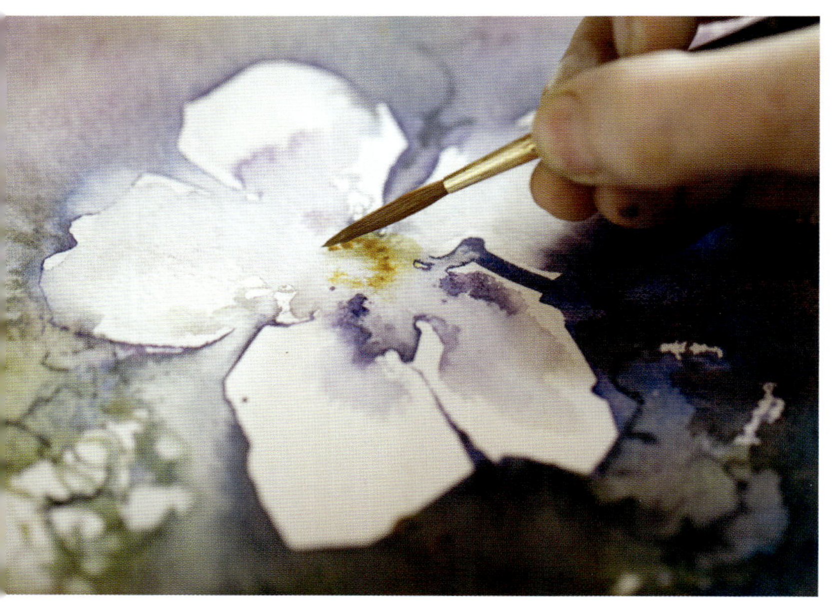

Adding details

Once you have established some soft colour in your centre, use a fine-pointed brush to dot in small amounts of more concentrated pigment. I normally recommend holding your brush loosely, high up the handle, to achieve flowing brush marks but it is better to grip it lower down and more firmly when you need more control for details. Stamens can also be added using a rigger brush.

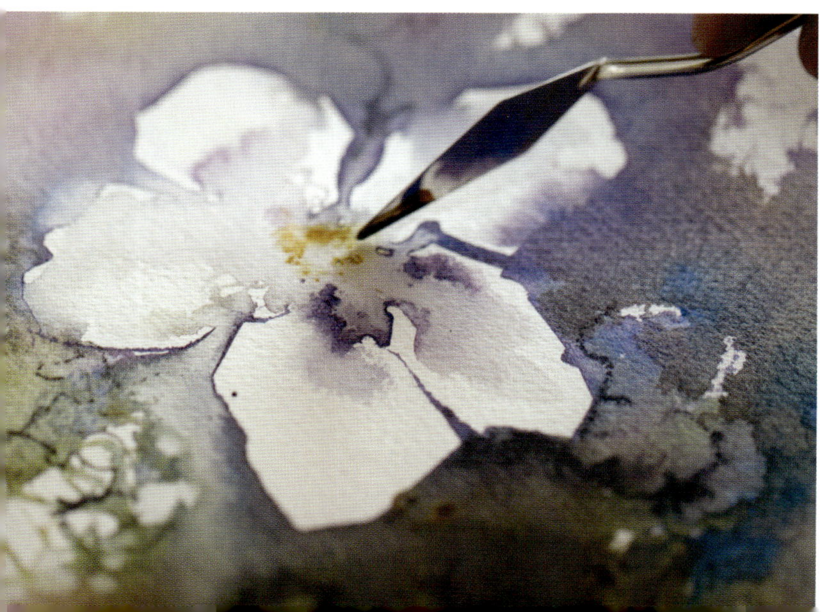

Stamens

For a loose interpretation of the stamens, apply ink or paint with the edge of a palette knife dipped in pigment. You can draw linear marks first then add dots by splattering with the palette knife (see page 31). Do protect the painting with bits of paper to control where these marks go! Compare the finished centre of *Blossom 2* with the one in stage 7 of the previous demonstration to see which you prefer.

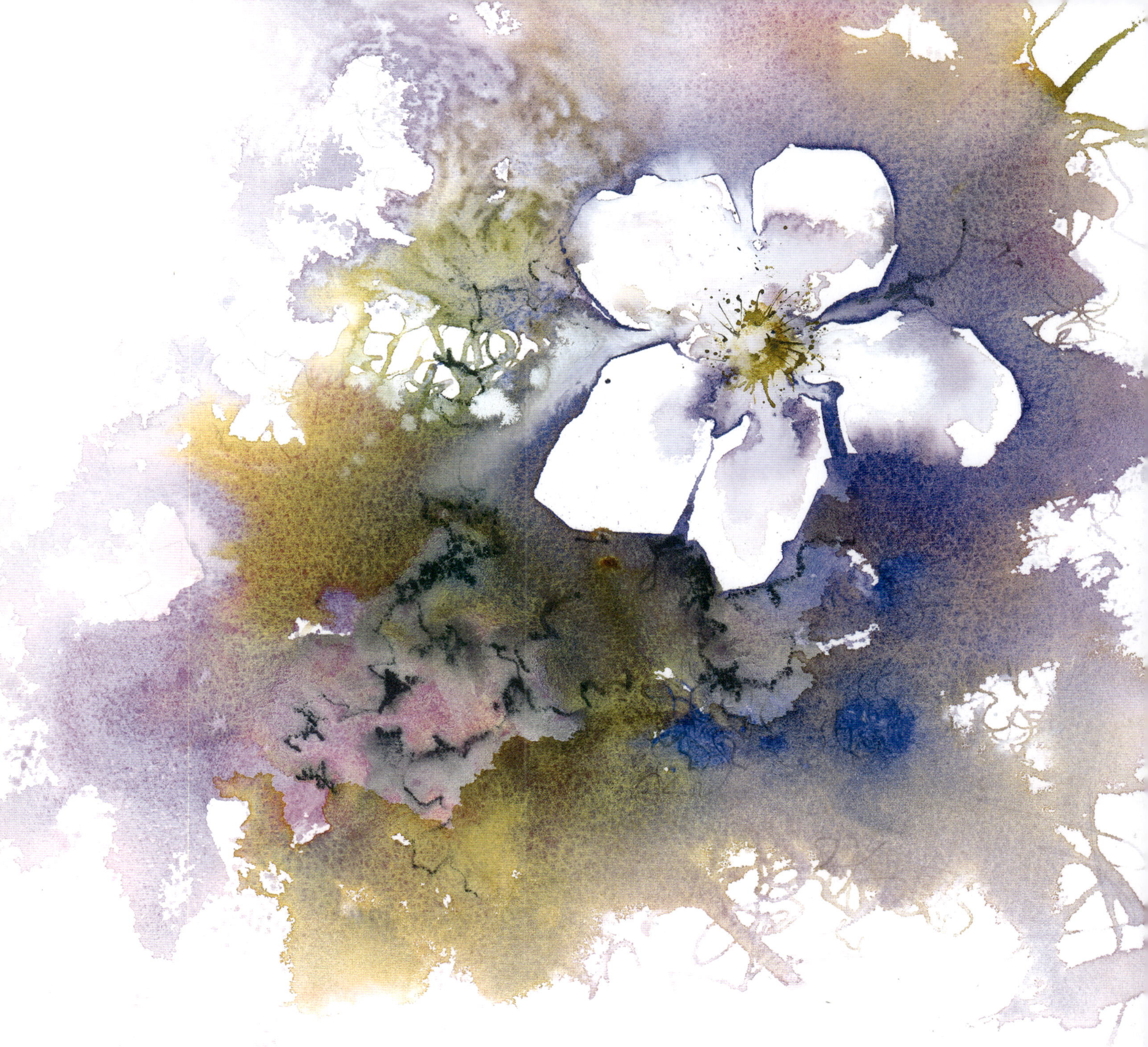

In this interpretation I changed the mood, using a different technique to paint the centre. I also used another blue so that there is a subtle change of atmosphere and temperature. The effect is more shadowy, especially where the background wash has run inwards, creating cloudy effects in the petals. Pencil marks scribbled in the background suggest other flowers such as lilac and salt textures intensify this idea.

Experimenting with different surfaces

The surface you use has a major effect on the finished appearance of your picture. Finding one you like is an important aspect to watercolour painting. You may value the flow of silky-smooth textures, or you may prefer the more rugged effects of a rough paper. It is worth buying single sheets of various paper types and brands with different characteristics and doing similar interpretations on each of them to see which you prefer. Even when you do discover a favourite, continue exploring other options to avoid getting stuck in a rut. I still love Saunders Waterford paper but have recently also experimented with different kinds of board. I am really enjoying the novelty and excitement of seeing the watercolour react on a surface in new ways, forcing me to adapt how I apply the paint.

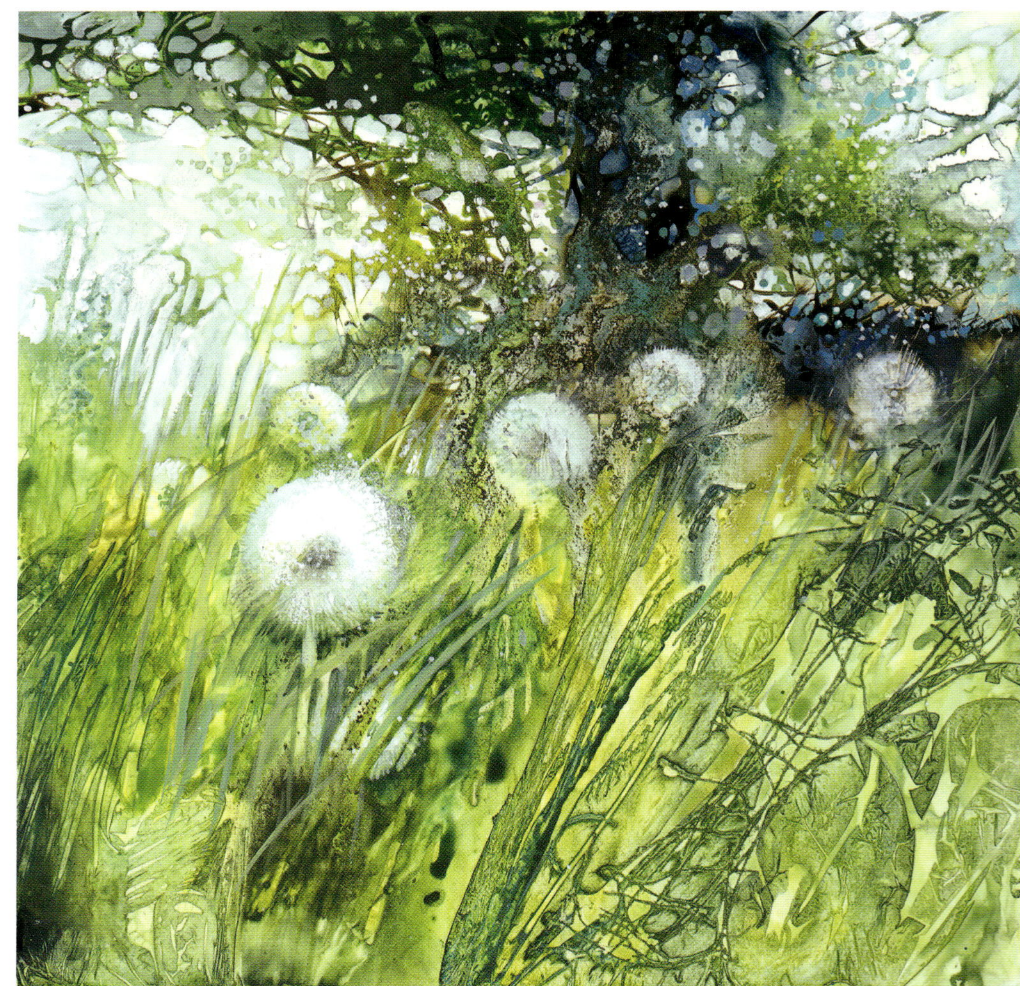

▷ Meadow Time

This interpretation was made on Ampersand Claybord. I found that the paint slips around on the smooth, non-absorbent surface but textures are intensified, with more contrast than usual. The surface is great for depicting a pale subject such as a dandelion clock as it is easy to wipe away the watercolour back to the off-white board.

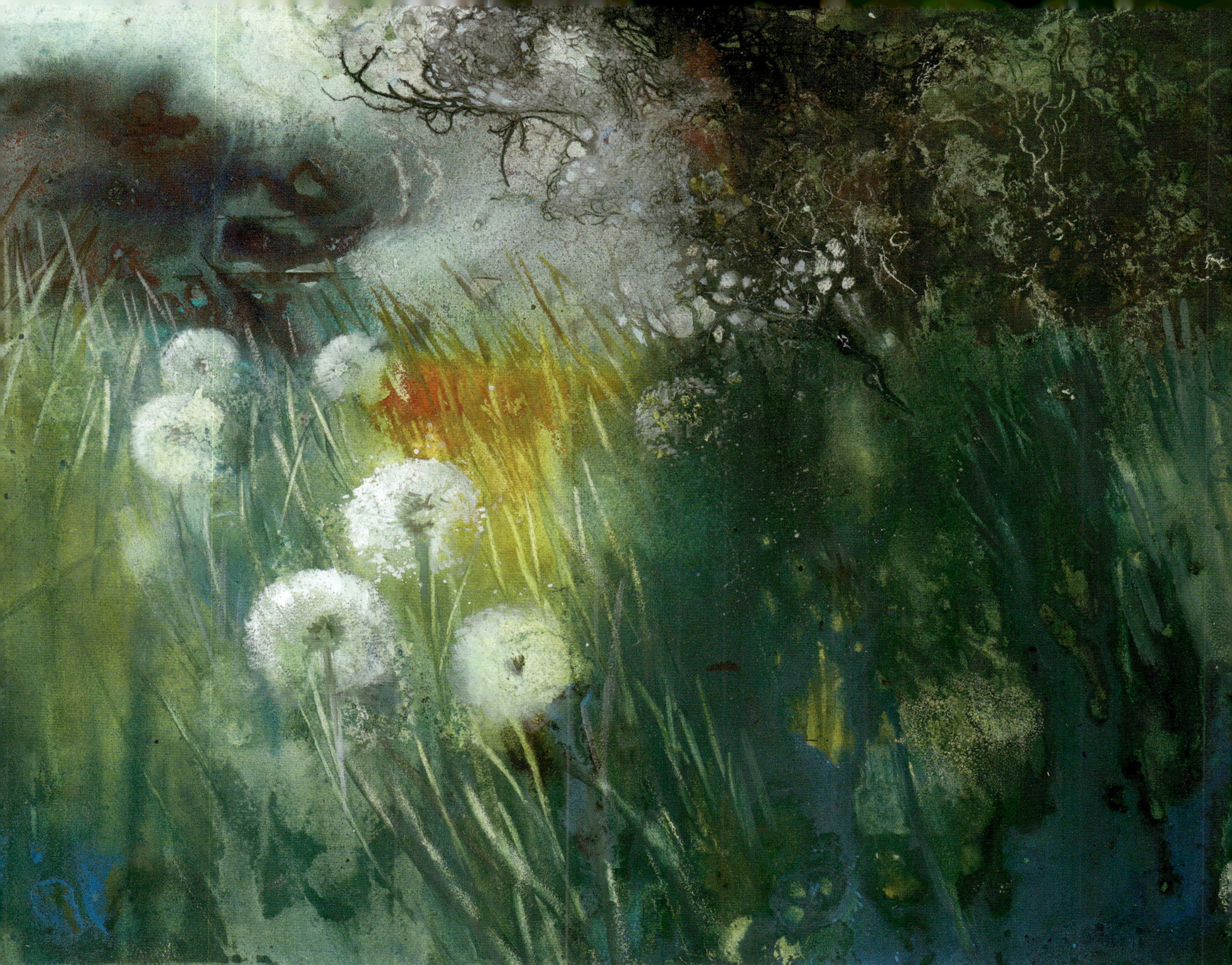

△ Clockwise

The subtly absorbent surface of the
Ampersand Aquabord lends itself to many
layers of really misty, dreamy washes of
colour that can be built up in a way that
would be difficult on traditional paper.
I lifted some colour away to create the
clocks but made the shapes whiter with
added gouache.

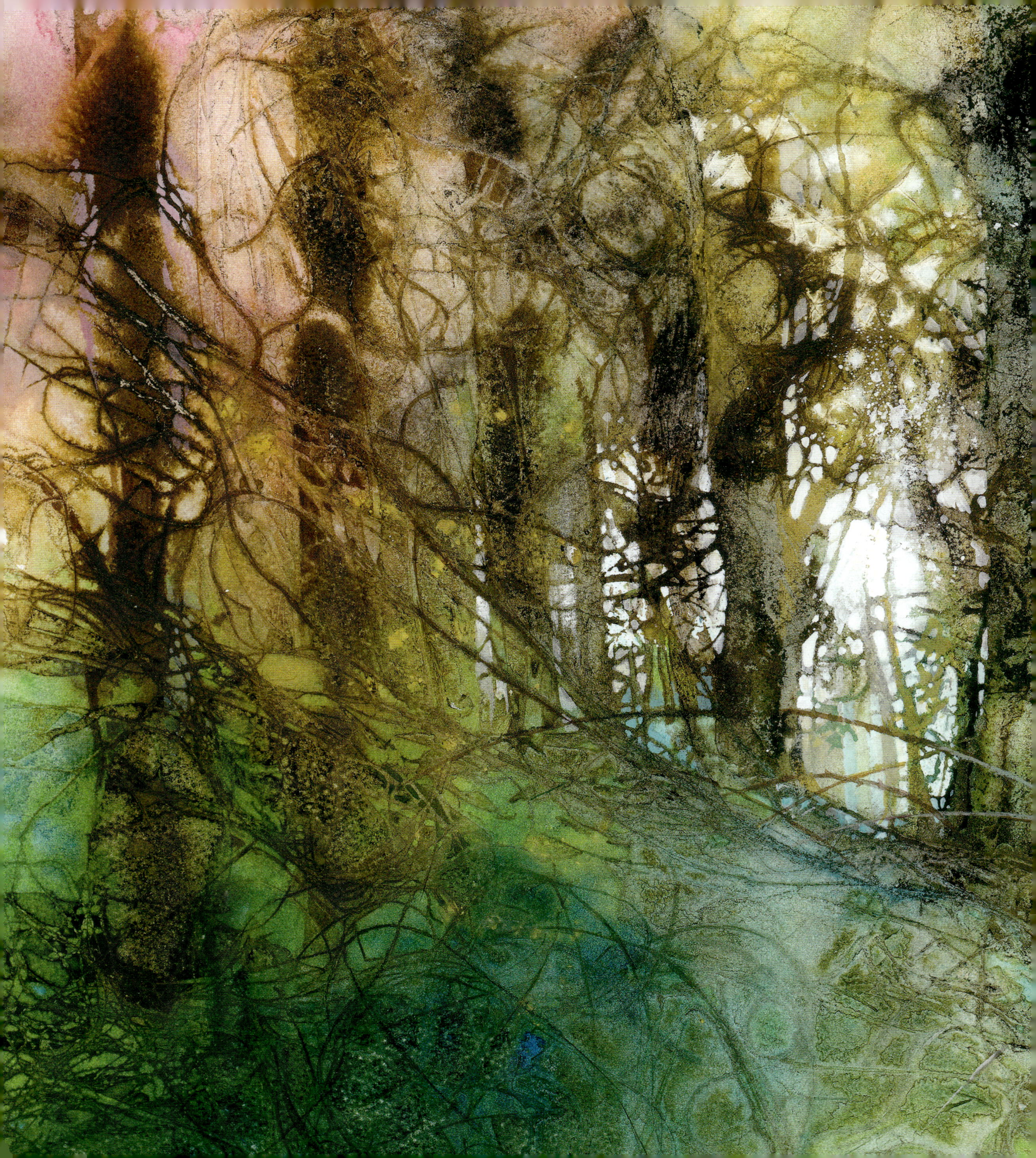

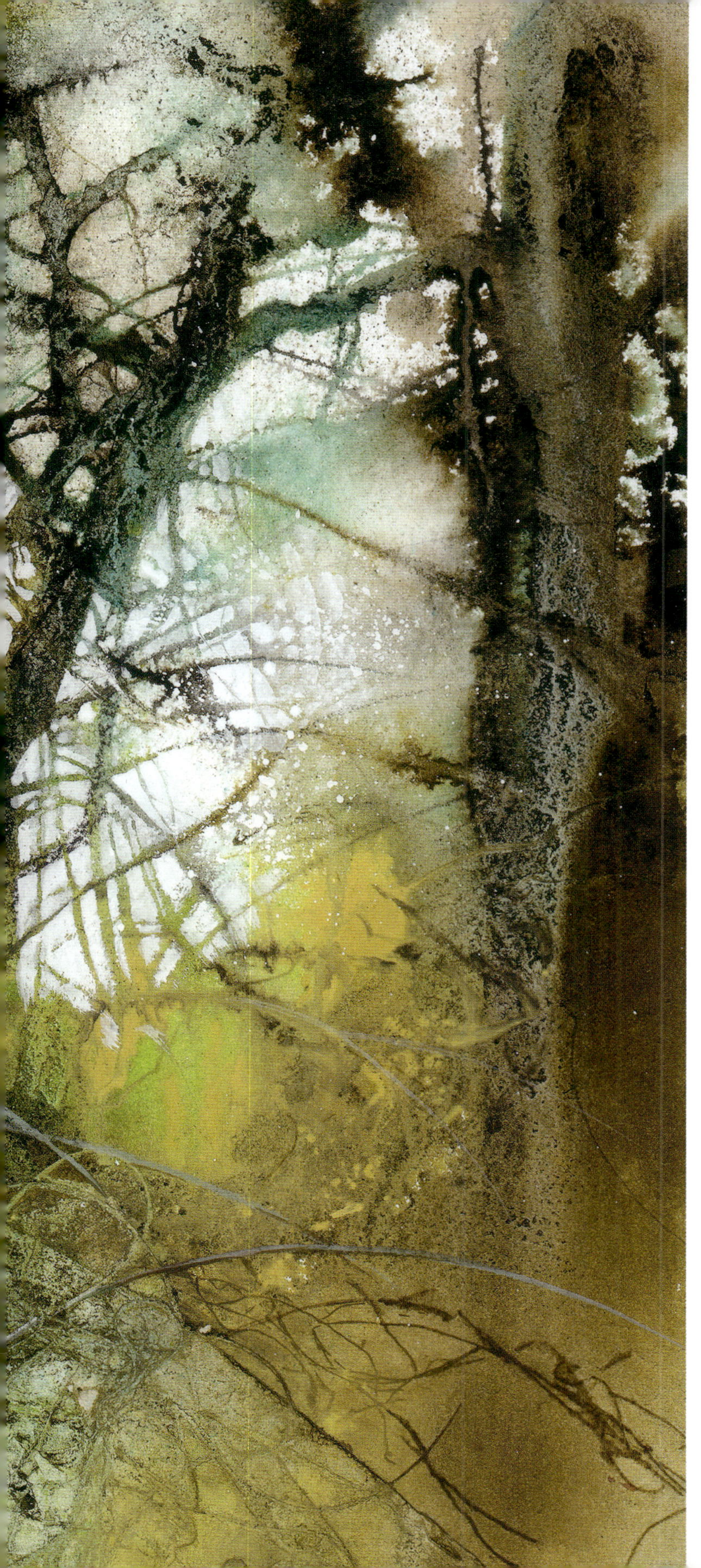

Trees and hedgerow

The organic shapes and patterns that are found in trees and hedges provide us with wonderful opportunities to play with textures, flowing paint and mark-making. Tune into nature and let it feed your branches of imagination and nourish your creative roots. I have designed this project around the kind of trees that grow in the countryside where I live and the ancient hedgerows that edge the farmland. Explore your local landscape and translate these thoughts to fit your own world. In Britain, trees vary throughout the seasons but even without these seasonal changes you can transform your interpretations. Use scale, shape, colour or the moods of dark dusk or pale dawn – and remember that 'mighty oaks from little acorns grow'.

"WHEN I JUDGE ART, I TAKE MY PAINTING AND PUT IT NEXT TO A GOD-MADE OBJECT LIKE A TREE OR FLOWER. IF IT CLASHES, IT IS NOT ART."

PAUL CÉZANNE

◁ The Tangled Wood

Project: AUTUMN HAWTHORN

Make a habit of planning your colours before you begin painting. When choosing the colours to use for a tree it can be helpful to have some natural reference material in front of you alongside any photographs or sketches, especially when painting indoors. The colours I used in my loosening-up exercise of an autumn hawthorn tree were based on the hues of the leaves and berries picked from the tree itself. If you create records of colour in this way throughout the year it will help to keep you connected to your subject if you have to paint it out of season.

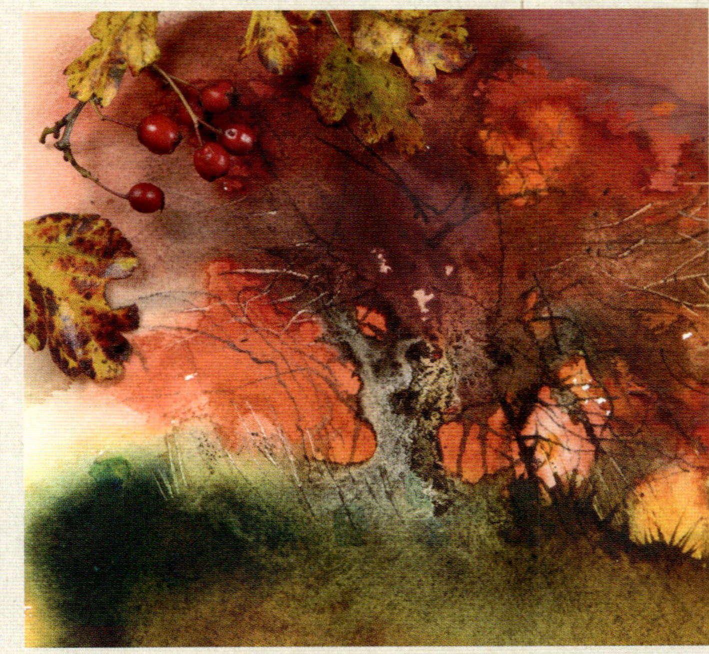

1   Choose combinations of colour to represent the sky, tree and land. Remember that the sky does not have to be blue and the colour of the land can also be invented. To enhance a warm autumn theme, try using warm yellows and golds for the sky or a paler shade of pink than the tree itself. I used Quinacridone Gold with Perylene Maroon and Perylene Green. The colours will all move, blend and change as the picture evolves. First, roughly establish each area with colour washes, not worrying if you lose edges and definition at this stage. Allow the colours to flow from one area to the next. Try to keep the paint moving and fill the whole picture so that the washes do not dry in hard-edged patches.

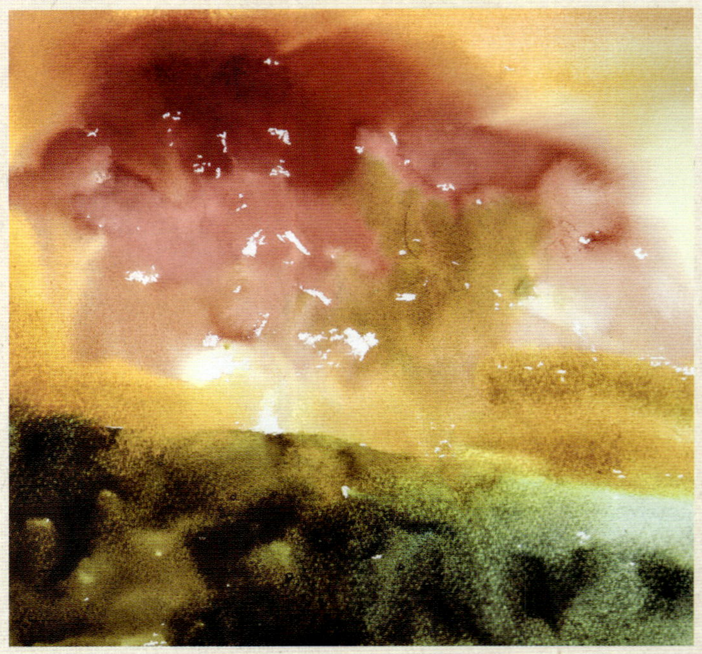

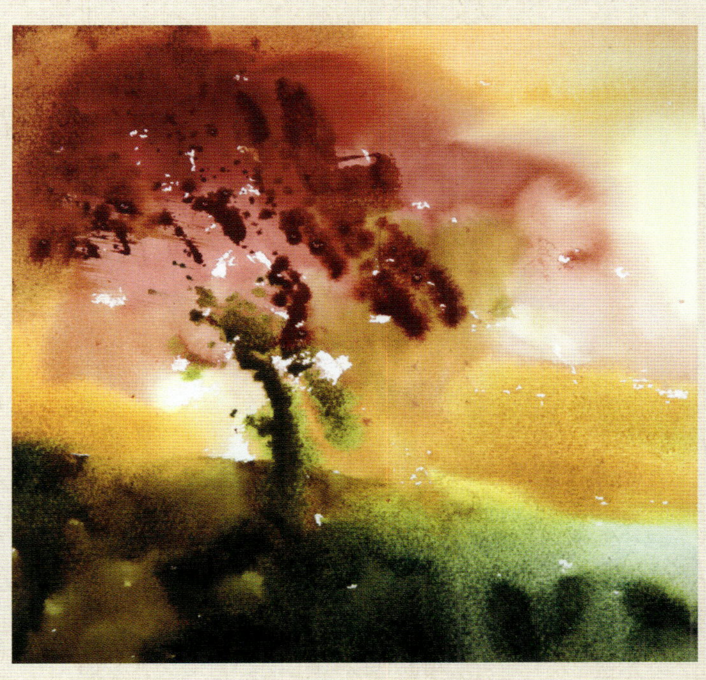

2 While the first rough wash is still damp you can go back on top with stronger colour to begin defining the autumn foliage and basic trunk shape. Keep the watercolour rich but wet enough to allow you to splash paint in loosely. The first wash was slightly more dilute and it has run down the page, creating interesting paler patches. Keeping the paper on a board and tilting it will facilitate this flow. If you want to keep things under more control let the first wash dry before adding the next layer and soften the edges of any new shapes manually rather than allowing the paint to blend itself. To avoid watermarks your first wash should be either wet or completely dry when you apply more paint.

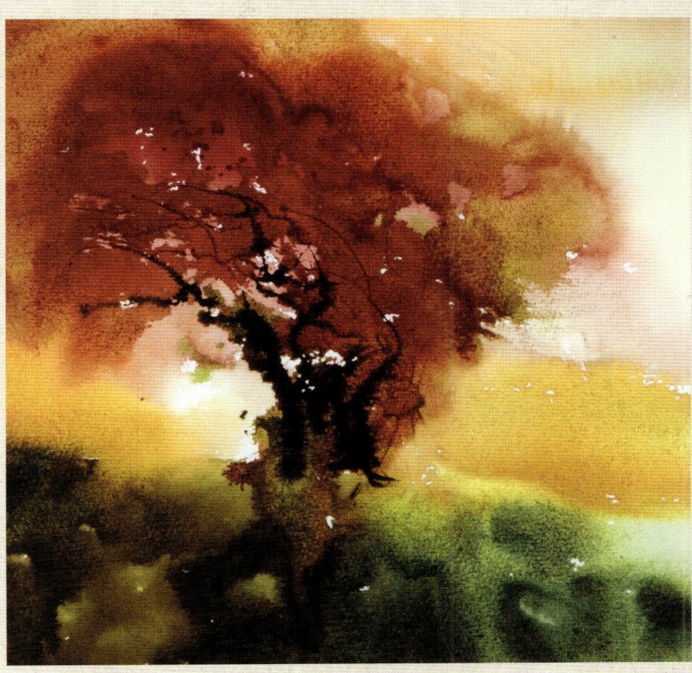

3 While the previous layer is damp, add the trunk and branches with ink. Try to keep some loose movement in these marks and have thin and thick lines to keep the branches natural. I used sepia acrylic ink by Daler-Rowney to get the specific texture I was hoping to achieve in the next step. Alternatively use a dark granulating watercolour; the Daniel Smith range is good for these. If your original wash has dried, try dampening areas first where you want the ink to go. If the ink has gone mad and spread everywhere, don't panic! This may happen if the wash is a bit too wet and although the effect may not replicate what is shown here it will be atmospheric and loose. In this case, allow it to be part of the overall texture, working in a more traditional way on top when it is dry.

4 Drop a little granulation medium into the wet ink and let it flow through, breaking it into granular textures. Manoeuvring the unstretched paper will help you to coax it in the direction you want. Let gravity help to re-create the meandering dribbles and patterns of nature. If you use granulating paint rather than ink, water should be sufficient to create more subtle texture. Where the paint is still damp you could sprinkle salt to suggest mottled foliage. The shiny areas here indicate where the paint is still wet and the matt areas are dry. Learning to judge the moisture level is a major key to successful watercolour painting, whatever the technique.

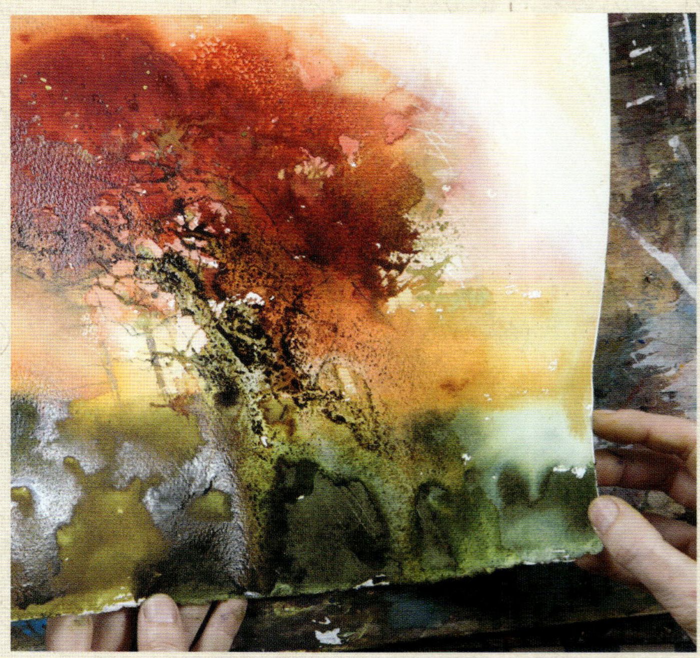

5 The paint can be left to dry now, so there is time for reflection. Stand back from your work and decide what needs adjusting. Paintings do not need to be finished in one go. You might try another version and come back to this one later, even much later, when you will see it with fresh eyes. In this piece I decided to use white gouache to add a milky texture to the sky while tidying up some bits that even I found messy! Changing to the opaque medium would create unity as I intended to use it in the next stage as well for added definition. I am pressing quite hard here with a round brush and almost scrubbing the paint so that the edges are broken with the underlying colour peeping through. I advise using an inexpensive brush for this method.

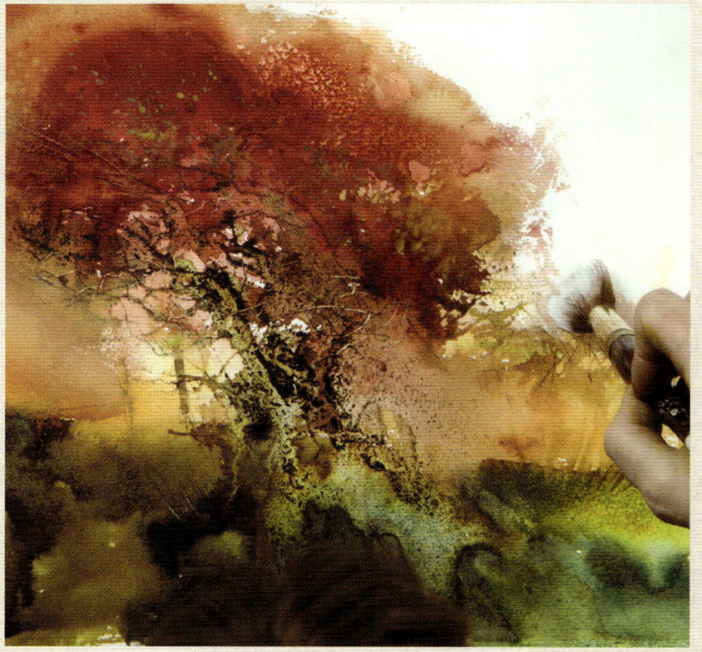

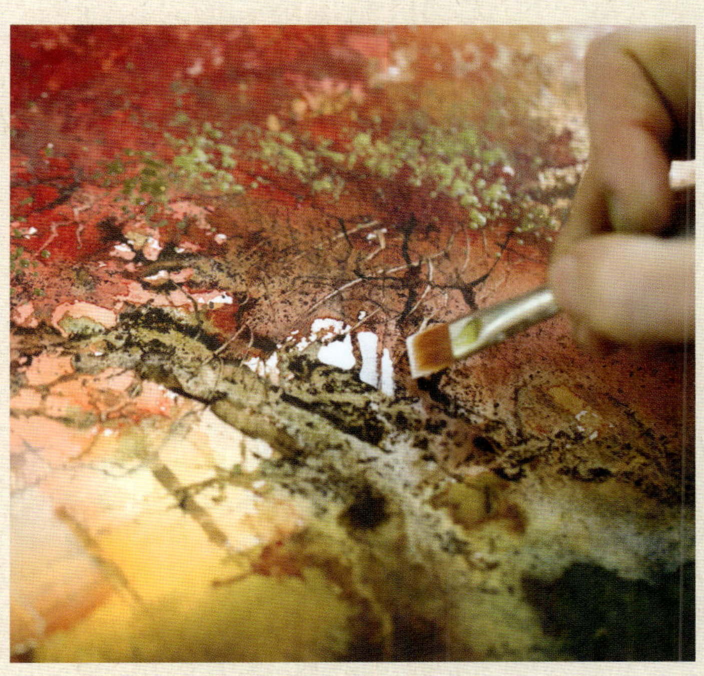

6 The structure of the tree needed work and I used the gouache again to paint shapes in between the trunk and branches. This is a kind of negative painting but using pale paint on top of a dark background rather than the usual dark on light. I have used white but you can choose any colour or add white to a watercolour pigment you have already used to make an opaque paler version of the same colour. If you would rather not use gouache you will need to plan more carefully in the previous stages so that the tree structure remains defined throughout the process.

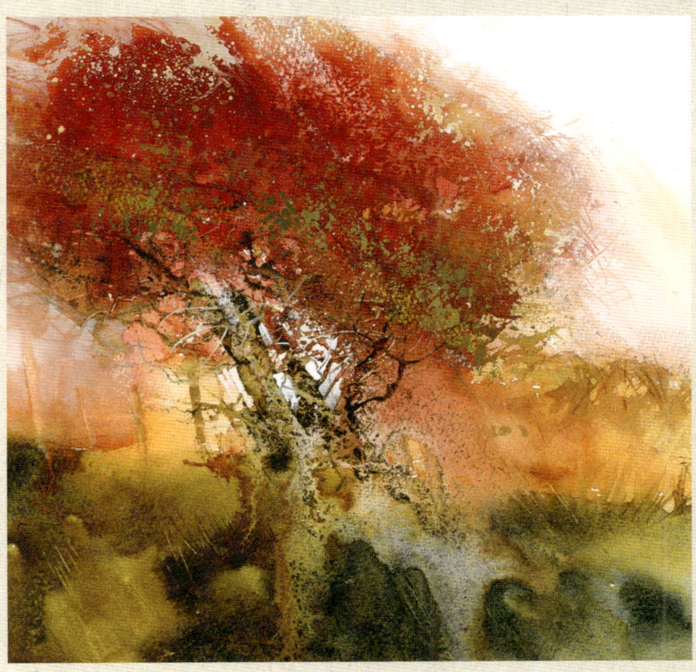

7 I scraped through the damp gouache around the tree with a scalpel, revealing lines of the original wash. These helped to break up the solid gouache and suggest branches and movement. I skated over some of the edges of the tree with dry gouache to further link the areas and add a bit of shimmer. A few splatters of paint were also added. You could indicate berries, blossom or foliage in this way. Here I used Derwent's coloured Inktense blocks on their side to catch the raised surface of the paper and suggest further texture. Any opaque crayon or oil pastel would do the trick and you could also use them to add dots or highlights.

Techniques

Adding ink

If you add ink you can apply it with a brush in the normal
way or use the pipette from the lid of a bottle. If your ink
has not got this kind of lid you can buy plastic squeezable
applicators that will do the same job. The ink is a lovely
liquid mark on top of the damp watercolour. A thin layer
will not work so well. Conversely, too much may spread
too far so judge it carefully. It is a case of trial and error.

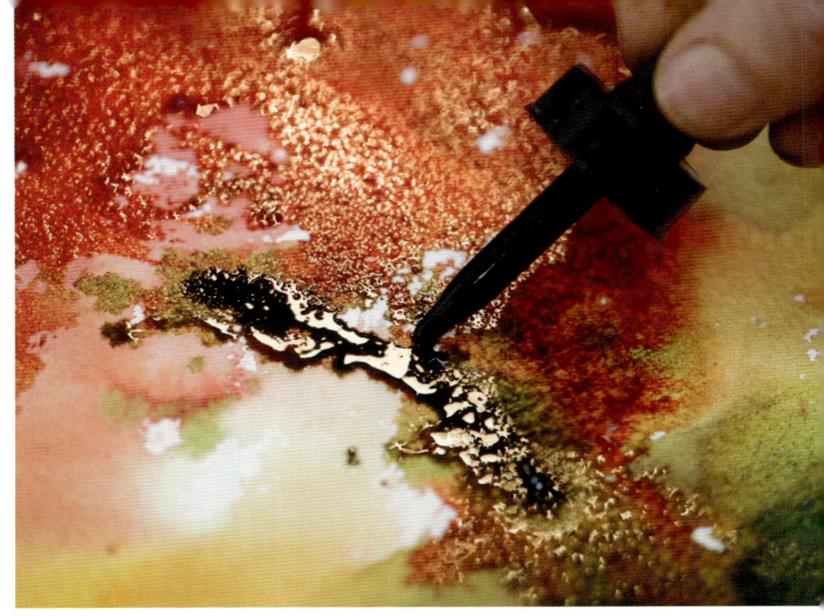

Adding granulation medium

The granulation medium has been added immediately
but carefully to specific places on top of the ink or
watercolour. You can see it breaking through the
mediums here. This picture makes me want to race
for my paints. It looks so juicy and tempting I could
eat it! I hope it makes you feel the same way. Let the
fluids move around the paper but try to coax them in
directions that suit the subject.

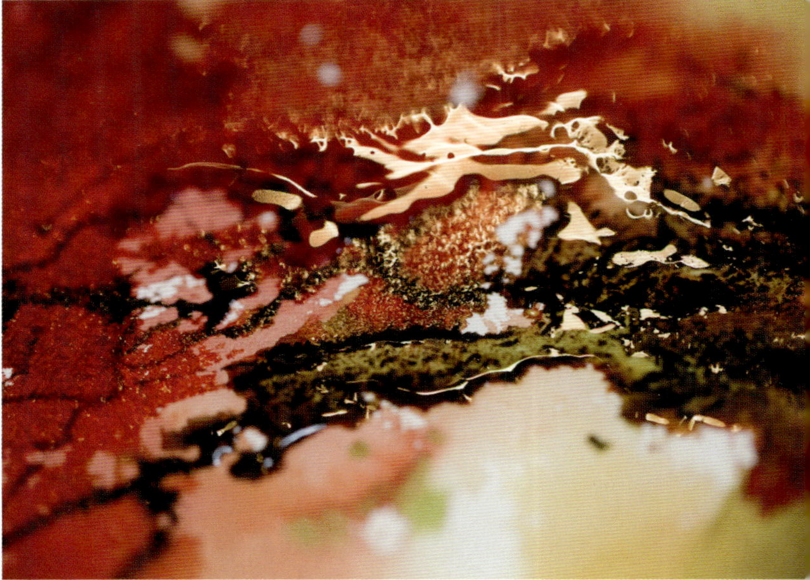

Using a flat brush

In the demonstration, I added a few details of fence
posts under the tree. These were simply applied using
the straight edge at the tip of a flat brush. Dip this
into paint and literally print a line with it, holding the
brush perpendicular to the paper. If you drag the brush
sideways you can pull the paint into a thicker mark. Use
a brushstroke for a short post or repeat the brush print
to build a longer post.

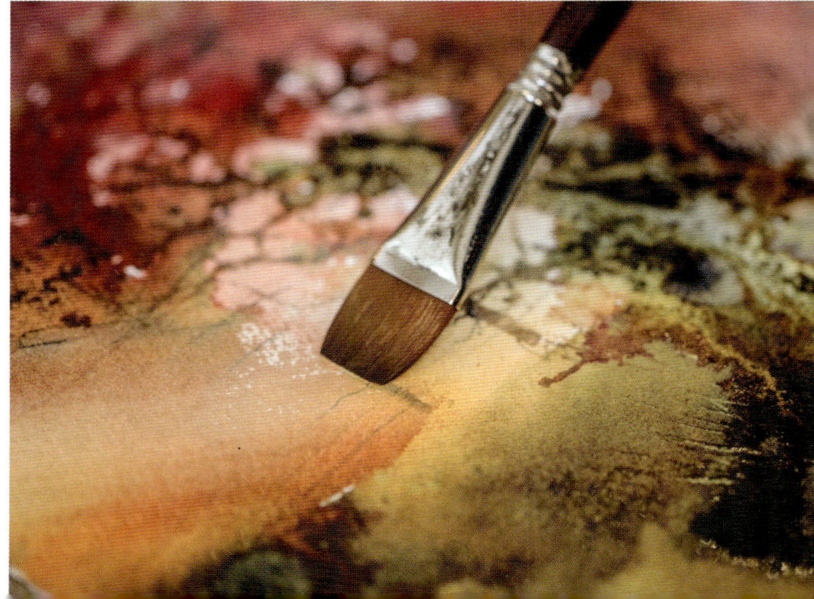

Fence post detail

You can see the fencepost that I made using a flat brush in detail here. Look at page 100 for alternative ideas about painting geometric shapes. I also added some squiggly lines with a watercolour pencil to suggest delicate branches and used a scalpel to scrape away lines of still-damp paint to describe pale twigs.

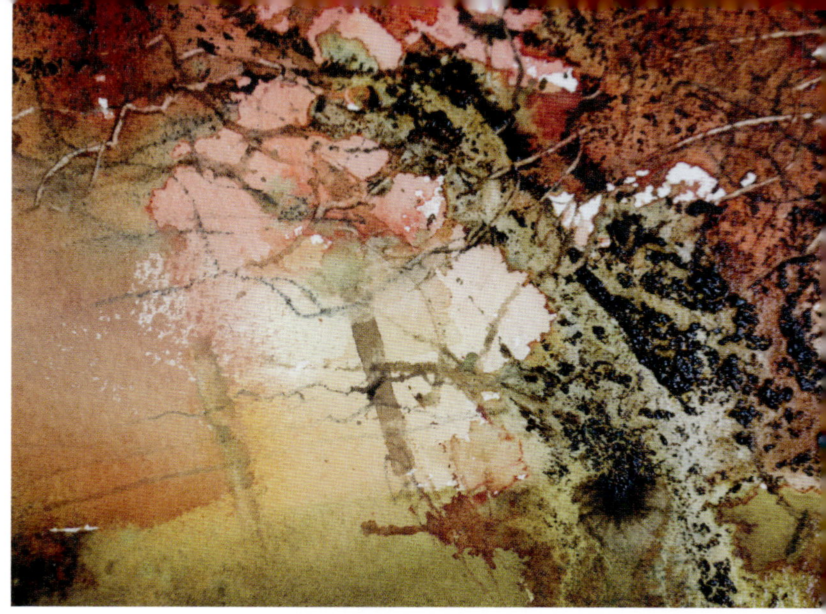

Adding details

I linked the posts with some wavering pencil lines to suggest loose fence wires. Look how loosely the pencil is being held. You have more control if you hold it near the lead but that will encourage a tight rather than relaxed line. This is a watercolour pencil which gives a smudgy mark when used in wet paint.

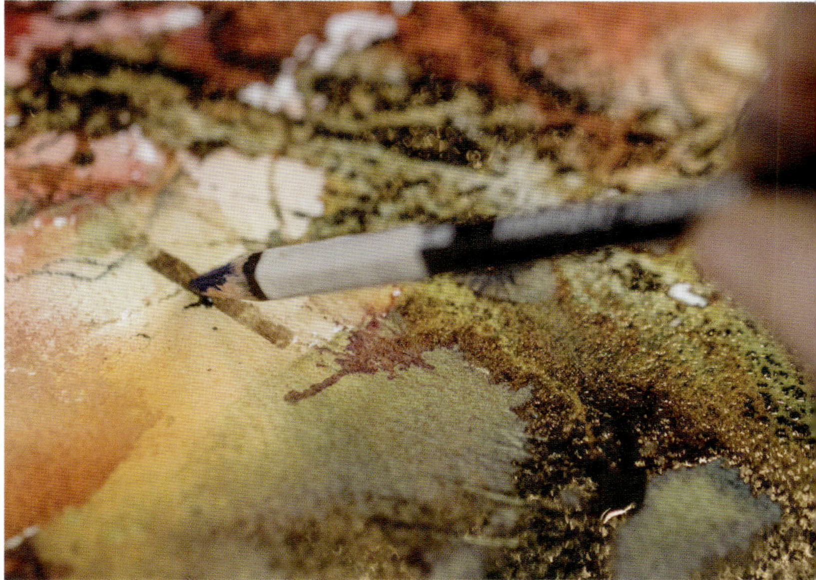

Scraping out lines with a scalpel

One way to make pale lines in a dark background is to scrape away some of the dark paint, revealing the paper. Use a scalpel or similar sharp tool. It is easier to avoid digging into the paper if you choose thick paint to work into. I have selected a damp, concentrated patch of colour from which to scratch lines and hint at grasses. A different kind of line can be made using a rigger to apply pale opaque watercolour on top of your dark wash.

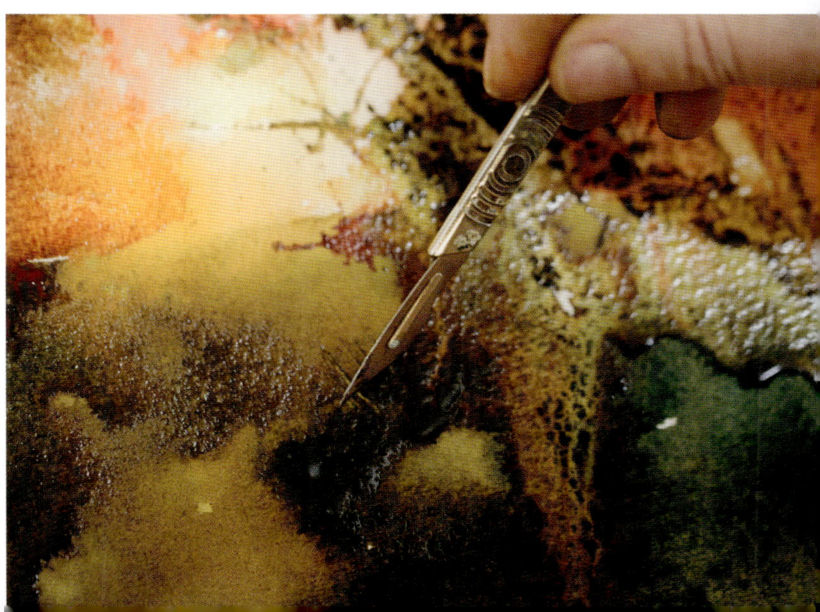

Techniques:
TWIGGY MARK-MAKING

Crayon

Thick crayons make it easy to draw branches. Block-shaped ones such as Inktense blocks are good for obtaining chunky or thin marks, depending on whether you use the edge or corner of the square end. They are also water-soluble so can be easily smudged and blended into a wet wash.

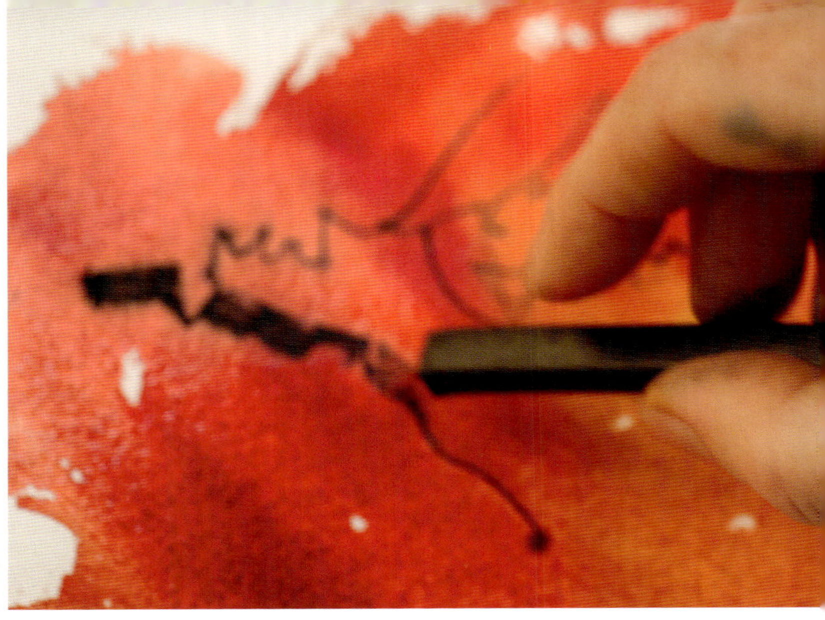

Lead pencil

Draw delicate twigs with a variety of pencils. The hard 'H' pencil shown here is engraving the soft, wet paper, making the paint sink into dark lines. 'B' pencils make softer, wider marks for bigger twigs.

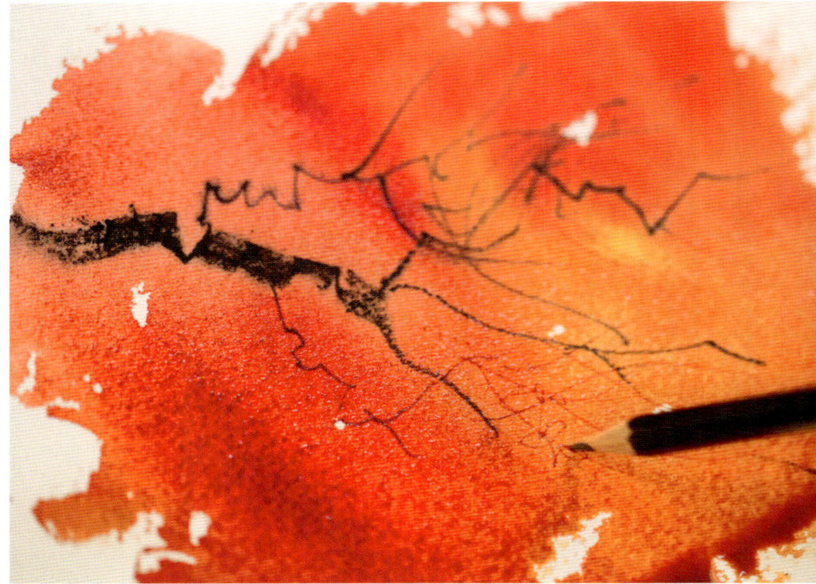

Watercolour pencil

You can draw really intense marks with a black watercolour pencil. Use browns and softer colours for a more subtle effect. Hold the pencil loosely for relaxed lines. Press hard for dots.

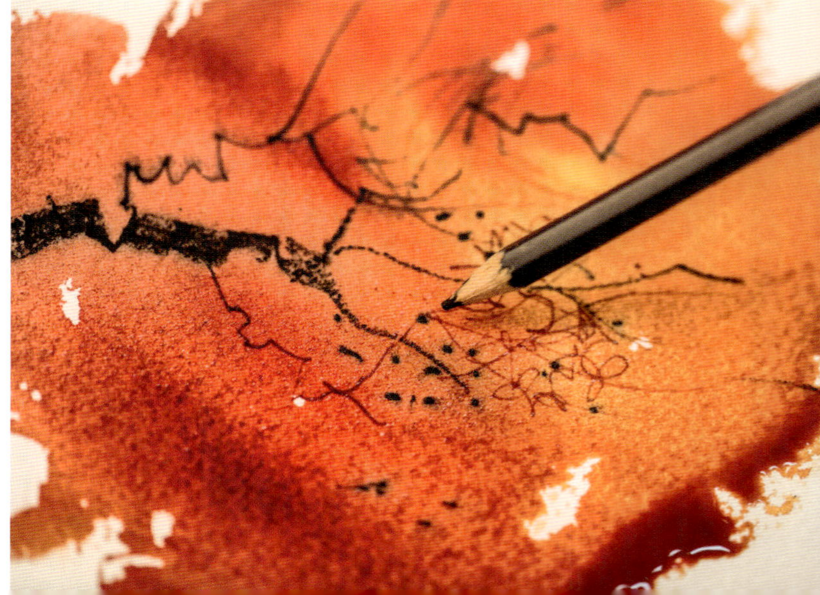

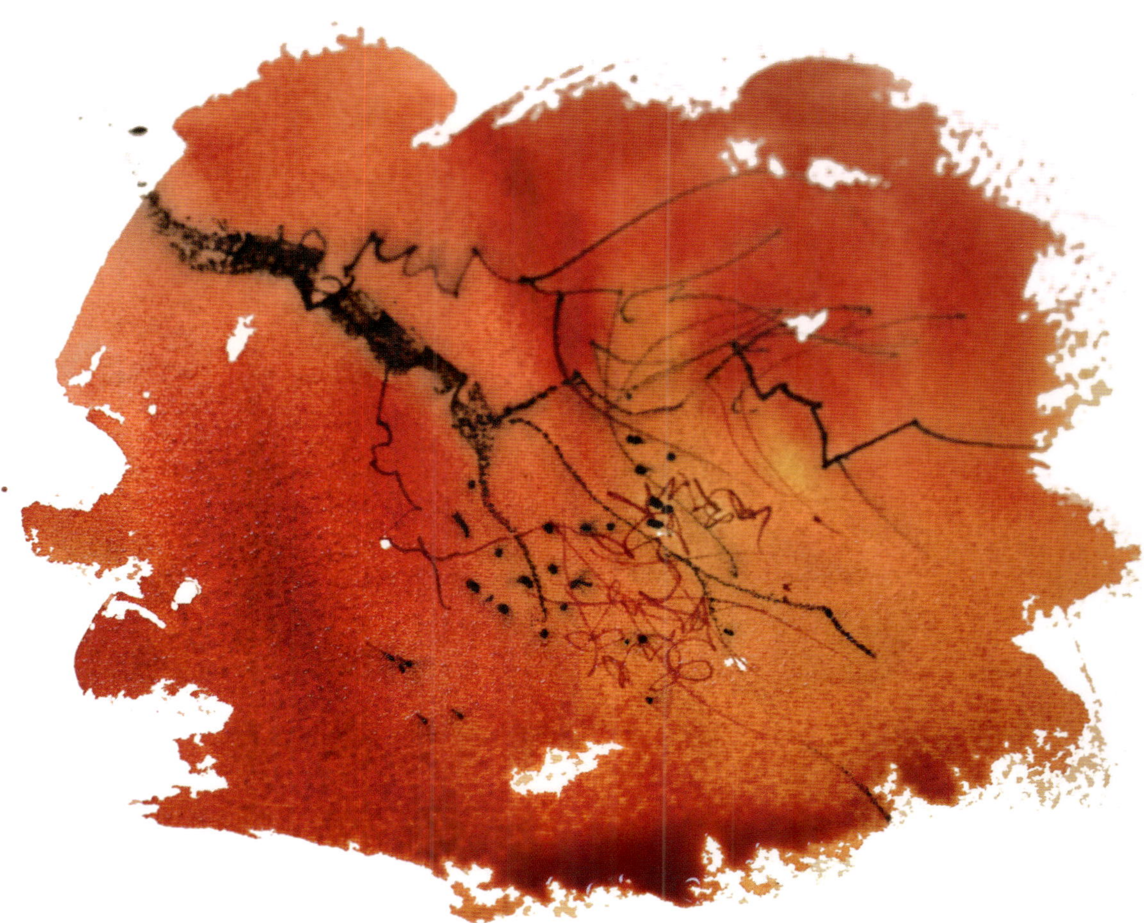

◁ Combine different qualities and widths of mark and line when you paint twigs and branches to echo what is happening in nature. The pencil lines illustrated were worked into a wet wash. Explore the difference that working on wet or dry paper makes.

▷ Use twigs, stems and stalks from the plant you are interpreting to draw into your work. Simply dip the end into paint or ink to make your marks on paper. Try to echo the character of the plant you are using as your tool in the representation.

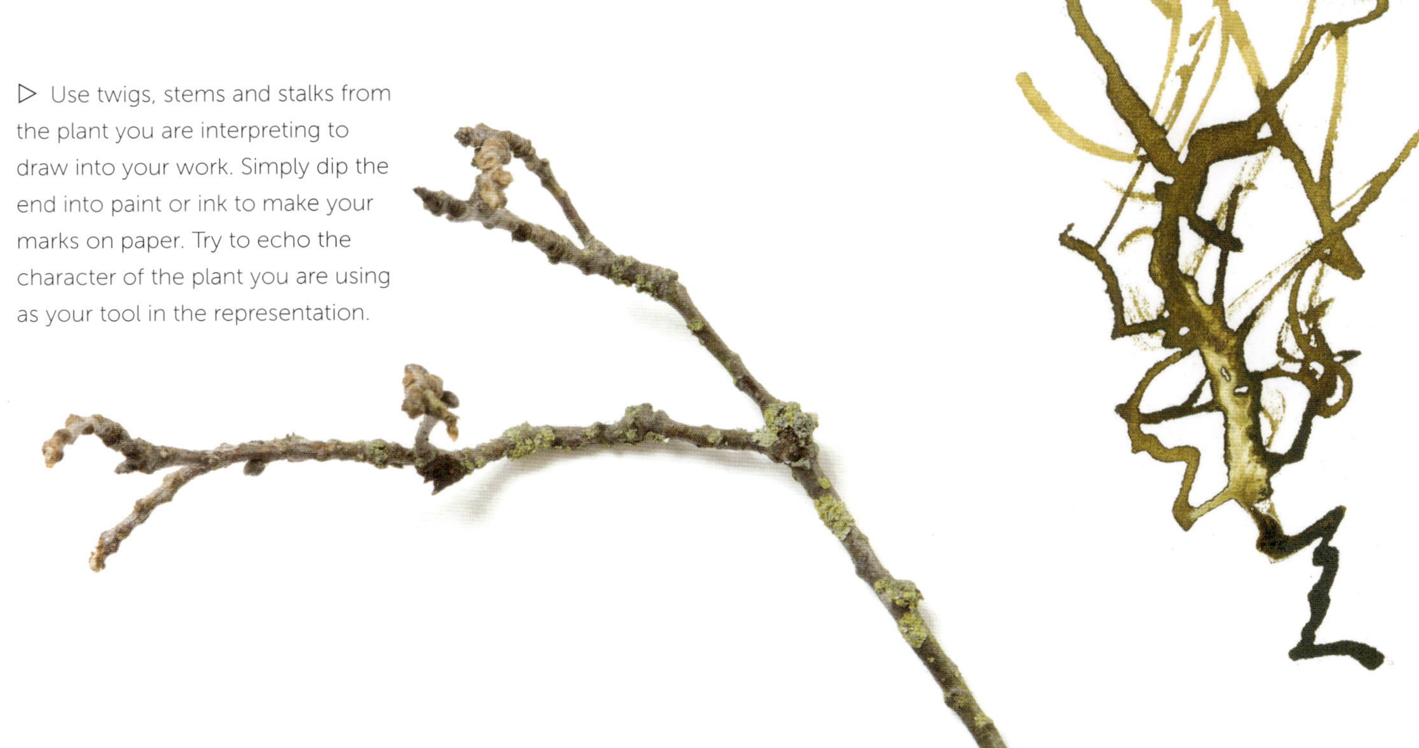

Taking it further:
USING GESSO AND TISSUE PAPER

Very different kinds of marks can be made by preparing your surface first with gesso alone or in combination with craft tissue paper. The raised effects of thick ridges of gesso or the creases and crumples of collaged tissue are very useful for many kinds of texture but seem especially appropriate for the twigs and branches of trees and hedges. You can apply this technique on mount board but you must cover the whole area as the unprimed surface is not suitable for watercolour. Working in this way on heavy watercolour paper gives you the option to prepare only a section, enabling the paint to flow in a normal way on the untouched parts of the paper. When the prepared surface is dry you can paint on top. Do not expect the paint, especially watercolour, to flow on this non-absorbent gesso surface in the normal way.

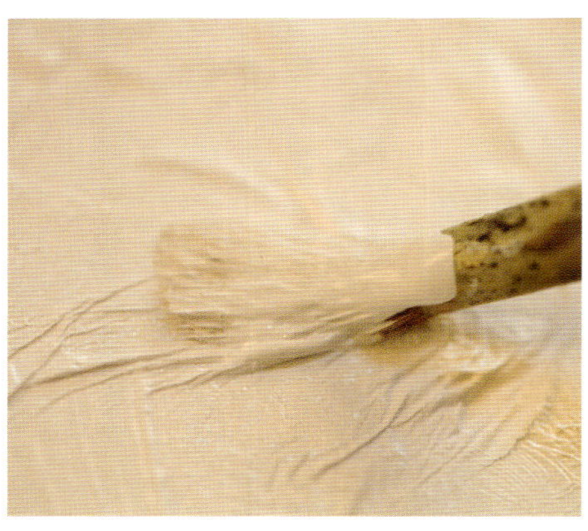

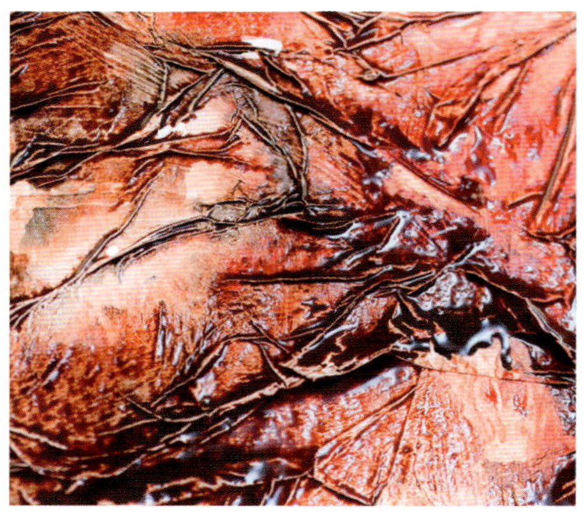

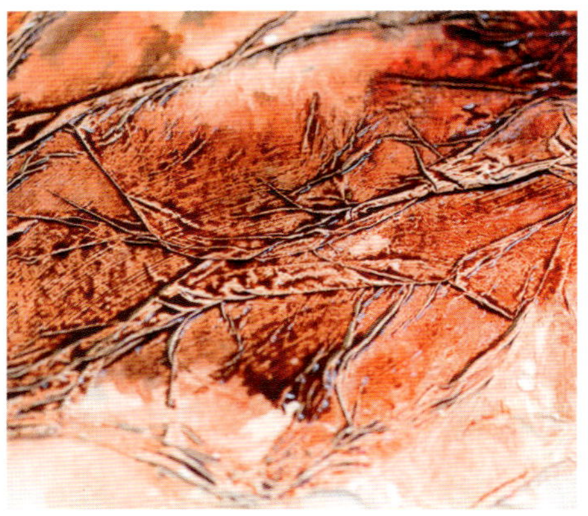

Use an old brush to apply gesso thickly on your surface. Place pieces of lightly crumpled tissue paper on top. Use the brush to press down the ridges of paper firmly, using more gesso to stick down loose bits and seal the whole surface. The tissue should not have any hollows underneath or it may tear when painted.

When the prepared surface is dry, apply a creamier consistency of paint than normal so that it 'sticks' better. Pigment will settle in the cracks and crevices alongside the raised areas to suggest branch-like marks. Apply the wet paint gently as the surface is fragile and easily damaged.

When the paint is dry it is easy to lift it off the gesso surface if you wish. If you gently wipe over the ridges with a soft damp cloth or paper towel it will increase the contrast of the textures. Only wipe once as the tissue can easily rip even though it has been sealed with gesso.

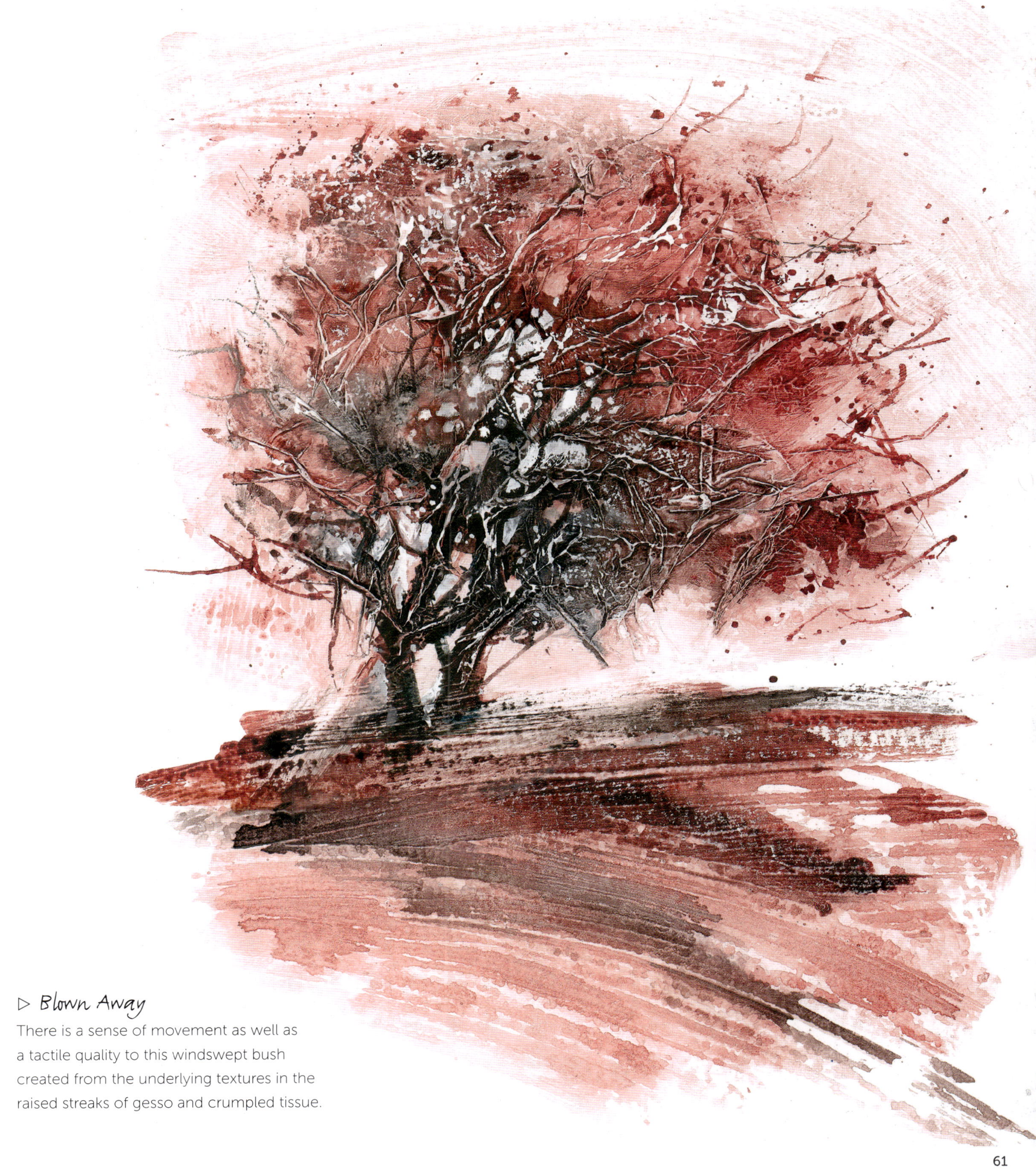

▷ *Blown Away*
There is a sense of movement as well as
a tactile quality to this windswept bush
created from the underlying textures in the
raised streaks of gesso and crumpled tissue.

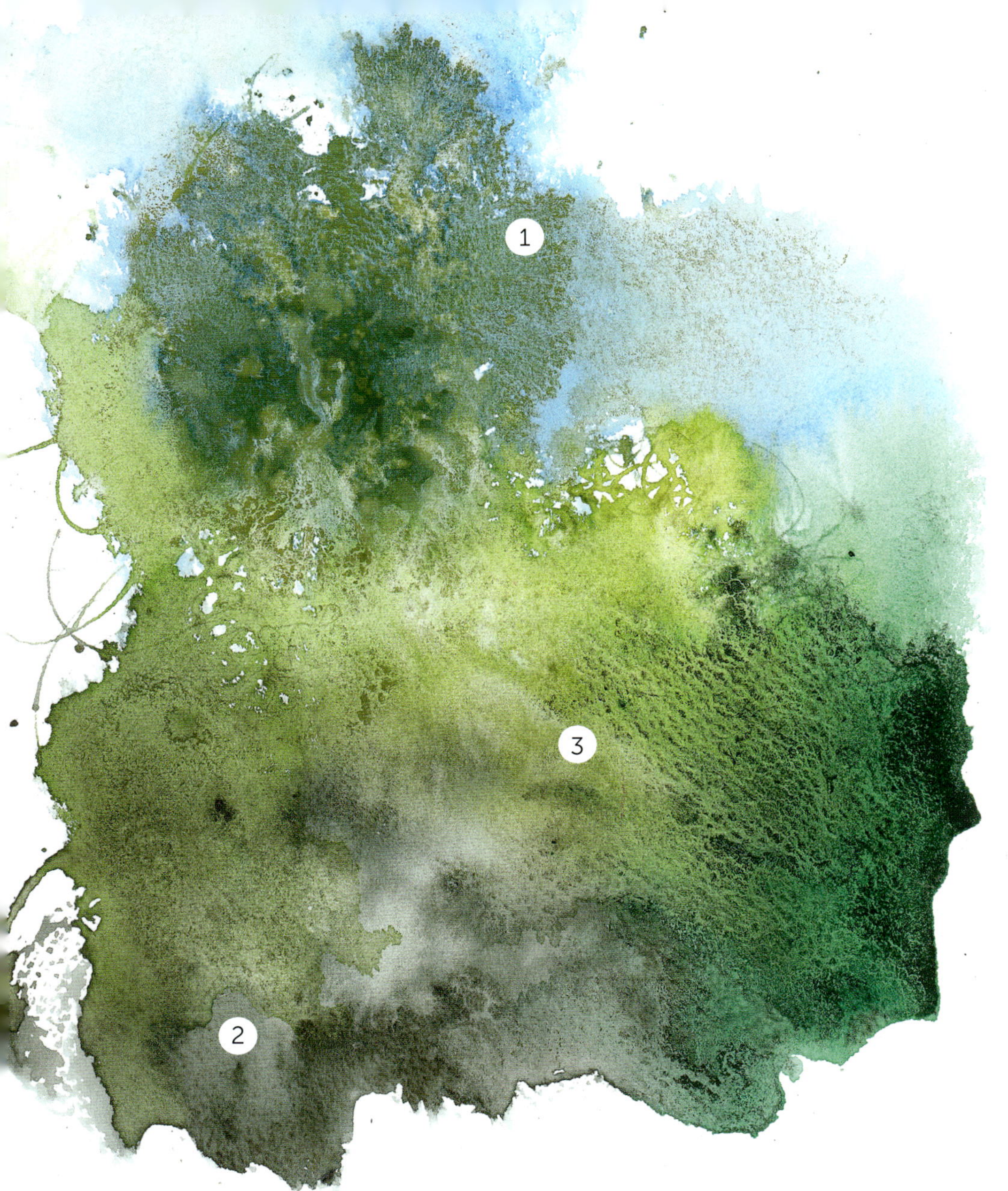

Ready-made greens

1 **Daniel Smith's Cascade Green** magically splits between green and blue after it is applied.

2 **Perylene Green** creates rich, moody darks which are useful for shadowy areas.

3 **Daniel Smith's Jadeite Green** lends an air of nocturnal drama with its rich veins of granulating darks.

Creating interesting greens

Having looked at warm, rich, autumn tree colours in the project, let's move on to the bigger challenge presented in spring and summer – that of creating variety and interest within the predominant greens. In early spring, leaves are fresh and new and only lightly dust the trees. Build up layers of shimmering speckled texture with clear bright greens and flecks of complementary colours such as mauve and yellow. Later the foliage becomes more solid, so experiment with variations on a verdant theme using either ready-made greens or mixing different blues with yellows. You can also jazz up boring greens with punctuations of other hues. For instance, add swathes of pink to suggest dawn light or a flush of wild roses rambling through the leafy branches.

Mixed greens

1 Mix **Phthalo Blue**
   with different yellows
   for clean, flat areas
   of green.

2 **Cerulean Blue**
   makes a very
   granular green.
   Here it is mixed
   with tiny amounts
   of **Green Gold**.

3 **French Ultramarine** is
   an essential blue for
   mixing greens. Note
   how the salt has lifted
   the mixed colour back
   to pale blue and how
   the greens are enriched
   by the complementary red.

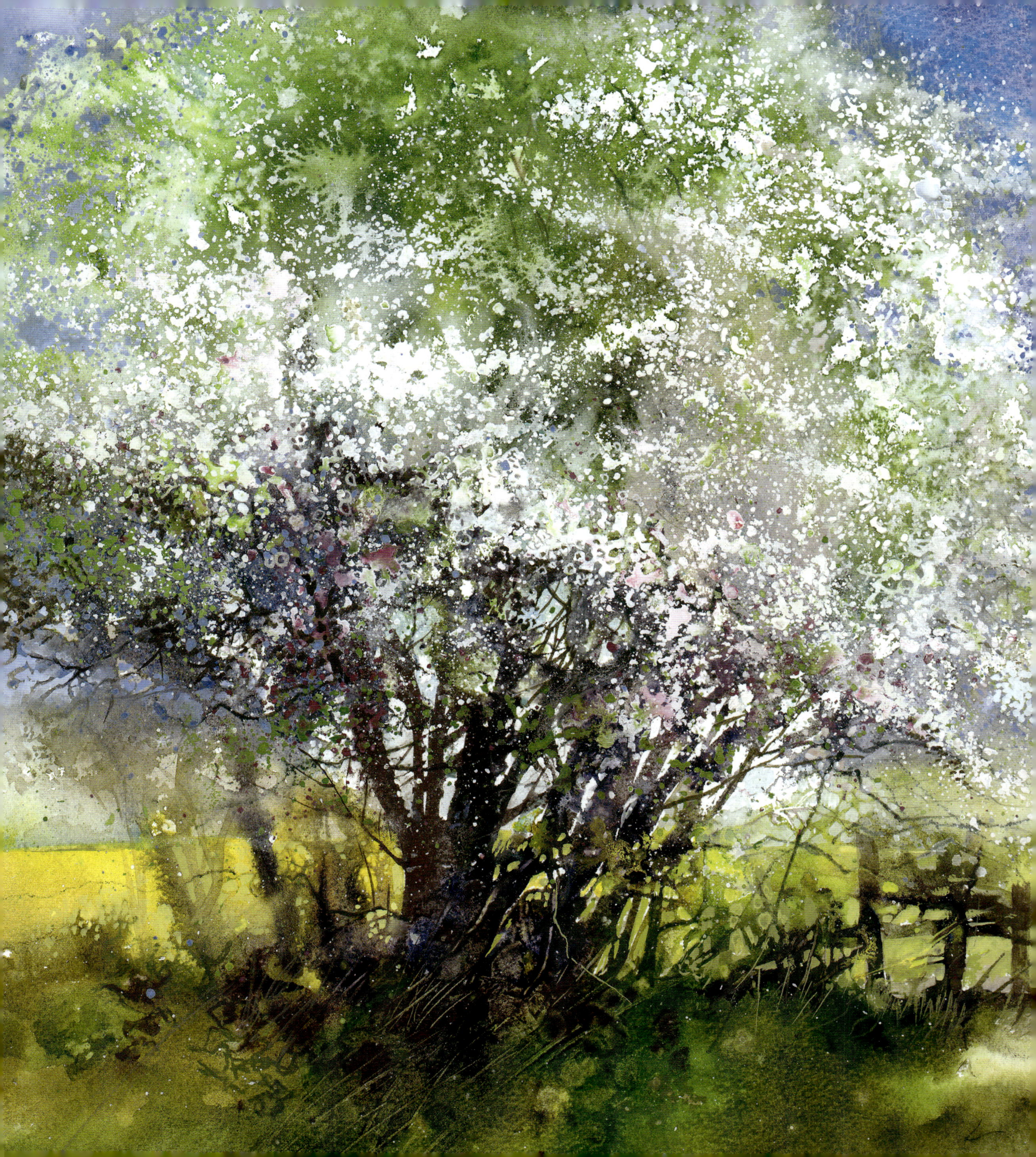

Through the seasons

◁ Spring Hawthorn

In spring, hawthorn is covered in clouds of May blossom. To begin building this multitude of pale speckles I splattered masking fluid over the blossom area then painted a fresh green wash over this when it was dry. While the watercolour was damp I sprinkled in a little salt for texture, brushing this and the masking fluid off when it was all dry to reveal flecks of white paper. I built up the blossom further with exuberant splatterings of white gouache and added lively spots of mauve among the dappled green foliage.

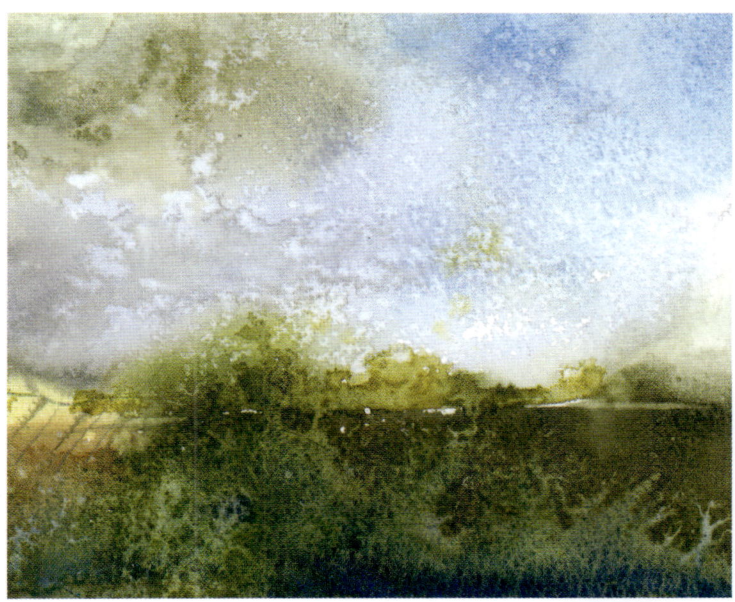

△ How Green is the sky?

This tiny picture shows a blur of distant hawthorn hedgerow. Perylene Green, Quinacridone Gold and Cerulean Blue keep these summer greens atmospheric rather than dull. There is even a hint of green in the sky. It is effective to inject a surprise element into your paintings sometimes.

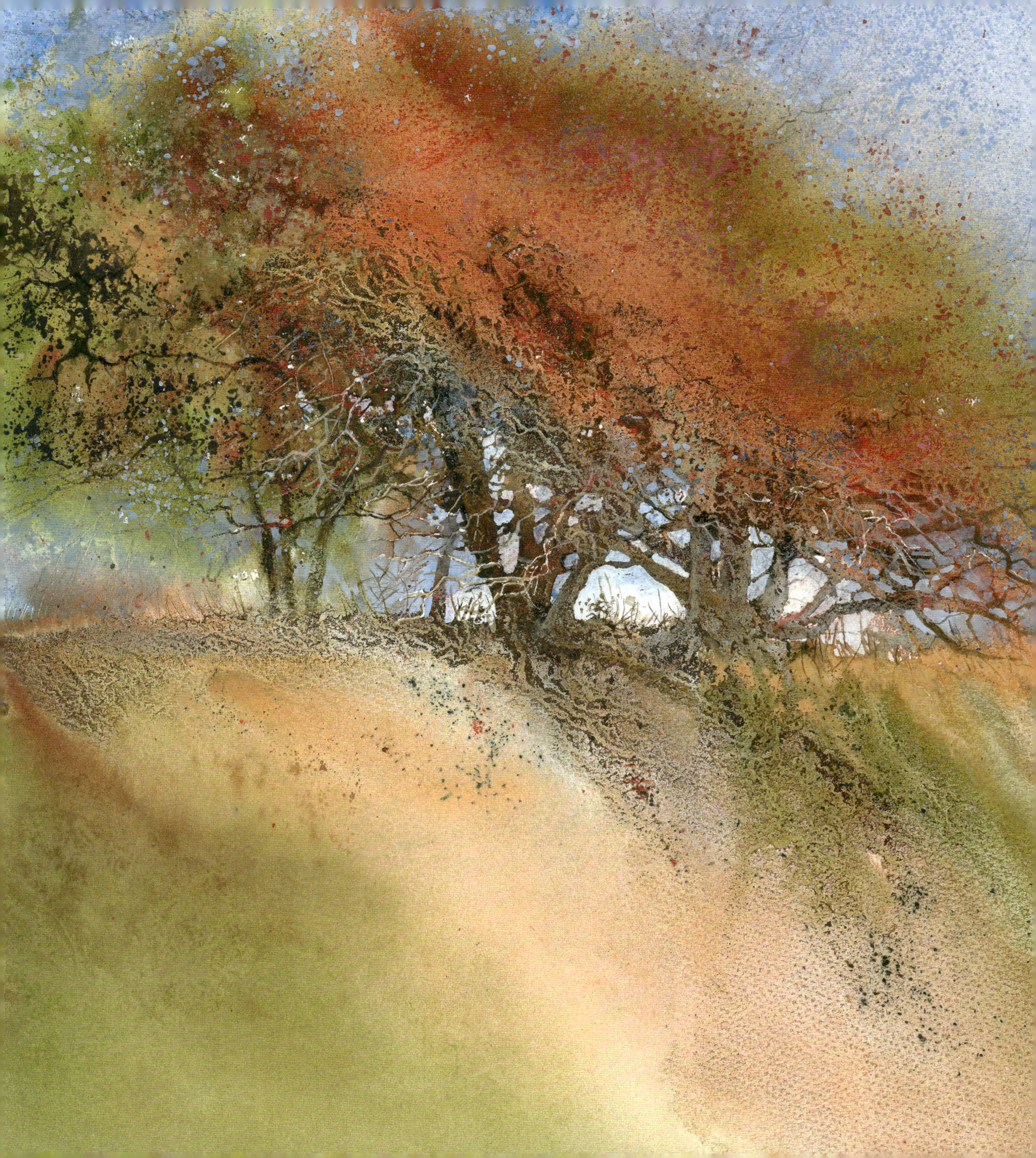

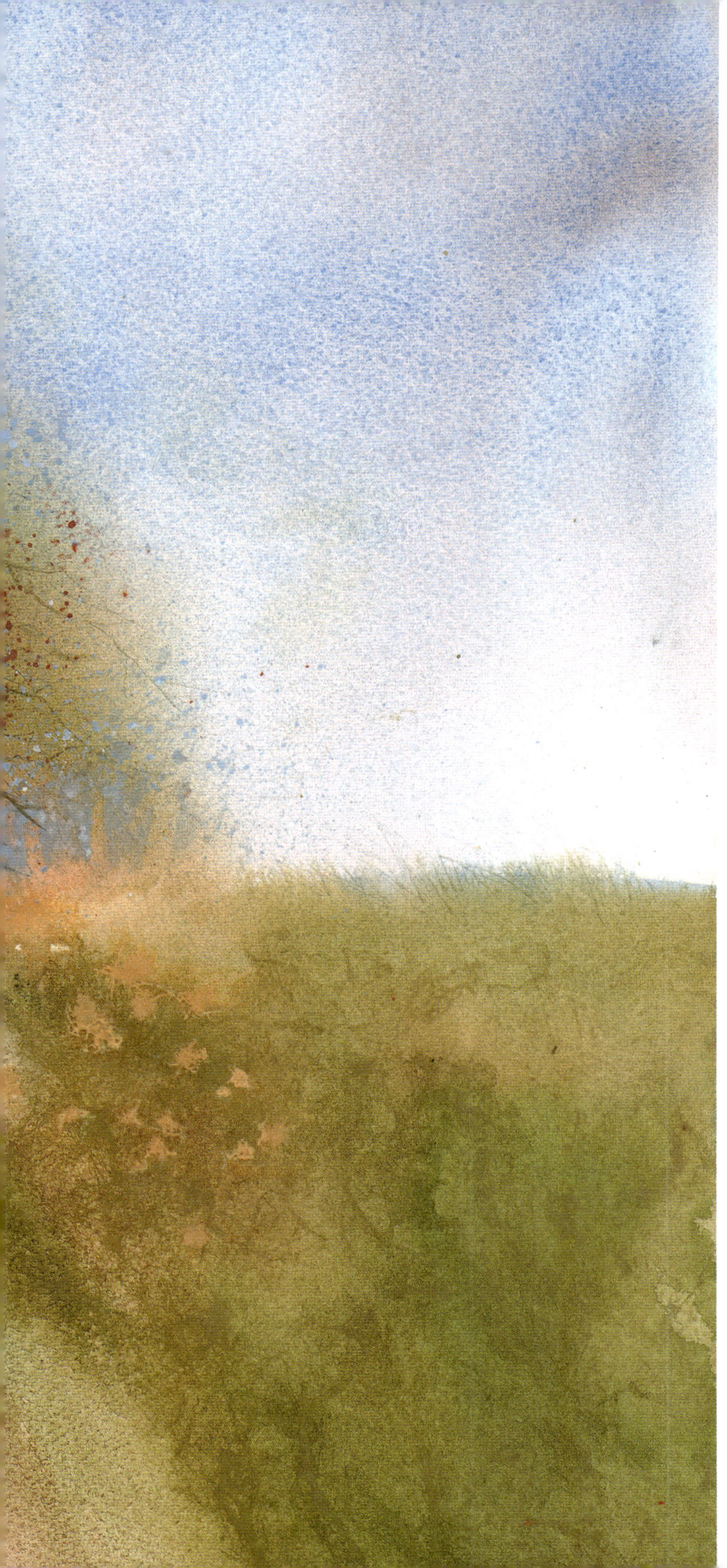

◁ **Fiery Hawthorn** (detail)

This interpretation is similar to the project demonstration but larger and painted in my own time without the restraints of performing for a camera. The aim in both pictures was to capture the fiery colours and speckles of the autumn leaves and berries and in this version I chose a contrasting Cerulean Blue sky to emphasize the theme.

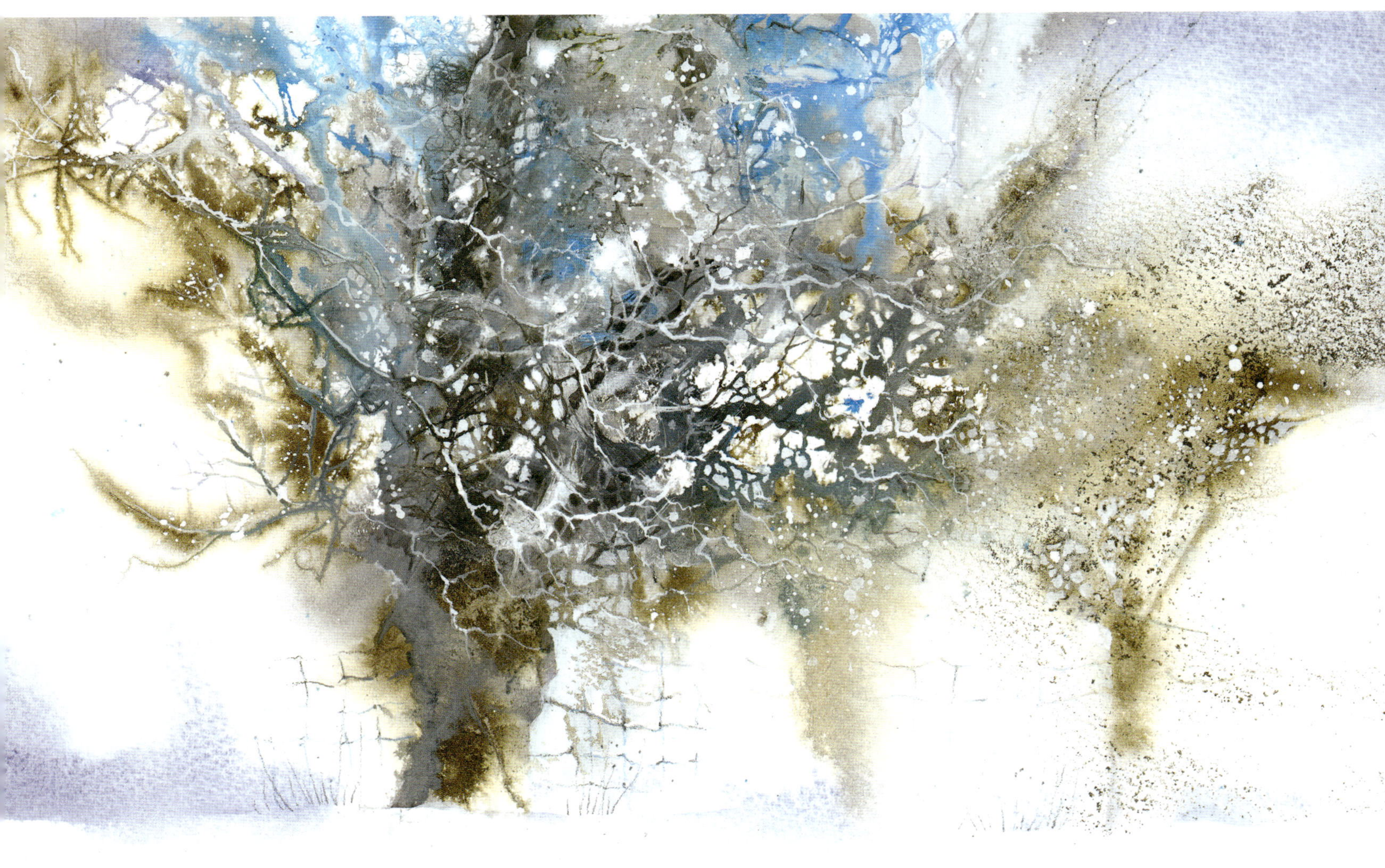

I aimed to keep this snowy scene simple and clean while also introducing an air of misty mystery. The first element was dealt with by using only Cobalt Blue watercolour and very white paper. Creating the atmosphere was achieved by choosing softly blurred washes. The addition of ink and its grainy textures added a bit of grit to avoid sentimentality. Snowy branches and snowflakes were added with white gouache. Finally the fence was drawn in with a pencil and some delicate rigger work.

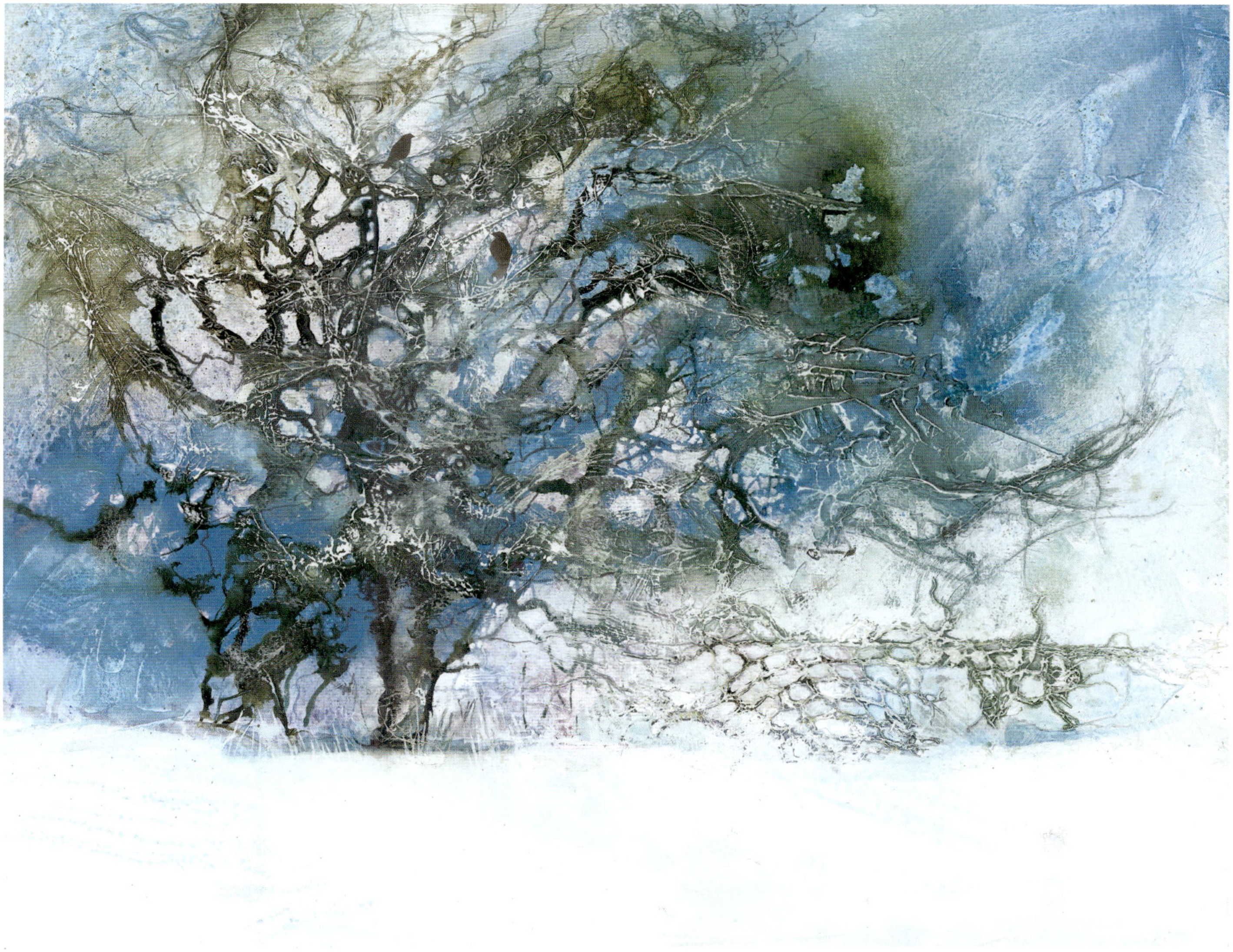

△ Wintry Hawthorn

I applied gesso to paper with a palette
knife to build slabs of texture. I also used
an old brush, retaining some of the brush
marks. Thick areas of gesso can act as
a kind of glue to stick down collage
material. I tore up part of a mesh bag that
had contained oranges and embedded
this into the gesso to represent a wire
fence. Watercolour ink in cool colours
went on top of this textured surface to
create a wintry tree.

▷ Wintry Hawthorn (detail)

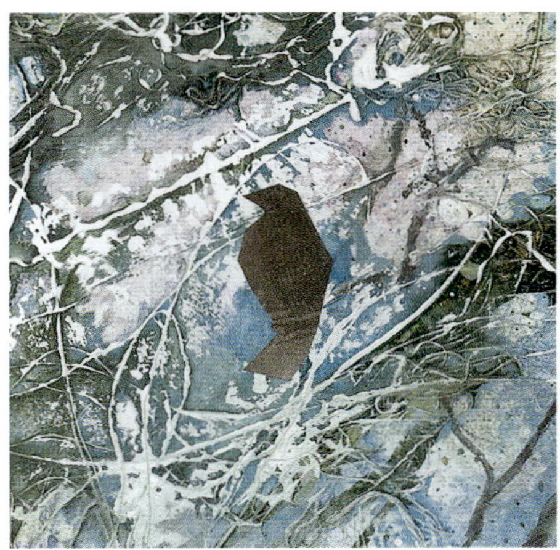

This snow-speckled hawthorn tree
needed a focal point, so I cut out
some birds from black paper and
stuck them on selected branches,
keeping the shapes angular to avoid
them being too 'pretty'.

Making a statement

When you paint a subject it is not a record but a
statement about what particularly interests you as an
artist. This might be the colour, texture, light, tone, edge
values or pattern. It can be anything at all and only you
know what the ingredient is. I am convinced that we
know these things subconsciously – even if we have to
delve a little to uncover it. The statement might reflect
your personality or you might want to surprise everybody
by expressing a different side of yourself in your pictures.
Loose paintings are no more valid than detailed, tight
ones. Pale and delicate renditions are just as special as
loud and dramatic ones. It is also OK if your statements
vary within your work but as your artist voice grows
stronger an identifiable link will emerge.

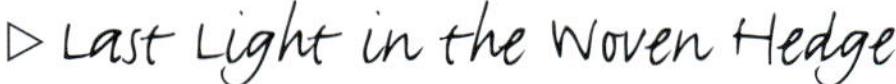

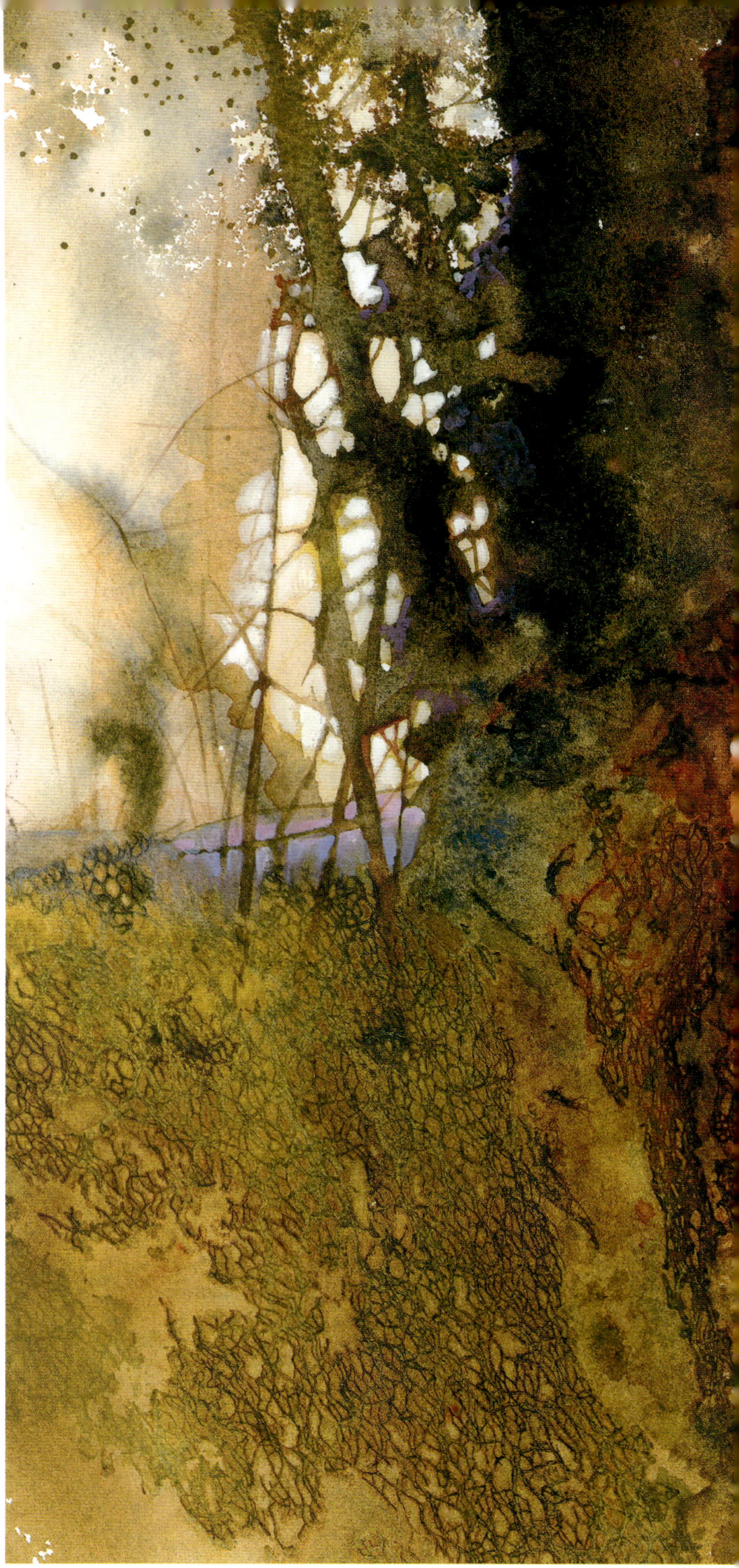

▷ **Last Light in the Woven Hedge**
I have become obsessed with the theme of the setting sun
dazzling through gaps in the semi-abstract tangles of hedgerow.
The effect of light is intensified by changing the colour of the
branches that crisscross over the sun. These branches are tinged
with pinks, reds and golds but in the shadows they are muted
shades of brown.

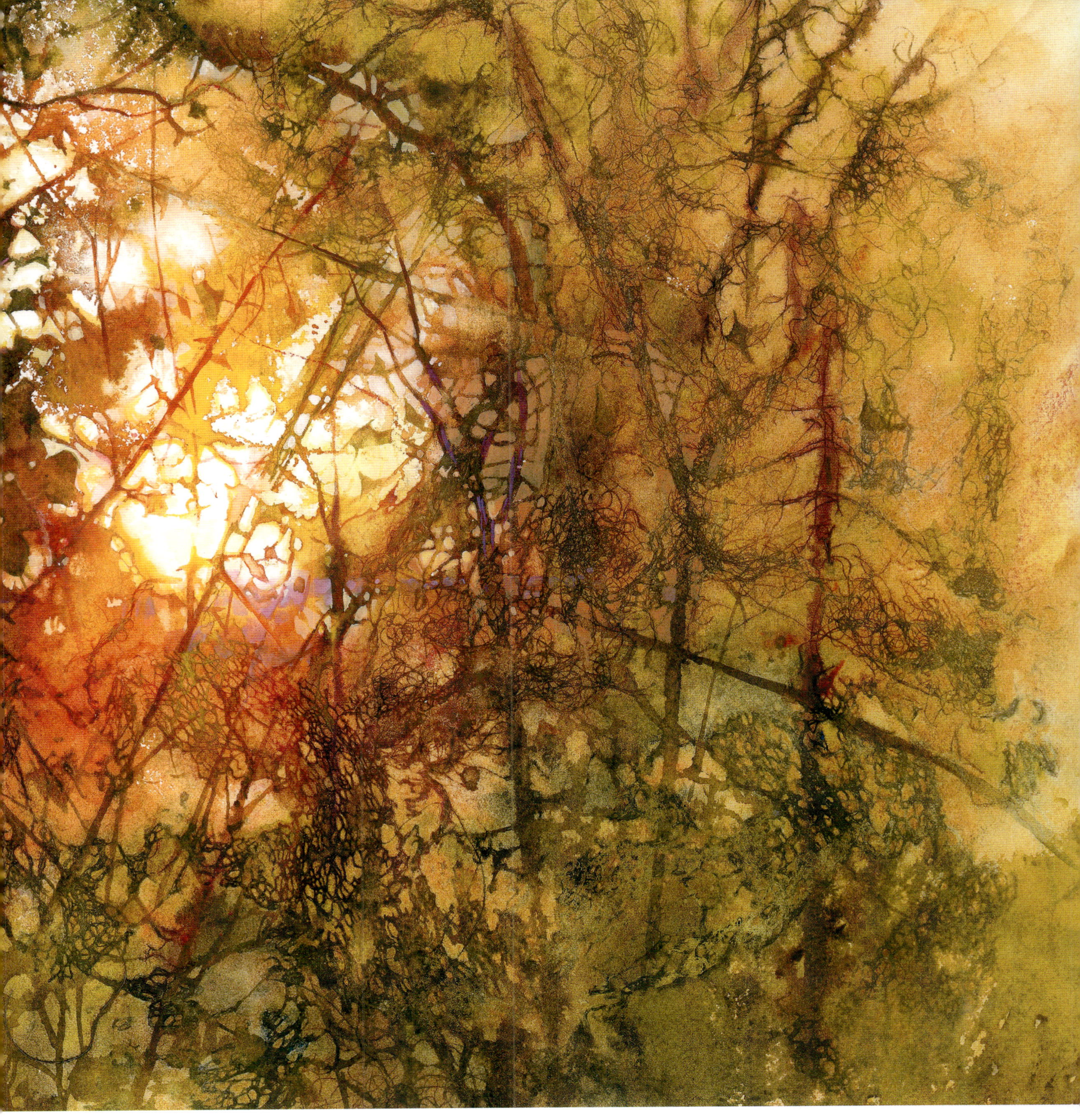

Creating mystery and mood

In painting terms it is easy to equate the words 'atmospheric' or 'moody' with soft, misty edges. However, there are many different kinds of atmosphere and each of these develops from a combination of sensations and perceptions. The cacophony of syncopated birdsong in the rookery; the trembling of the willow over rippled water; the sweet scent of honeysuckle on a dusky evening; the hypnotic hum of honey bees in the laburnum tree – these phrases are about sounds, smells and movement but still conjure visual imagery. We use all our senses to create a visual picture about mood and atmosphere. I often write words down in my sketchbooks to remind myself of these. Leaving something to the imagination also helps to create ambience in a painting. Your watercolours will naturally become more atmospheric if you do not explain every mark. However, it is important to keep your visual gestures meaningful and when it is relevant let your painterly decisions be influenced by these other kinds of experience.

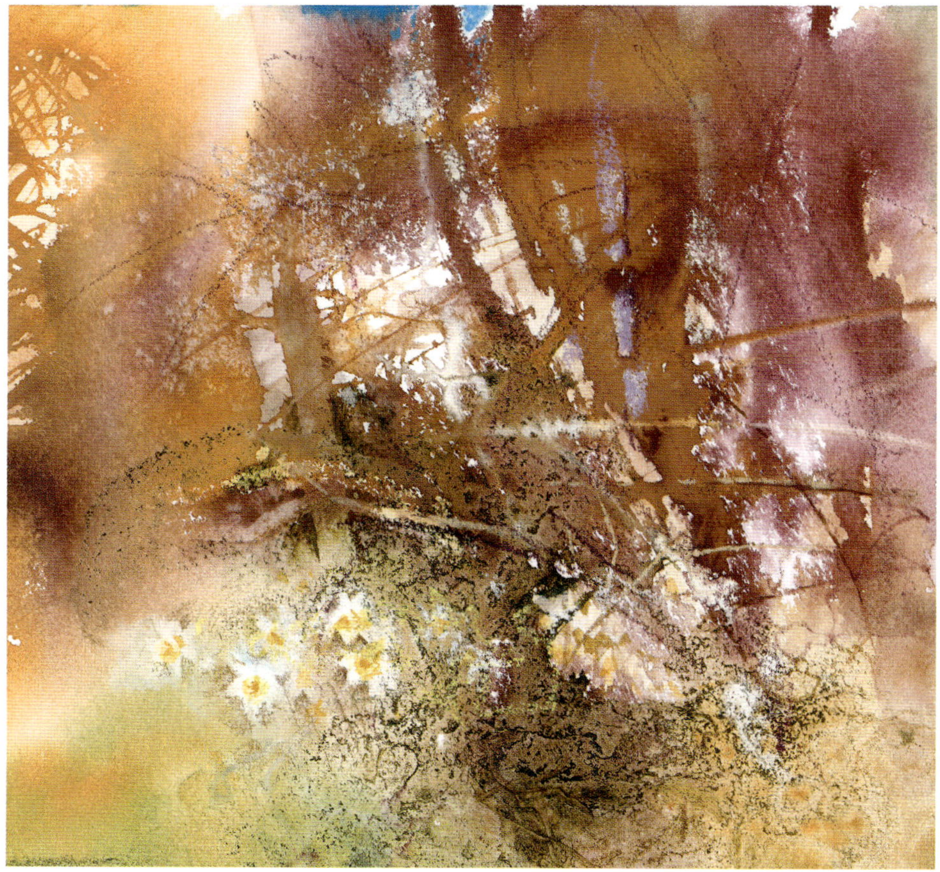

◁ **Daffodils in the Wood**
The soft light filtering through harmonious colours is atmospheric but the effect is heightened by its contrast with earthy textures and the fact that the details are merely suggested.

▷ **Silver Birch Light**
I continued my theme of light shining through the gaps between trees, creating a mood through my use of complementary colours.

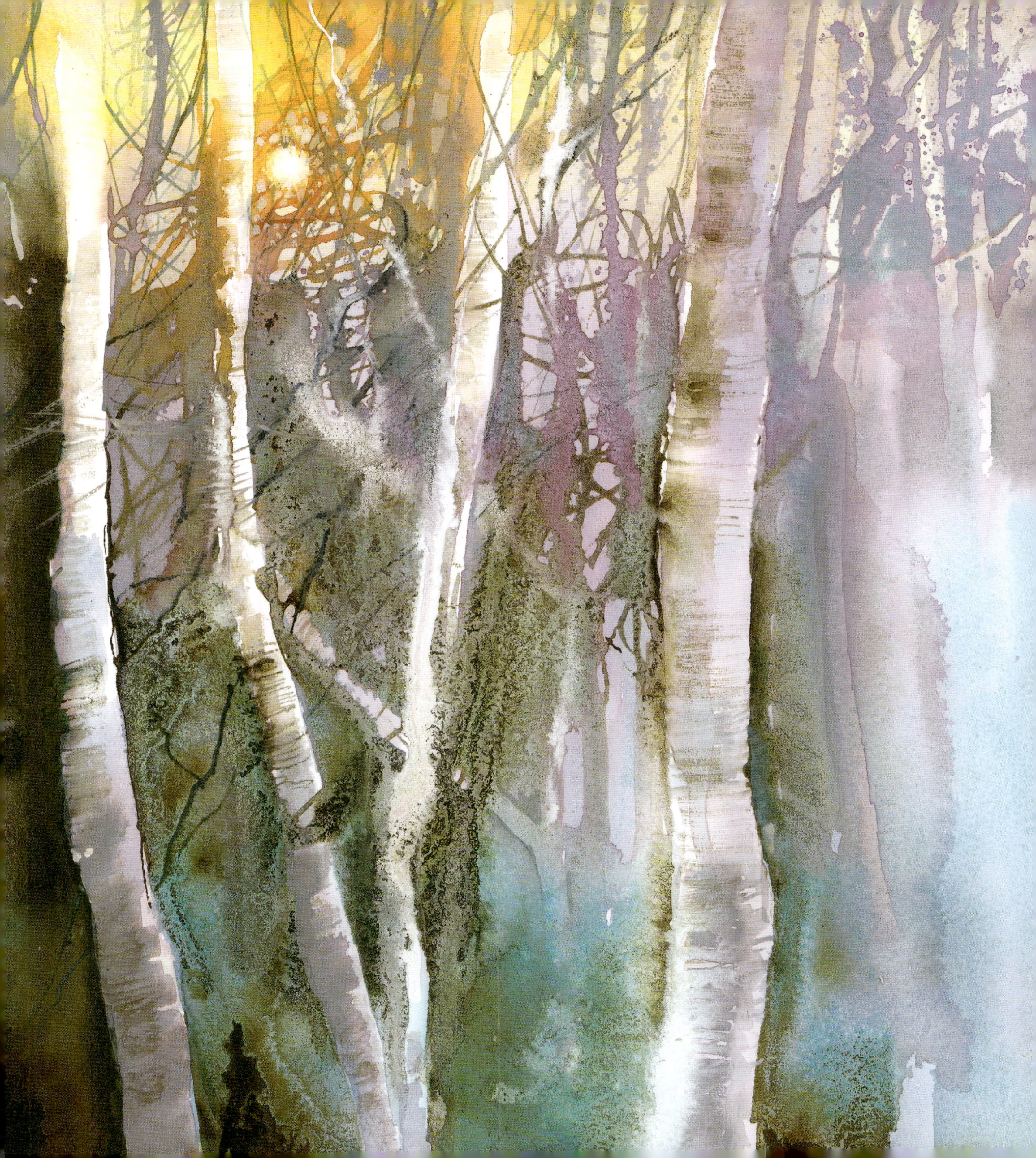

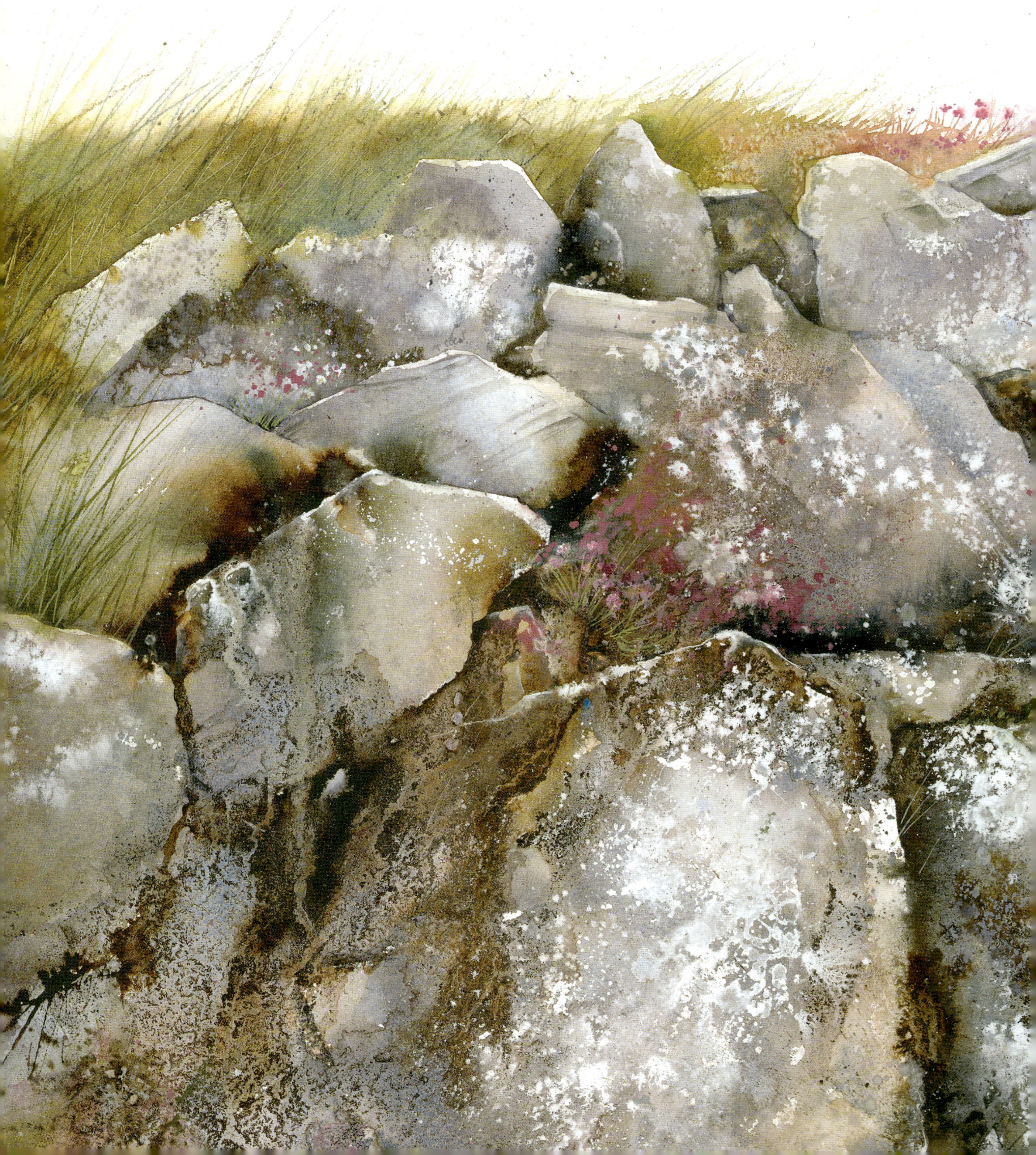

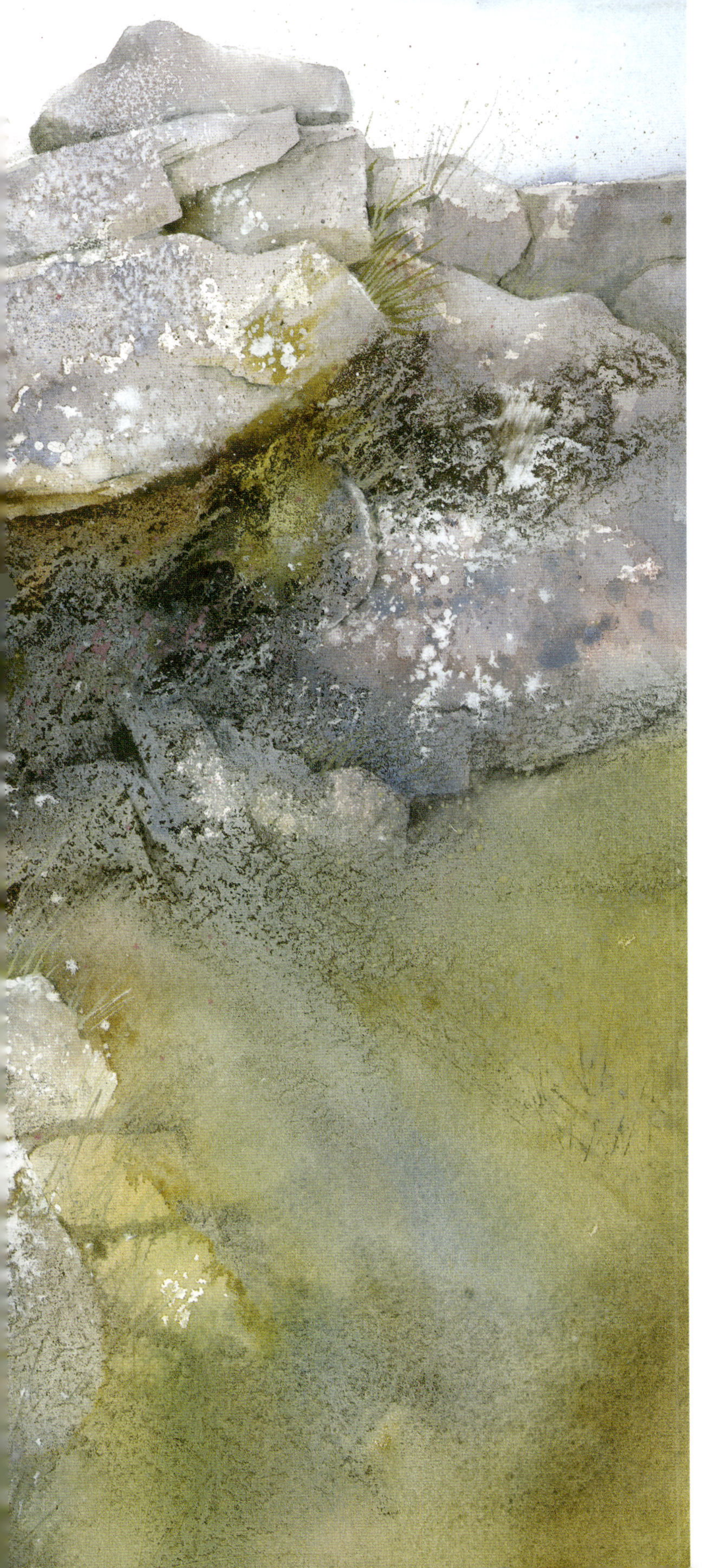

Landscape features

This section looks at some of the features of a rural landscape that tell a story or act as a focal point. Streams and ponds, country walls, rustic gates and fences as well as other manmade geometric elements add structure to the tumult of wild nature. Let's create poetic visual interpretations of these real objects and inject magic and imagination into our watercolour washes.

"PAINTING IS POETRY THAT IS SEEN RATHER THAN FELT, AND POETRY IS PAINTING THAT IS FELT RATHER THAN SEEN."

LEONARDO DA VINCI

◁ Of seapinks and Tumbled Rocks

Project: COUNTRY WALLS

I have chosen rustic walls for this project as natural stones offer an irresistible array of textures to explore. My wall interpretations are largely in close up but you might also choose to apply some of these thoughts to the bigger picture of a rocky landscape. Play with ideas as always before you start. I began by making some compositional sketches like the one shown here. The demonstration was painted as a portrait shape with more wall area than the background. It has been cropped to suit the book.

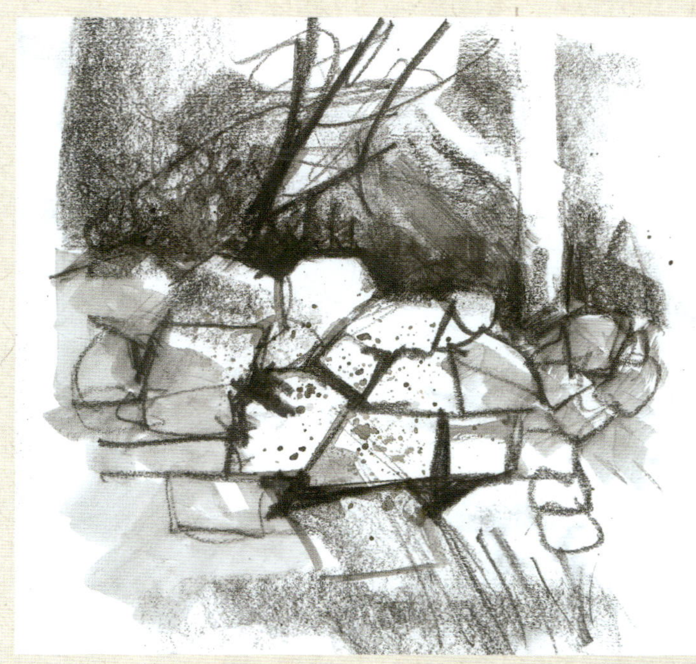

1 This is a simple composition, so it is important to position your wall and any added features carefully. For example, placing features off-centre can be more interesting than symmetry. Draw the wall profile first if you wish. Use a restricted palette so that attention is concentrated on the mossy stone-wall textures. I mixed different washes of Phthalo Blue and Raw Umber watercolour; use Quinacridone Gold instead if you prefer a sunnier palette. Begin with pale blues and greens above the profile of the wall, adding darker foliage effects while this is still damp. Continue painting around the stones, subtly changing the colour as you progress.

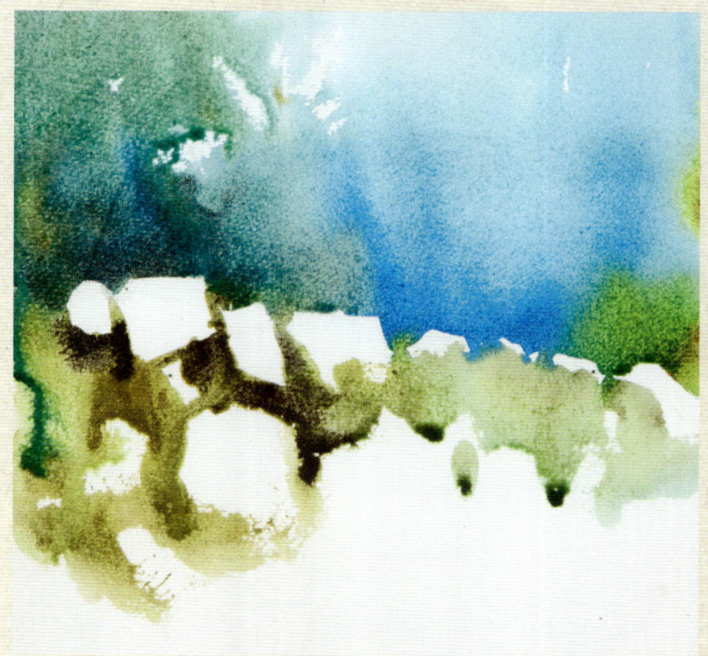

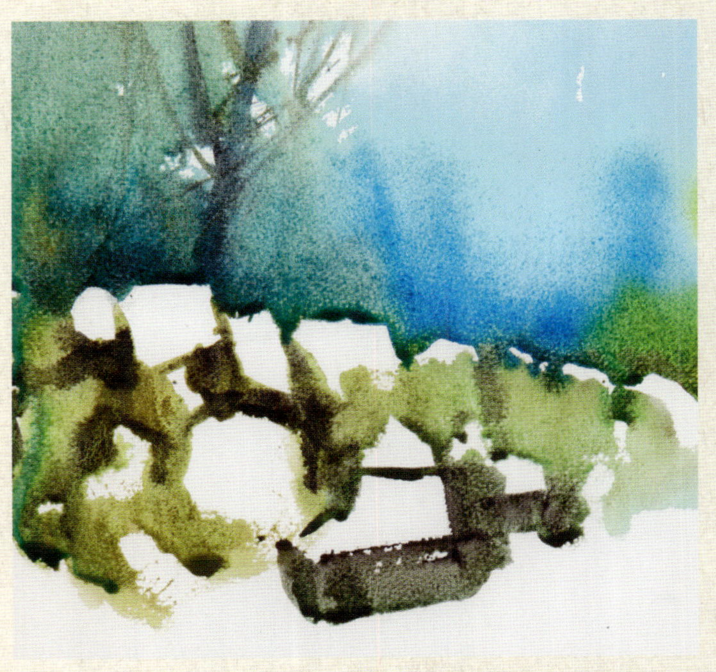

2 Use flat brushes for the edges of geometric rocks and round ones for more curved stones. Introduce some granulating darks such as Daniel Smith's Bloodstone Genuine and be bold with your application of shapes. You can see the paint gathering in small pools along the top of the wall and at the bottom of each small wash area. This shows you its consistency, which is strong but still fairly wet. Add trees to the upper part if it is still damp, using some of your dark colour. If the paint in this area is beginning to dry it would be better to add them later.

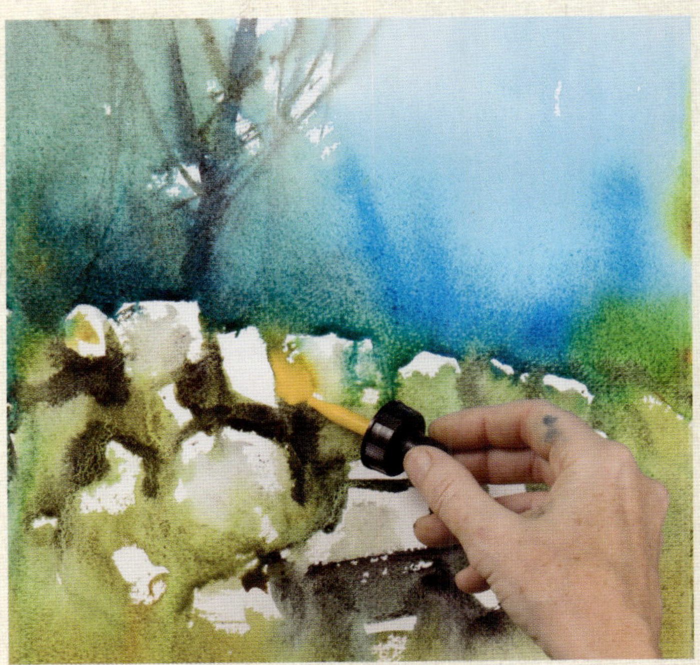

3 This illustration shows only the top part of the wall. Continue the wash down to the bottom of the paper below the wall. At this stage I added yellow and brown ink into the watercolour using the pipette in the lid. If you do not want to use ink you could add more dark granulating watercolour instead to accentuate the gaps between the stones.

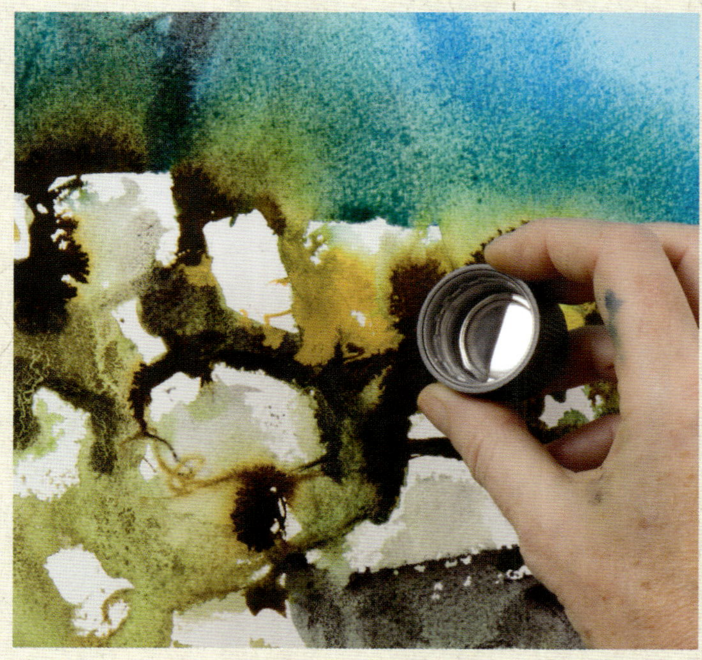

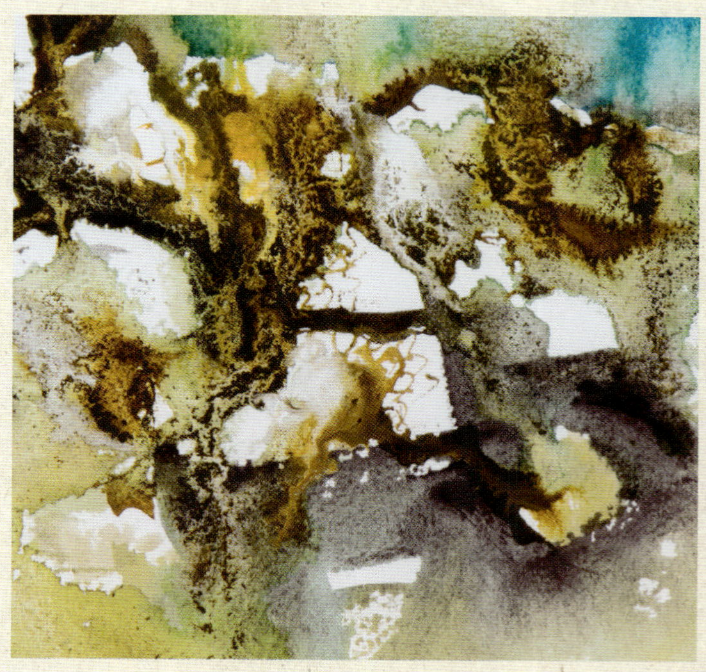

4 While this was wet I poured a little granulation medium into the picture and allowed everything to flow and separate into the rustic textures of the wall. If you are only using watercolour, just add a little clean water instead. I was careful about the amount I applied to avoid the colours spreading too far.

5 You can see the textures clearly in this detail. The white in the stones is just the untouched paper. If you prefer a less contrasted look you could blend some of the hard edges or drift a pale glaze of wash over the white areas when dry. If you want more detail you can add further cracks, crevices and plant details at this stage.

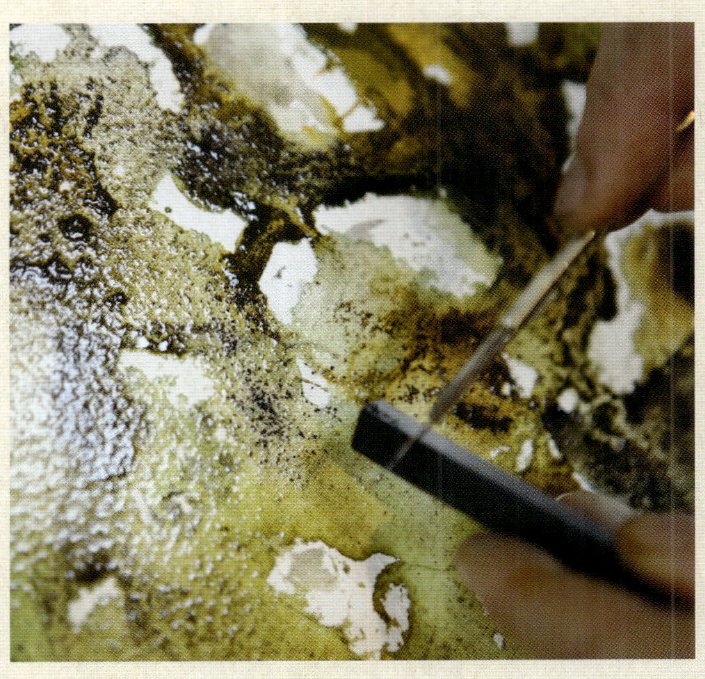

6 An alternative method to develop granular texture is to scrape colour off a watercolour crayon or pencil into a wet wash using a sharp knife such as a scalpel (I used an Inktense block). The tiny shavings will dissolve into the wash and are far more easily controlled into specific areas than other granulation methods. Speckles can be fine or chunky as required.

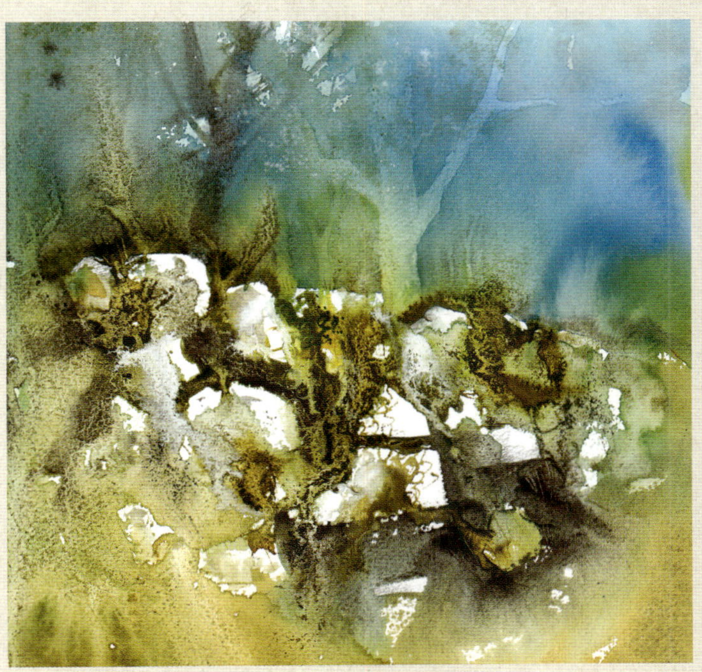

7 A good tip when you approach the finishing line is not to start filling every empty space. A basic rule is to keep things plainer in, say, one quarter of the design. I added a pale tree in the background with negative painting. Now follows the classic question – is it finished? Does the wall or background need further work? When making your decision, bear in mind that sometimes the intention to tidy up and improve your first spontaneous stages can mean losing some of their precious magic. Always err on the cautious side when choosing finishing touches; they can, after all, be added later, when a period of time has given you a fresh eye on your painting.

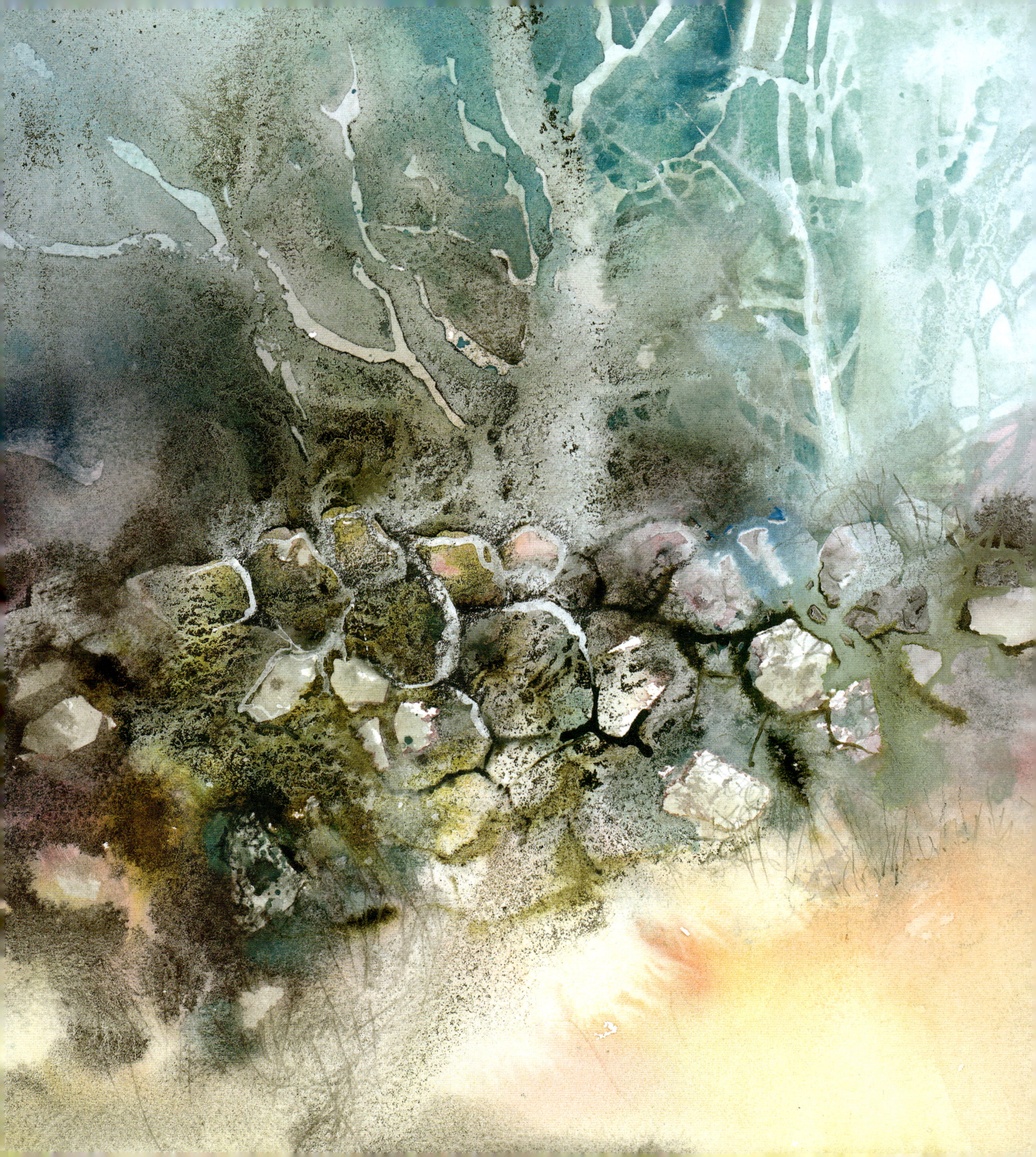

Taking it further: WALL TEXTURES

Rural boundaries are usually built out of the land they arise from, using the rocks, stone, earth or vegetation of the local environment. You will need to adapt your mark-making according to the specific colour, texture, size and shapes of the particular feature. Salt is useful for developing stony granular marks. You could also try using a piece of old credit card to scrape pale slabs out of thick paint layers to represent rocks.

Also think about how the gesso and tissue paper methods on pages 60-61 might be adapted to suit these new landscape elements. You might consider replacing the tissue paper with torn pieces of textured wallpaper or other collage material to get a tactile three-dimensional look. However, in the quest for fresh techniques do not forget about practising good old-fashioned brushwork. Dragging dry paint, stippling or scrubbing with old brushes all help to create mottled or patchy textures.

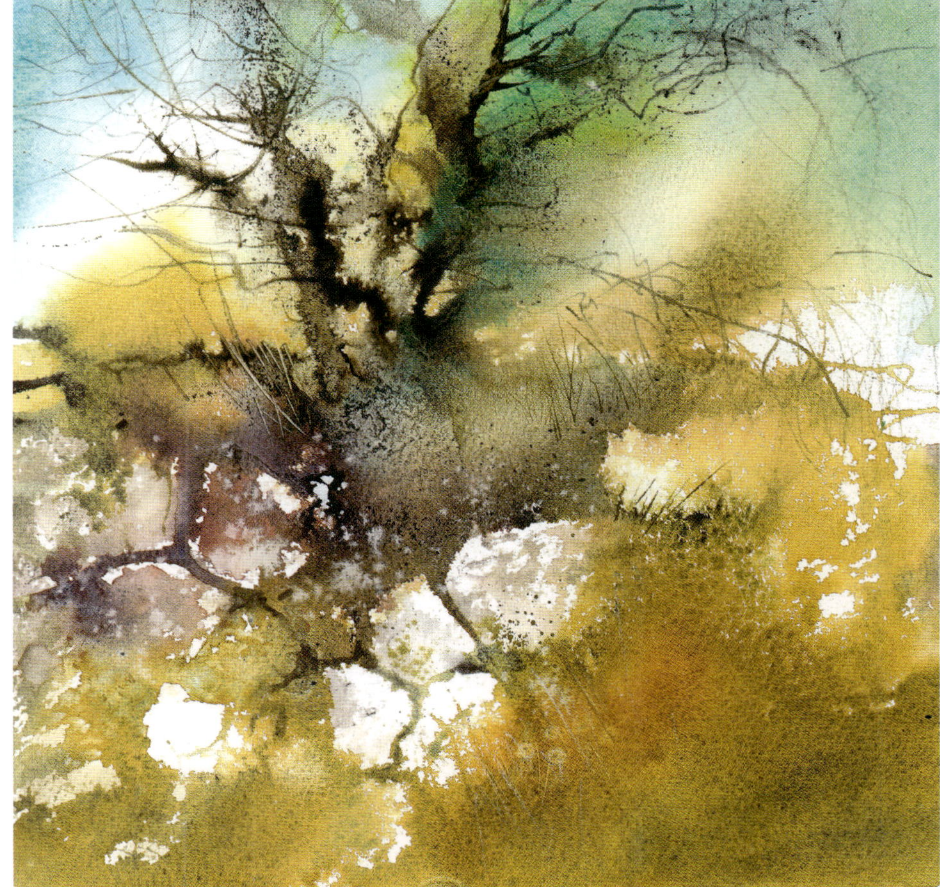

◁ *Dusky Wall*

These turquoise and indigo blues against whispers of pink evoke a mystical ambience made more potent by the misty background trees. I used black watercolour pencil for some of the shading in the rounded stones as this smudgy quality seemed in keeping with the mood.

▷ *Tumbled Wall*

In this sketchy picture the mottled effect within the rocks to the right was made by spraying the paper first and drifting colour into the globules of water. I allowed the paint to find its own pattern without the interference of brushwork in this area.

Developing your theme

Look at manmade landscape features in relation to the weather and seasonal changes of the surrounding vegetation. You can take ideas for colour and light using the natural environment as your inspiration and also borrow elements of the composition to lead the eye around the painting.

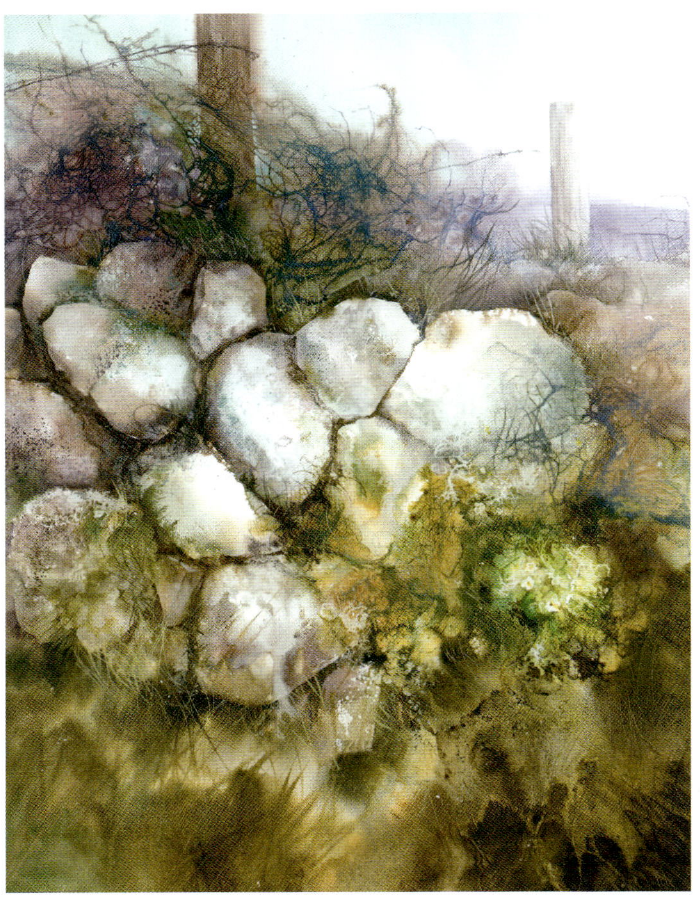

△ Early Spring Bank

The walls in south-west England are often part of a high bank combining stones with earth and plants. In springtime primroses nestle among the rounded stones. In this interpretation I was careful not to make the flowers too fussy but reflected their sunny colour in the wall to give a spring-like atmosphere. I chose complementary purple blue for the distant high land behind the top of the bank.

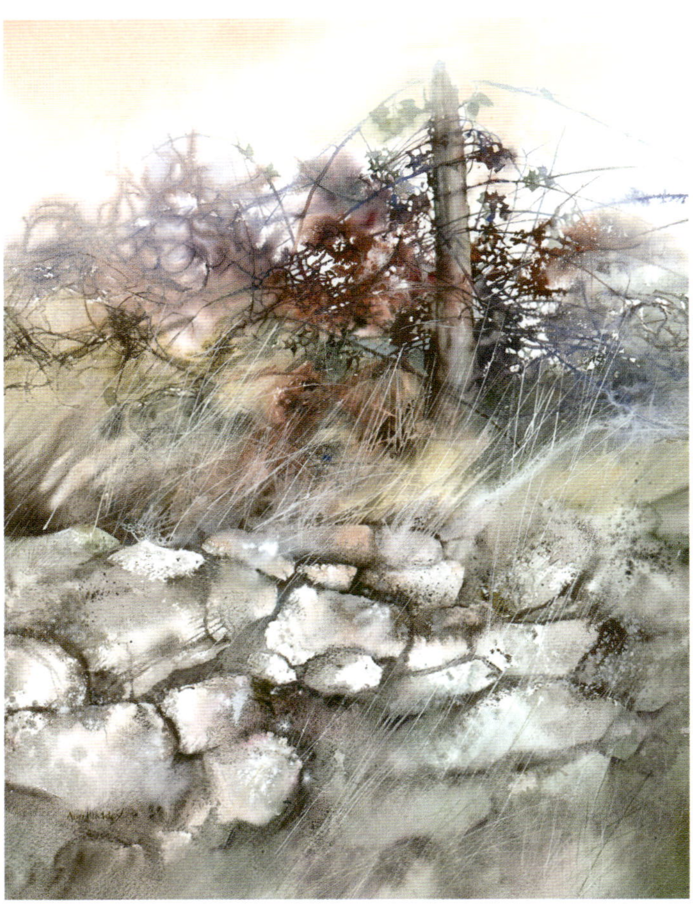

△ Tangled Winter Wall

This wintry interpretation employs tonal contrast more than colour to make its point. The wall itself is virtually monochrome and overall the palette is subdued and subtle. Interest is concentrated on the tangled textures and pattern of the winter undergrowth. The pale blades of dead grass are painted using opaque watercolour on top of the background in directions that lead the eye to the fence post that is the focal point.

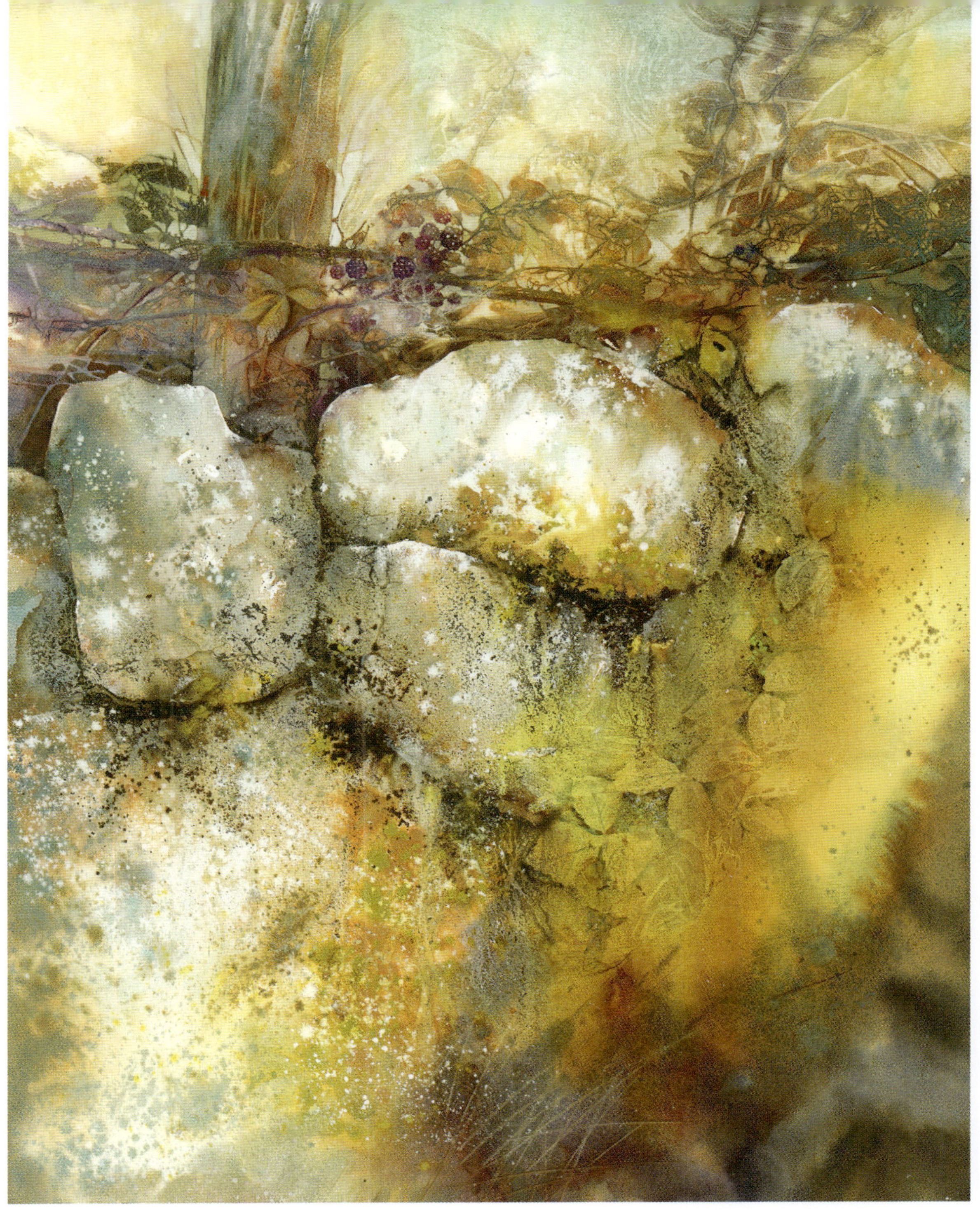

△ Autumn Wall

Here the wall was given a golden autumnal glow with a wash of Quinacridone Gold watercolour. I continued this into the background to emphasize the theme. Bramble leaves were merely suggested by negative painting around some shapes and one corner was left out of focus to concentrate attention on the hard edge at the top of the stones. These contrasting crisp contours lead the eye to a focal point of autumn blackberries.

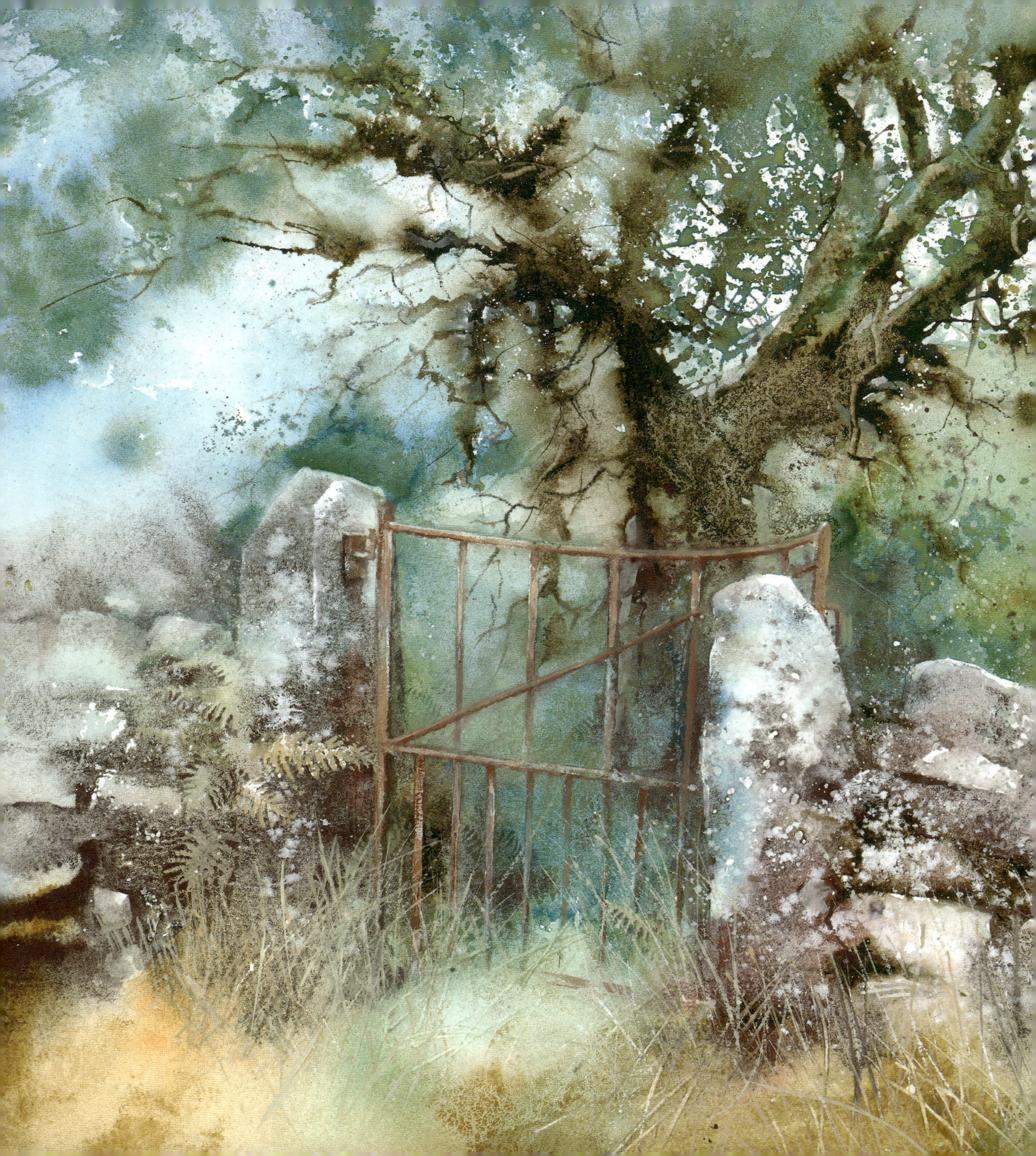

Gates and fences

Gateways, stiles and fences can be attractive features within the landscape, but the different qualities of their structures also make interesting subjects and focal points in themselves. These manmade elements play a role in telling a story, welcoming us through or blocking us from our path. When you keep a gate slightly open in a painting, it invites the viewer to look behind it. Adding hints of a different colour or light on the other side also tempts the eye to journey onwards.

The interpretations here have a fairly traditional approach. For ideas about how to represent geometric shapes and patterns in a more experimental fashion using printmaking and collage, see pages 100–101.

◁ *Beyond the Old Iron Gate*
I passed this fabulous gateway down a magical mountain lane in North Wales. The huge boulders used as gate posts contrast with the thin, bent lines of the iron gate and the delicate fringes of bracken and grasses. The gate is slightly ajar, inviting you through to explore the mysteries of the wild wood behind.

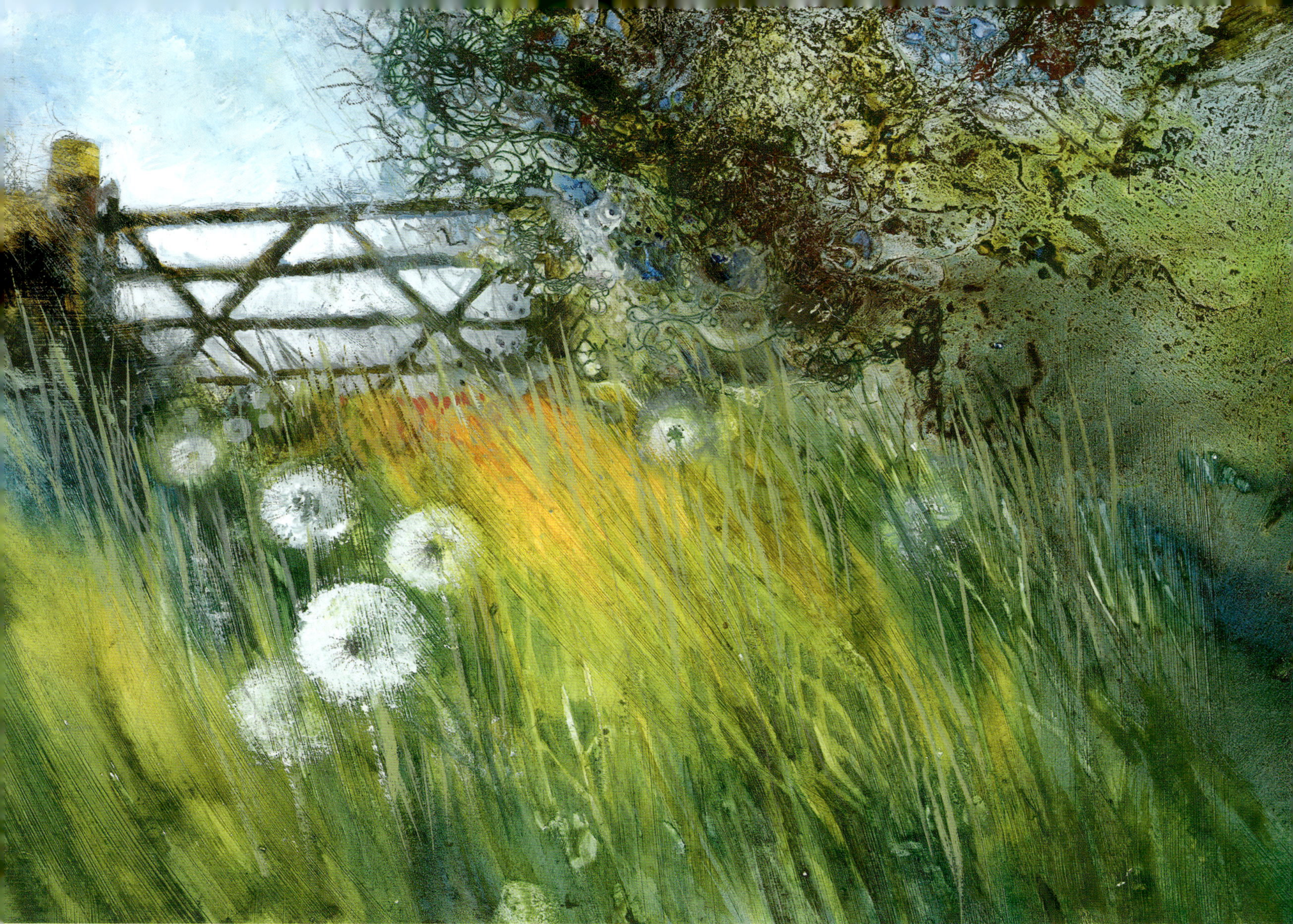

△ *Around the Clock*

This was painted on mount board coated in gesso. The glow
of orange in the grasses really leads the eye towards the dark
silhouetted gate. However, the lack of information about what
lies beyond makes us want to linger among the foreground
clocks. It is left to the imagination to translate what the orange
colour represents (see pages 48 and 49 for similar scenes on
different surfaces).

A hint of pale tangerine beyond the gate invites you to approach it. The broken wooden gate is painted in plain dark strips to offset the textures in the surrounding landscape. In this instance I did not get involved with the textural qualities of the woodwork itself but there is plenty of potential to explore this in further interpretations – for instance, using thick blocks of paint and scraping through it with a scalpel to get the effect of woodgrain or drawing woody lines into a wet wash with different pencils.

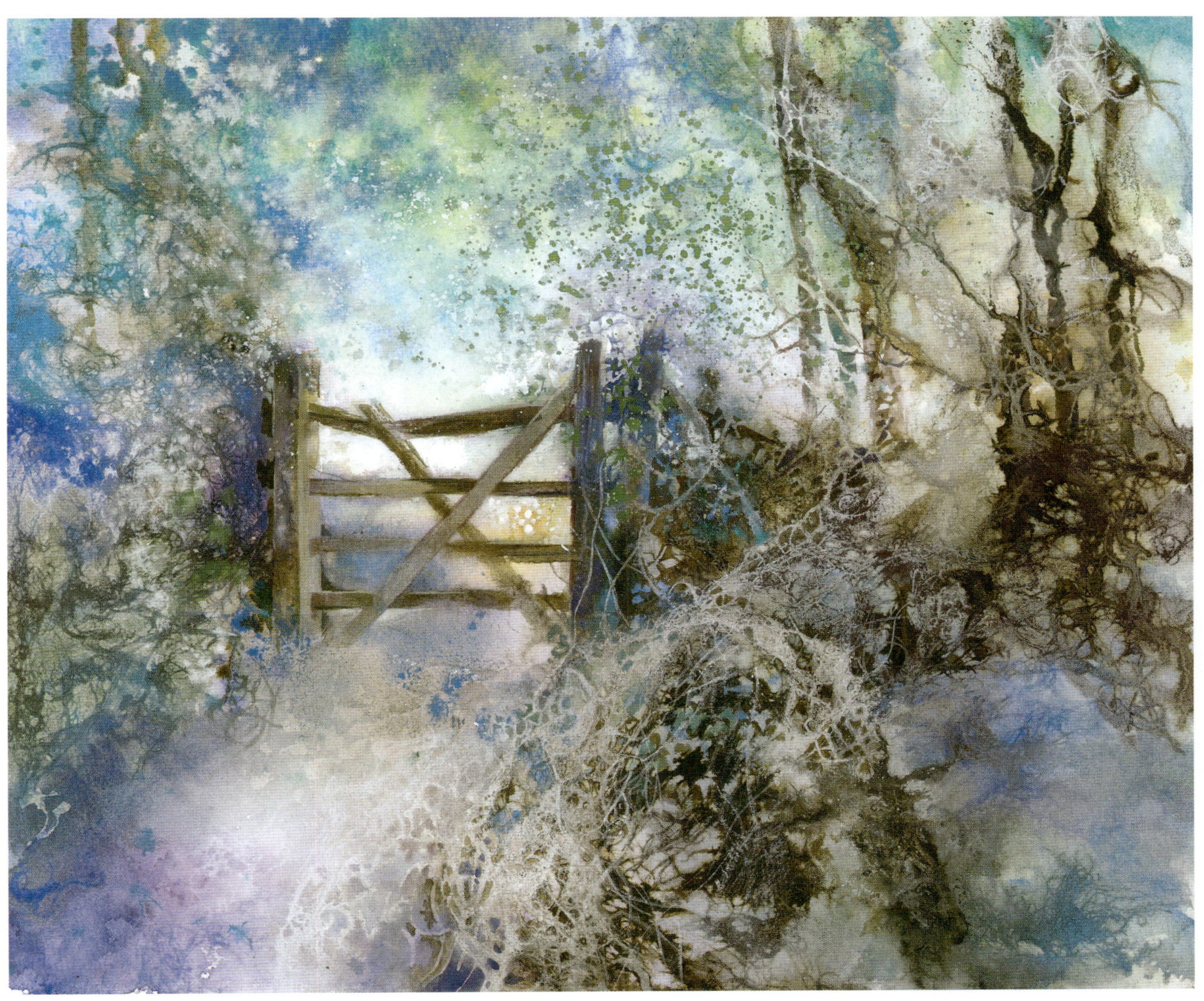

Painting water

Fluid, transparent watercolour is the perfect medium with which to portray all kinds of water – a natural, flowing feature of the landscape. You can almost allow the liquid paint to make its own journey down the paper and do the work all on its own. I am concentrating here on rivers and streams; I see these subjects on my daily walks and I am familiar with them, which I believe is important.

You would need a whole book to cover all the variations of this theme, so I have focused on two aspects of water. I have dipped into the technical issue of how to paint details such as ripples, reflections, splashes and movement in an exercise. The finished interpretations also demonstrate the bigger picture of the compositional role that a river plays within a landscape.

To paint water, take advantage of the classic qualities of watercolour and use them to the full. Choose translucent pigments and thin layers of paint. Keep plenty of crisp edges and leave bits of white paper to add sparkle and shine, but let the juicy paint flow into wet washes within each fluid area. Soften and blur edges to create movement but leave cleaner edges where the water is more still. Splash and dribble into the watery paint. In other words, echo what the water is doing in the landscape in the way you interpret it.

▷ Mountain Stream and Tangled Tree

In a magical Welsh valley a shining river zigzags its way between a jumble of mossy boulders and tangled trees. The shapes of the river are surprisingly geometric and angular as it finds its way between the rounded rocks. A juxtaposition of hard and soft edges emphasizes the rush of the water winding through. The pattern it creates leads the eye to the salmon-pink, sun-washed mountains glimpsed through the tapestry of branches.

▽ Ripples, Sparkle and Movement (exercise)

Explore mark-making devices to capture watery characteristics. Drag a loaded brush sideways in a series of random strokes, leaving gaps of white paper to help re-create rippled movement. Pieces of cling film stretched horizontally over some of the washes will break it into watery patterns. In other areas let the wet paint form back runs into the dryer riverbank. This blurred edge helps the effect of moving water. If the paint looks too solid when it is dry, lightly drag on streaks of undiluted white gouache to create shimmer. Splatter white on with a palette knife or splash with a brush depending on the size of the area that requires further sparkle.

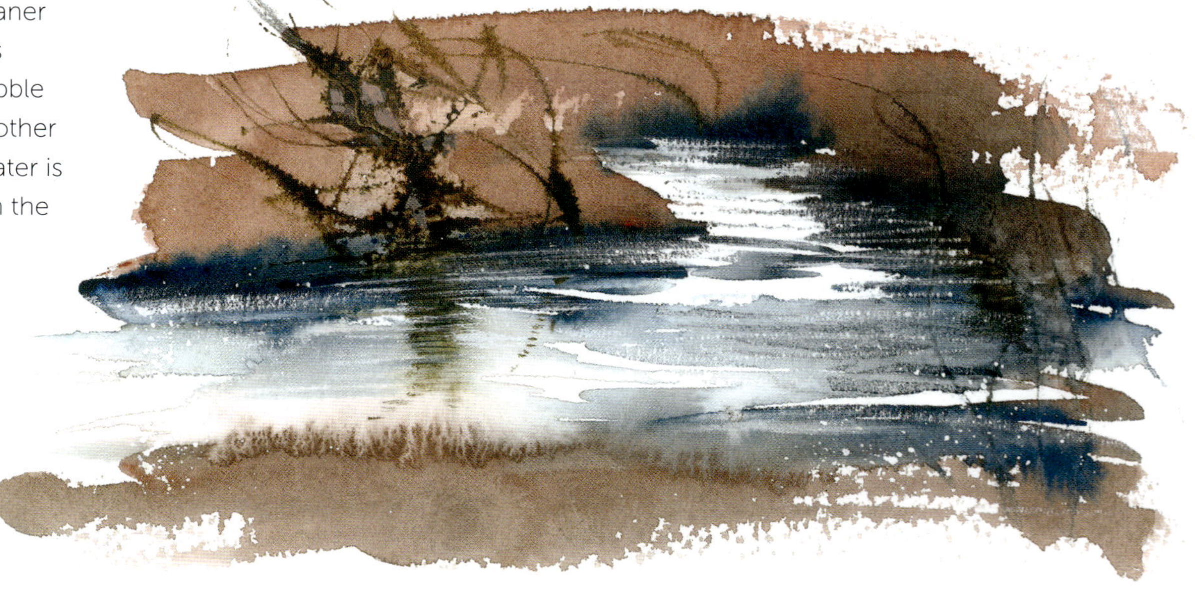

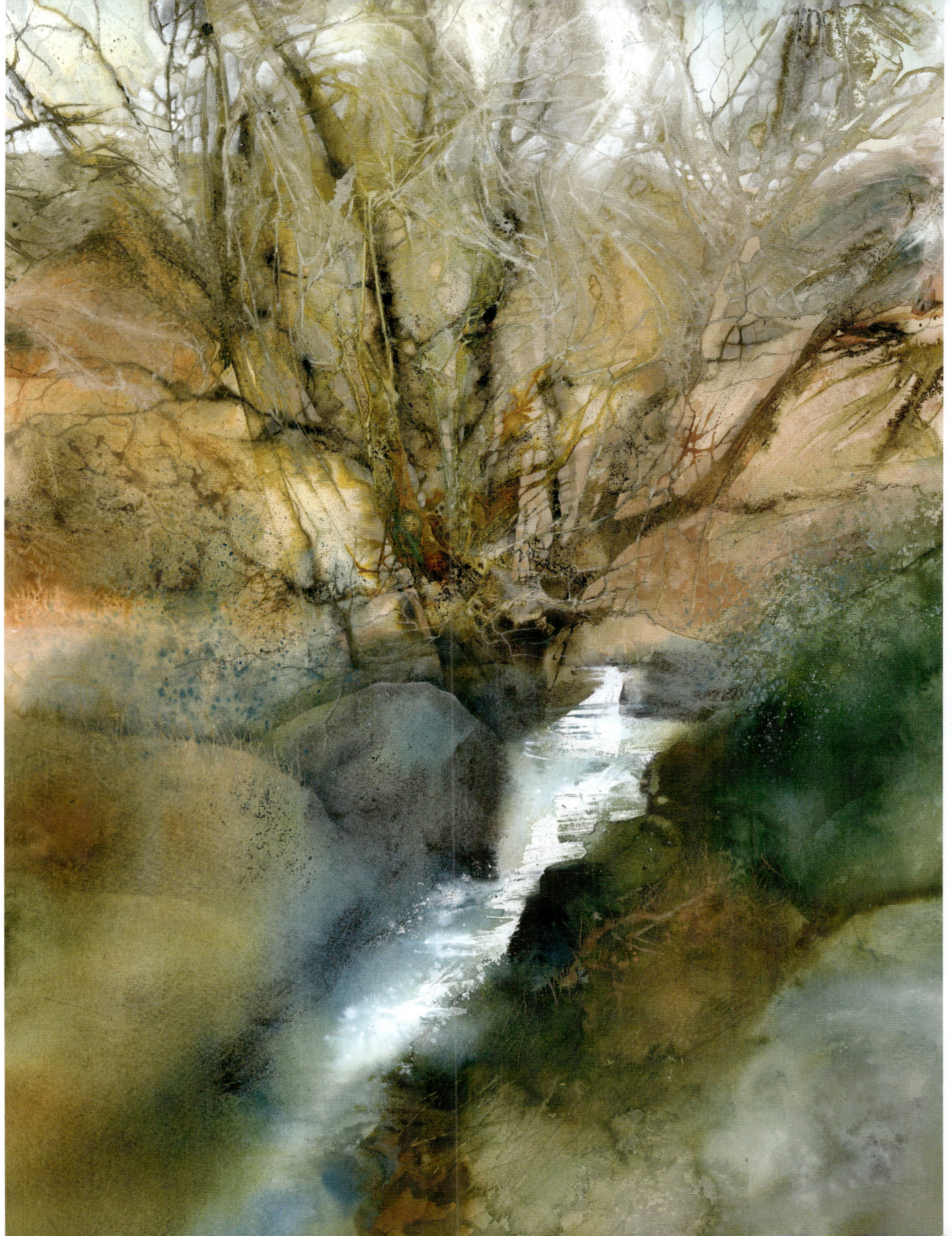

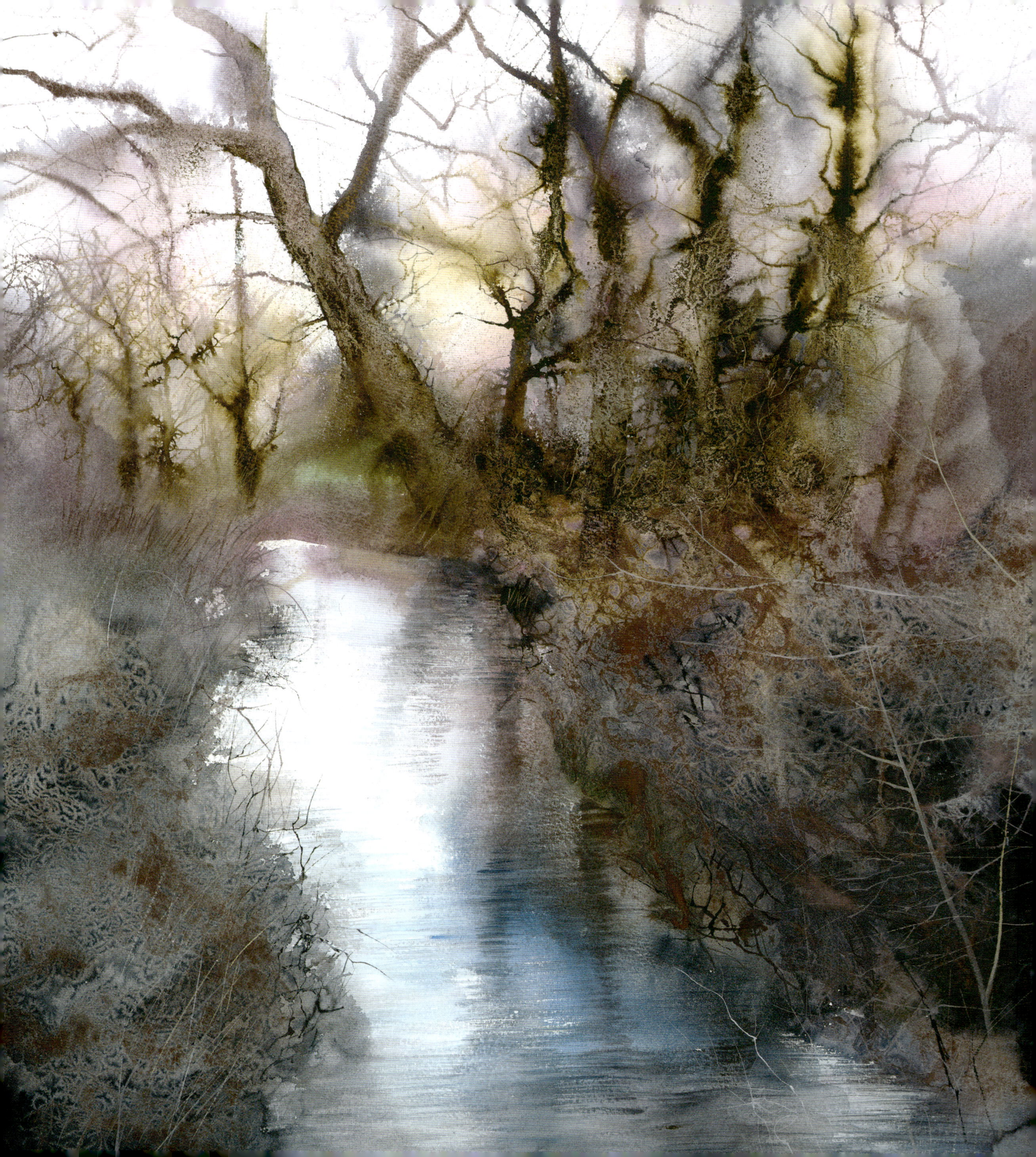

Landscape features such as rivers and pathways can be used as a compositional device to lead the eye around the painting and tell a story. The river here gently zigzags through the middle of the painting, leading the eye from the shadowy water at the bottom to the sharp bright edge where the river turns a corner. That little tip of light almost points towards the secret area where the water disappears, leaving an air of mystery as to what might be around this bend.

▷ Twilight River

This interpretation is the same scene as in *Lazy Hazy River* except that this time the river and setting sun are viewed from a subtly different angle. In this version the water goes straight up the page, ending in a more abrupt edge where it changes direction behind the undergrowth. This time attention is drawn up to the golden circle of the setting sun directly above which peeps through the trees. The change in composition alters the visual story. The plot is now about staying in the moment and concentrating on the magic of the twilight hour.

Willow Reflections (overleaf)

This is a new interpretation of a similar painting I did in a vertical format and smaller size for my book *Experimental Landscapes in Watercolour*. The picture shown here fills a whole sheet of watercolour paper.

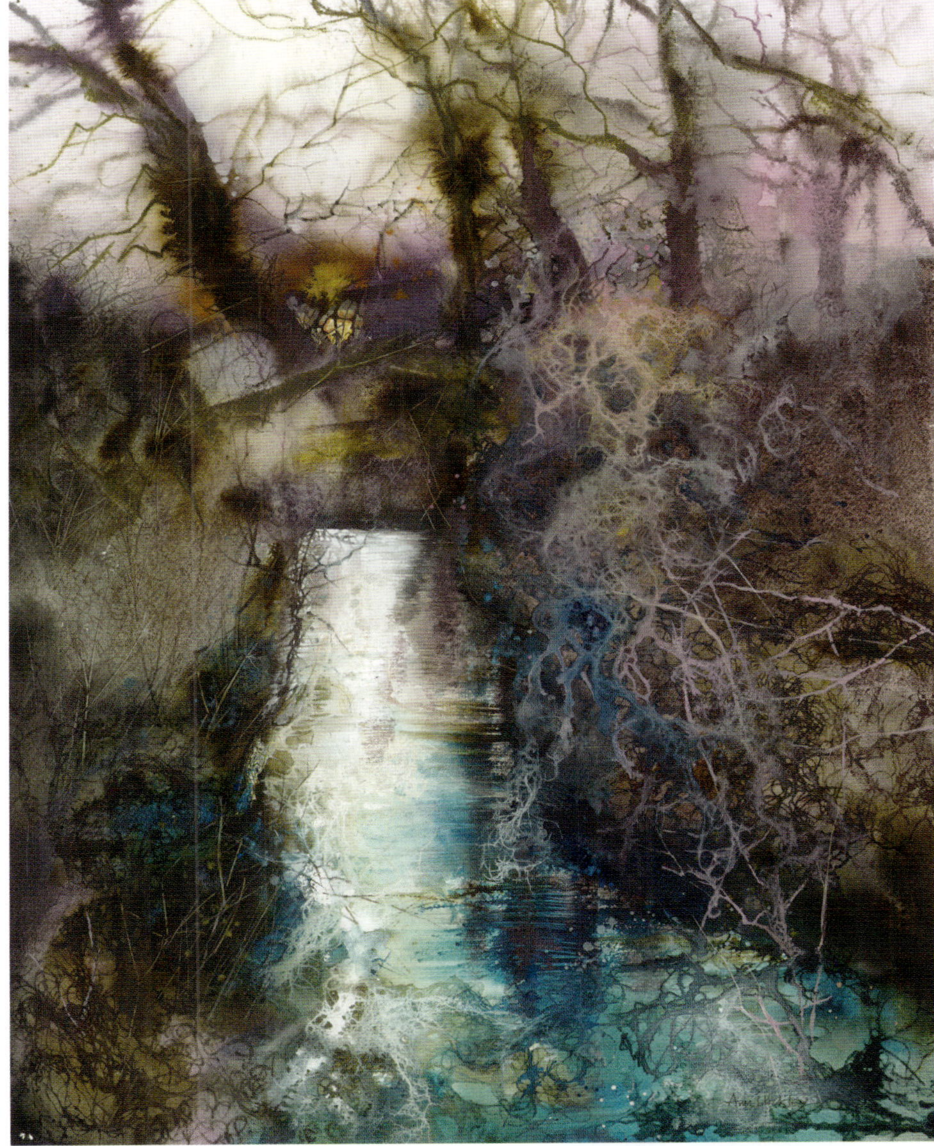

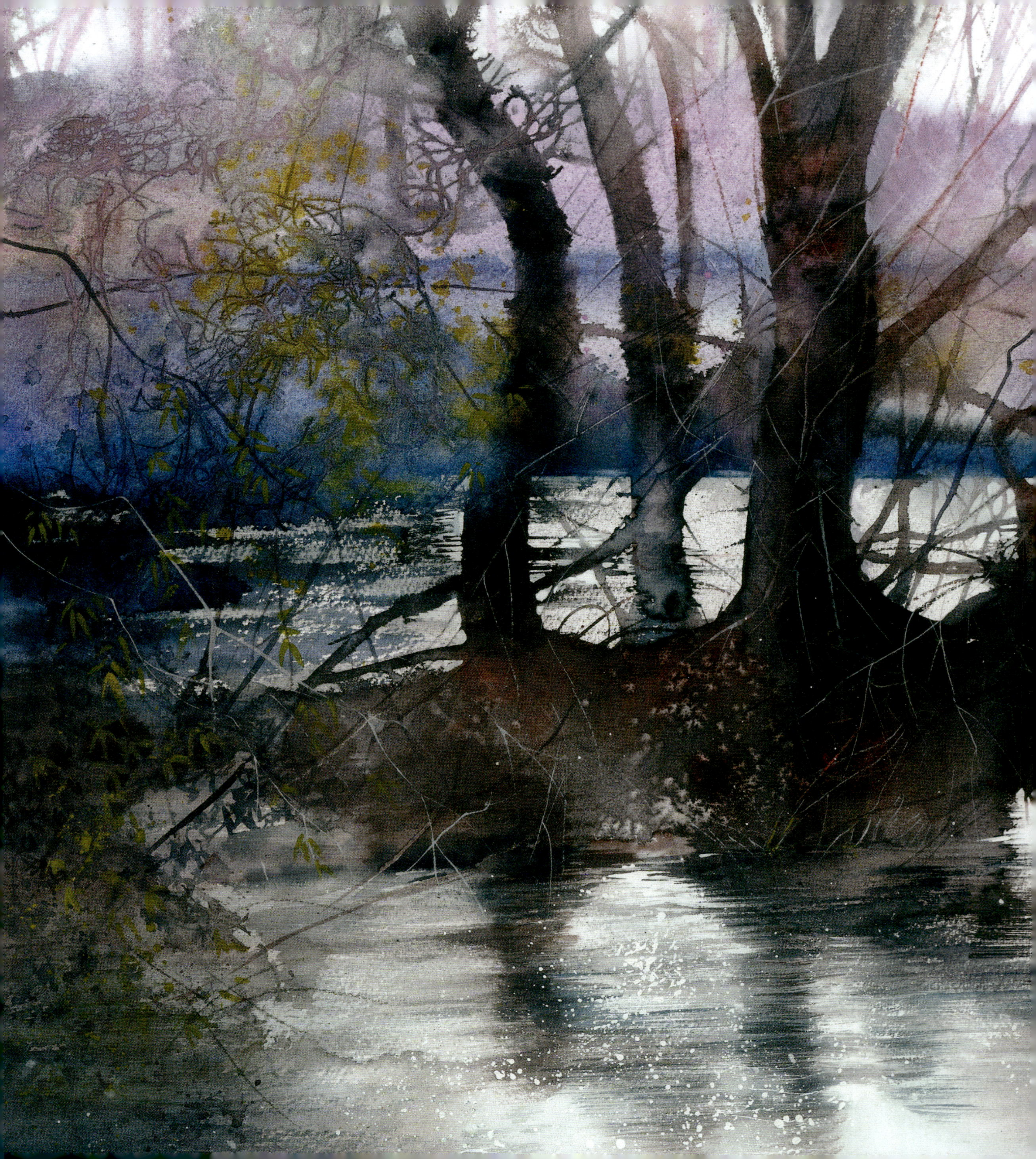

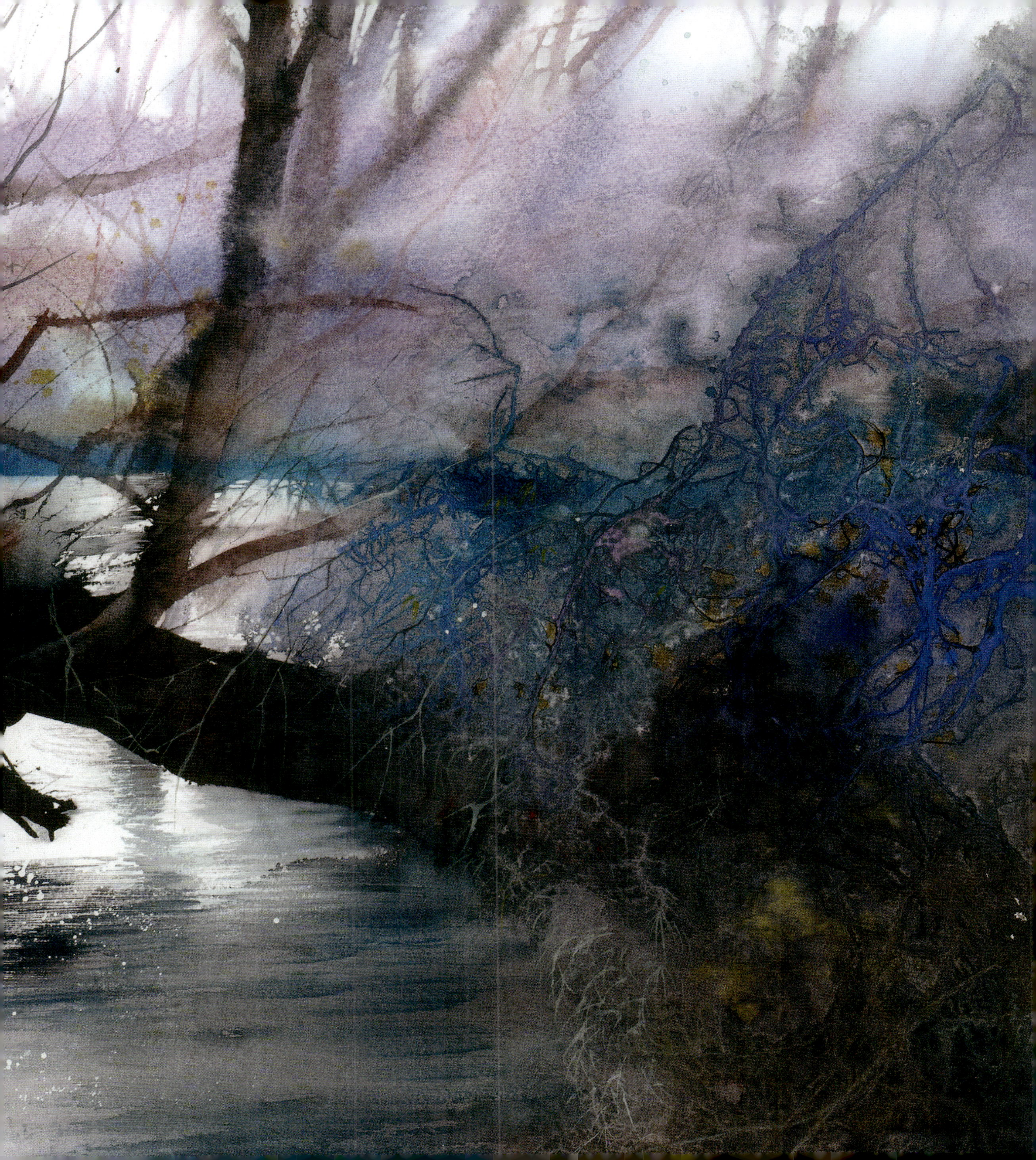

Project: BEEHIVE

In this project I have used a beehive for inspiration.
You could paint any geometric shape such as a
pale cottage in the mountains in a similar way.
I painted the hive from life as it sits outside my
studio but visually borrowed some rambling
branches from a nearby apple tree for my
composition. The photograph shows the different
view. It can be helpful to play with photographs
digitally to give you creative ideas about how to
interpret something. Here, I changed my colourful
snapshot to sepia and heightened the contrast.

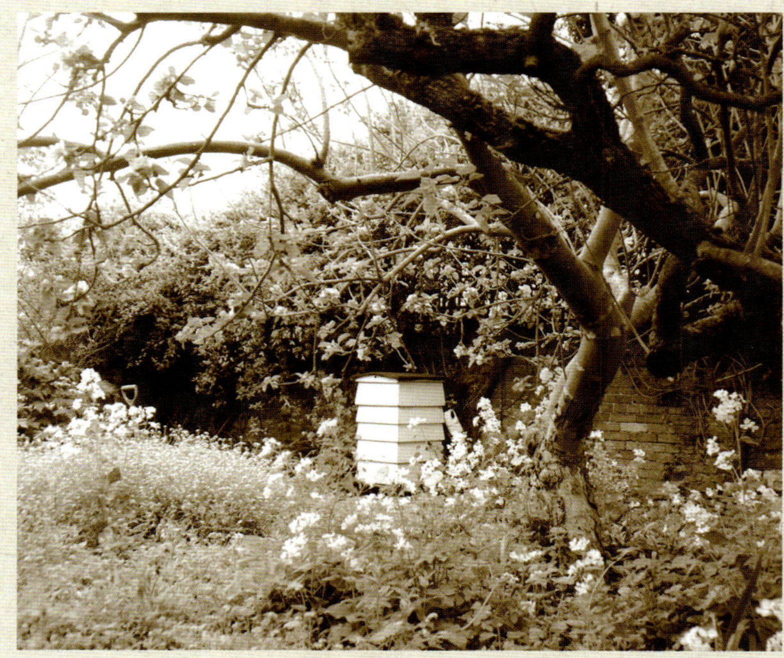

1   Try sticking to a very limited palette and
    concentrate on tonal values. I used only
    Quinacridone Gold and granular Bloodstone
    Genuine in this picture, inspired by the colour
    of honey bees. I began by painting around
    the straight edges of the beehive roof leading
    upwards into the branch tangles using juicy
    washes of the Bloodstone. It looks very abstract
    at this stage, especially as the illustration shows
    only a detail. Be confident and make bold,
    spontaneous brushstrokes.

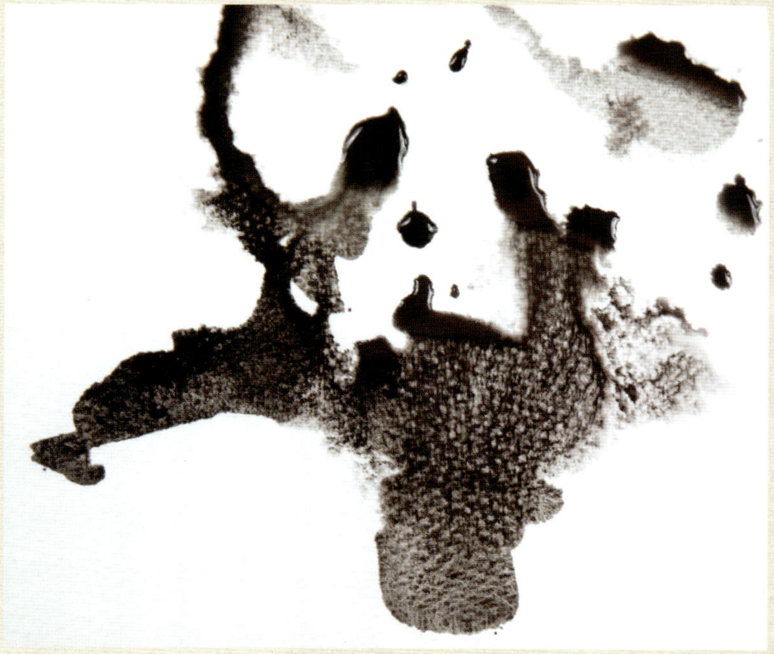

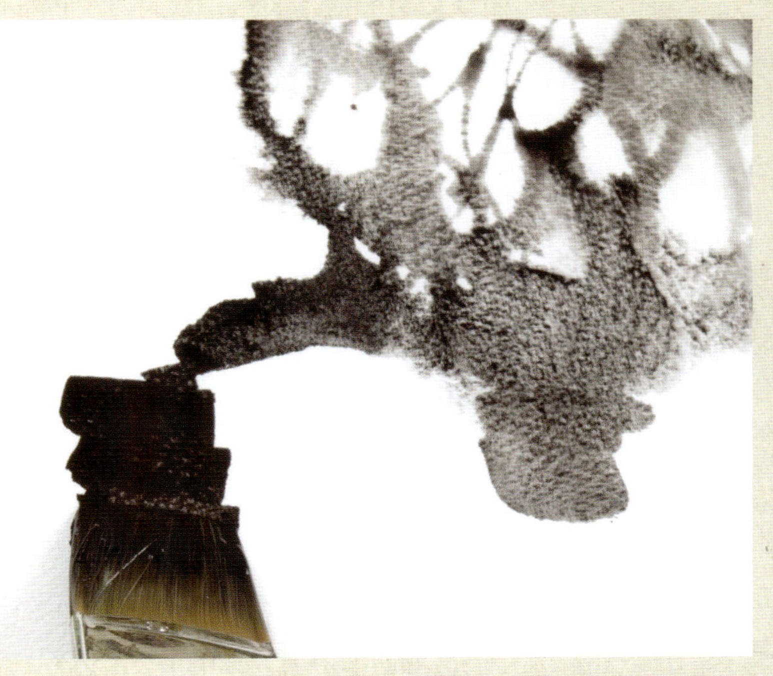

2 A flat brush is ideal for painting clean straight edges and useful for sharp geometric details such as the zigzagging side of the beehive using the square corners of the brush. If you are using a round brush, make sure it has a sharp point to keep these details crisp. I did this demonstration freehand, but drawing the important focal point first using unobtrusive pencil work can give you more confidence to paint freely.

3 Continue around the shape, diluting the watercolour to get paler tones, and introduce another colour to represent the ground. The two areas should be allowed to mingle. It is interesting to note my colours almost fighting for dominance, one pushing against the other. I feel this gives the picture a lively buzz. The edges stay crisp where the white shape is dry but soften when next to any moisture in 'lost and found' edges.

4 Complete painting around the whole subject, adding texture to the wash if you like. My beehive was still largely hard-edged, so I used a damp brush to borrow some of the surrounding wet colour to blur one of the hive sides. If your paint is dry you should still be able to dissolve and ease the soluble watercolour. If you paint a dark geometric feature on a light background instead, you would still soften some of the edges to link it with its surroundings.

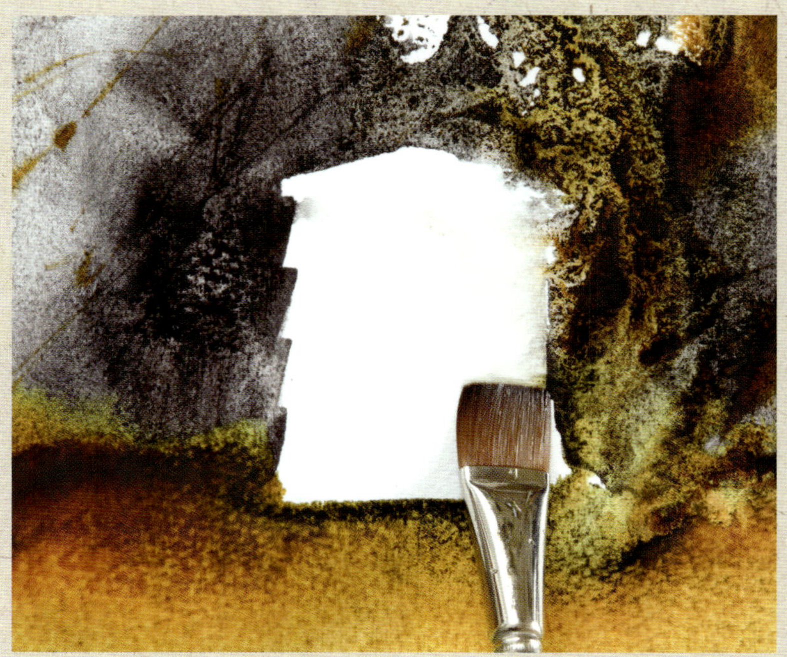

5 Features such as a beehive, building, wall, post or tree need to sit comfortably in their background. Even if you decide to retain a crisp graphic shape my tip is to at least soften the bottom of the subject into the ground. To take it further you can break up the shape by overlapping something in front of it. My favourite device is plants and I have gently dragged branches across the hive and pencilled some stalks in the foreground. You could integrate a building into the landscape by breaking up the shape with trees, fences or telegraph poles.

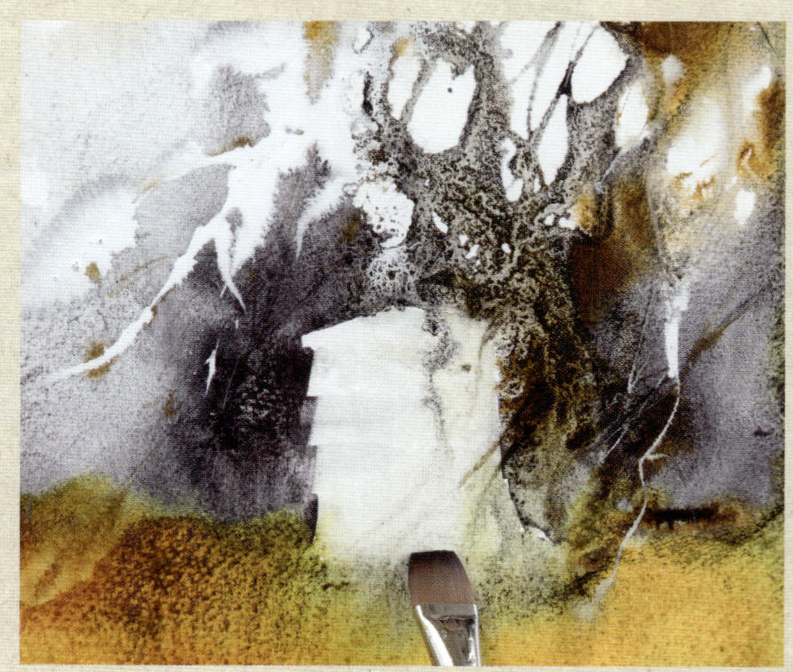

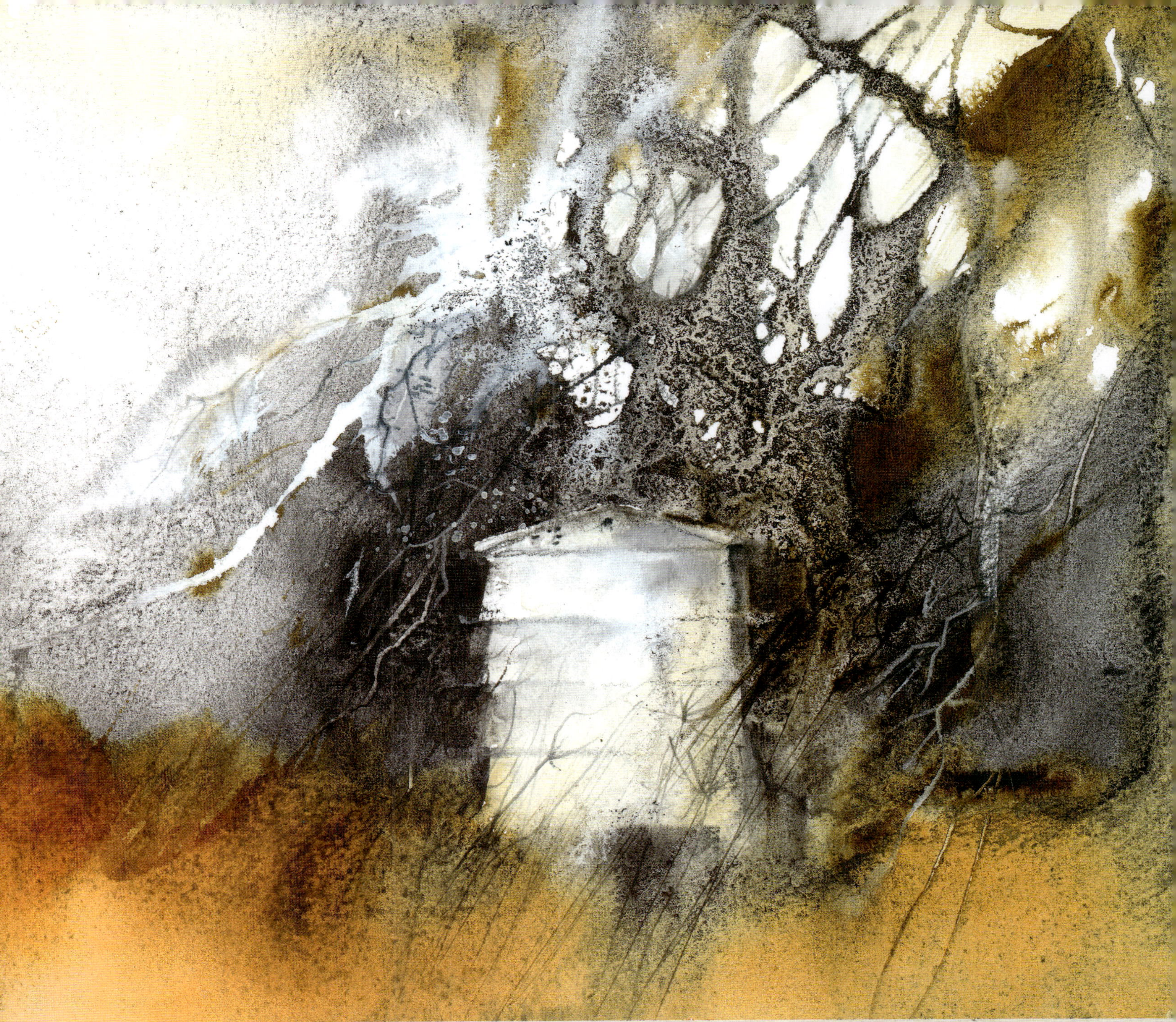

6 Add information to give form or context to your shape. I included shadowy details to describe the
stacked boxes of the hive and give it a three-dimensional quality. If you have chosen to paint a building
rather than a beehive be sure to treat features such as windows and doors in a similar 'lost and found'
way. Finally, the illustrator in me enjoyed adding some little black dots that I think might be our bees
flying home from their forays! It can be fun sometimes to keep a playful element in your work.

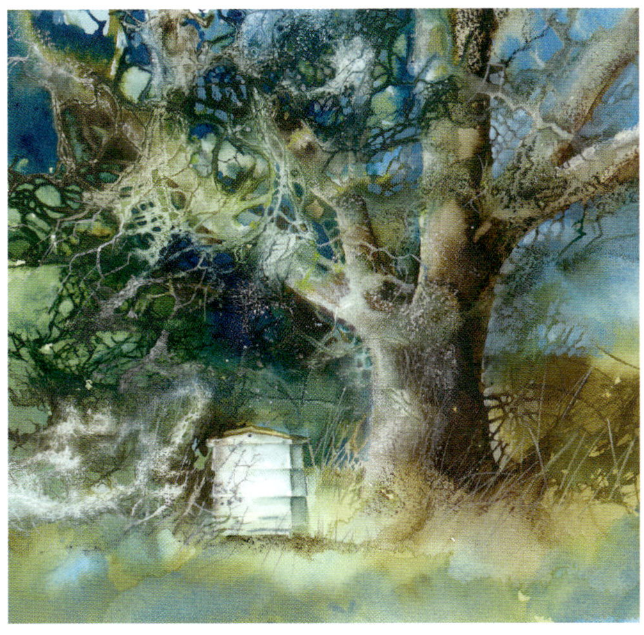 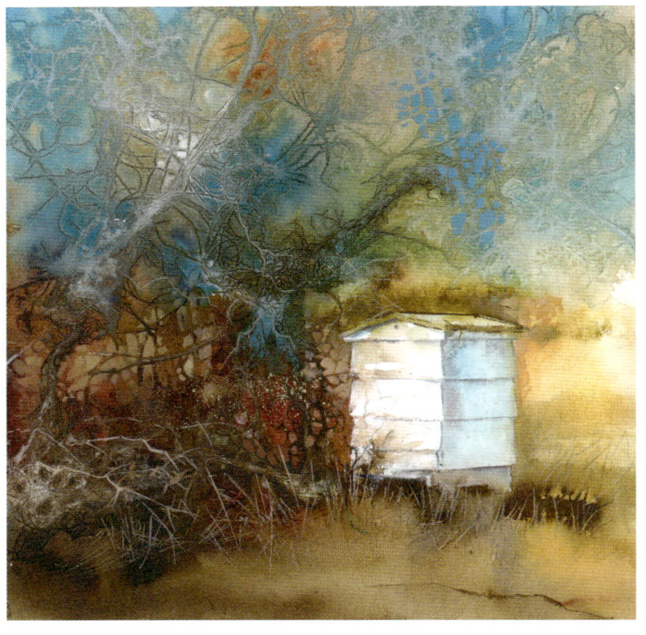

△ Under the Spreading Walnut Tree

One of our hives sits under a massive walnut tree in a wild, neglected field of brambles.

△ Among the Brambles

 I speckled some gold ink around this hive to create a magical buzzing shimmer of bees.

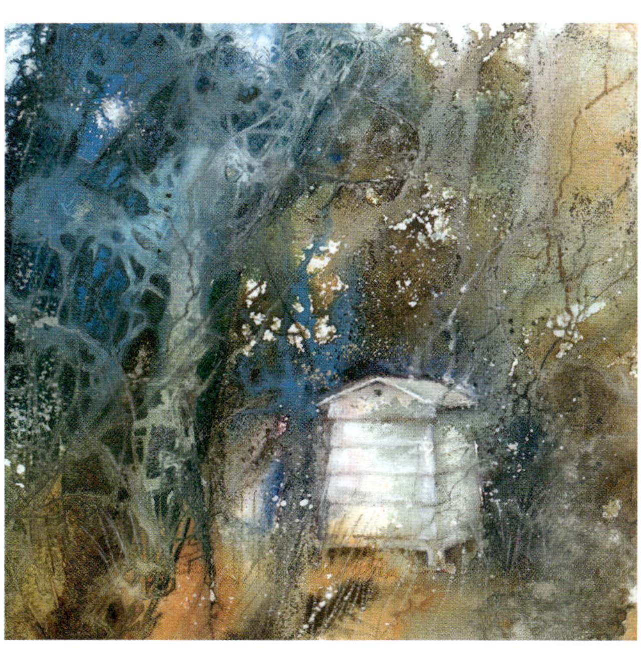 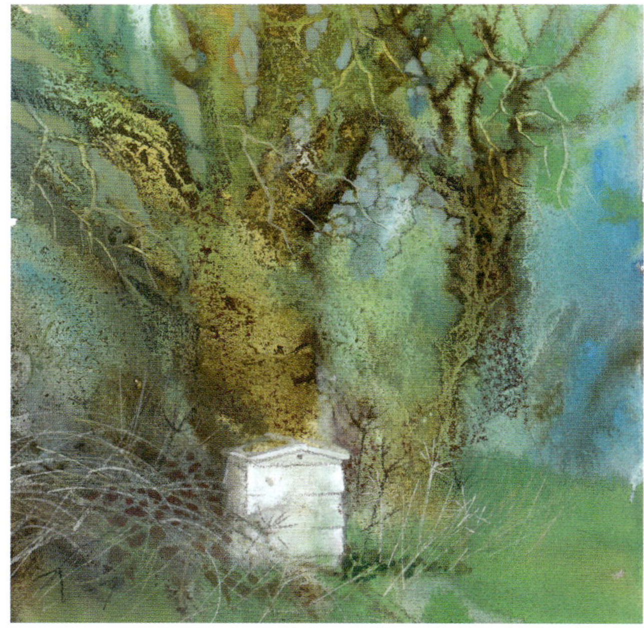

△ As Busy as Bees

Speckles of white paper and splatters of paint keep this picture alive and humming with activity offset by the brooding branches of the tree.

△ Beehive in the Wood

I deliberately kept this beehive rather smudged and shadowy so that it would sit very quietly in its secret corner of the woodland.

I loved painting this beehive theme. It is stimulating to try something new that is also very personal. My husband is a beekeeper and our garden seems to hold an almost mystical attraction to bees. In 2017 we had seven swarms in seven days! When you interpret a subject that is close to your heart it seems to have greater integrity and depth. I have only recently thought to include our beehives in a picture. Open your eyes to everything close to home and discover some fresh subjects. Remember that even the most unlikely or simple thing can be effective.

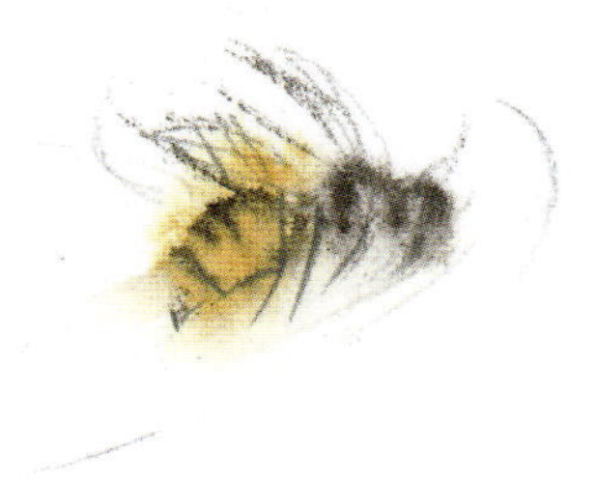

1

2

3

Techniques: GEOMETRIC MARK-MAKING

I am drawn to the free-flowing tangles of nature and shy away from anything involving a straight line! However, geometric shapes can act as useful devices to add elements of structure or a focal point to organic textures. You can mask or paint around such shapes if they are pale or add them on top if they are darker than the background.

Other methods may help you achieve a looser, quirky or more impressionistic effect. If you cut out and stick shapes on top of a background it enables you to paint very freely to start with, using your preferred technique. Marks made by printing instead of using a brush have an interesting quality. You can use bits of card to stamp lines or drag the paint sideways to create chunkier shapes. If the paint runs out and you achieve a 'hit and miss' effect it adds to the variety. When you print marks, make sure you do so using various lengths and thickness to avoid being repetitive. Below are three ideas to get you started.

1 Stick collage pieces on top of a wash to represent buildings, fences, beehives or other geometric shapes. The shapes do not need to be precise or real – they are simply expressive marks.

2 Try using the edge of pieces of card. Print to get a thin line or drag sideways for a thicker mark or chunky shape. You can print pale gouache over a darker wash or dark watercolour over a pale background.

3 Geometric lines and shapes can be printed or dragged on with the tip of a flat-edged brush.

I saw this barn on a trip to Australia. It was patchworked together from bits of timber and old tin. The bent and weathered fence posts in the foreground lead the eye towards the building. I decided to collage pieces of the photographed barn and bits of painted paper to represent the posts on top of a painted background. I felt that this paper patchwork echoed the ramshackle structure of the farm building.

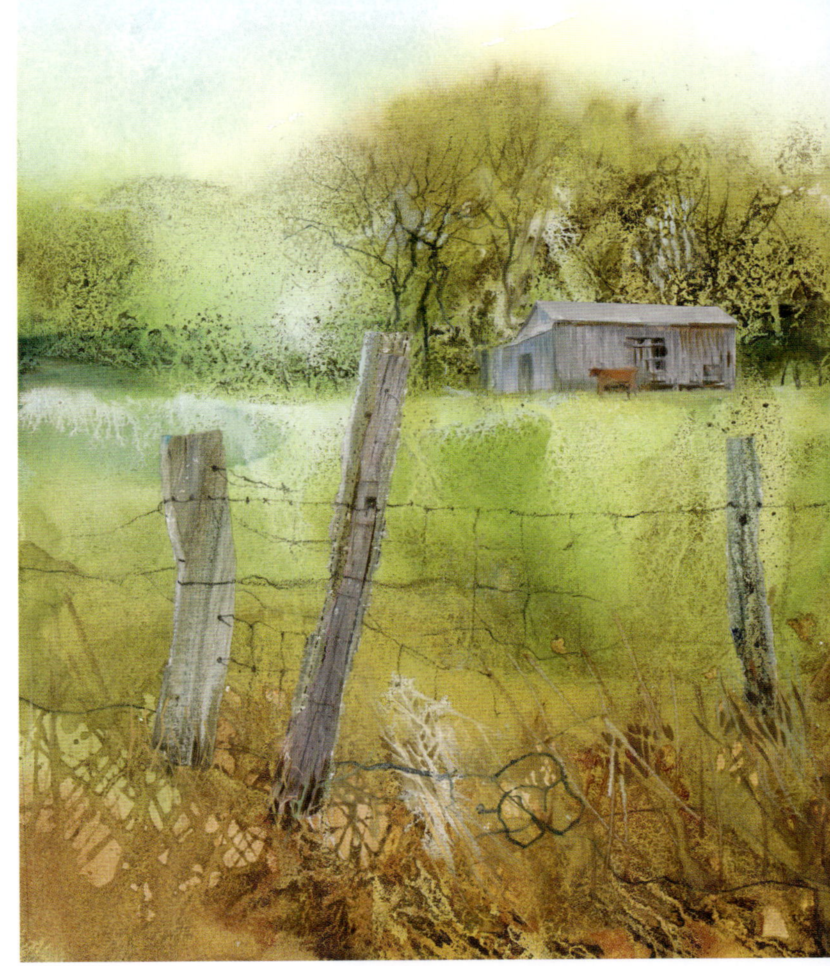

This watercolour also has collage elements. The rocks are made of scraps of torn watercolour paper stuck on before painting and the fence and bird were added on top of the watercolour background.

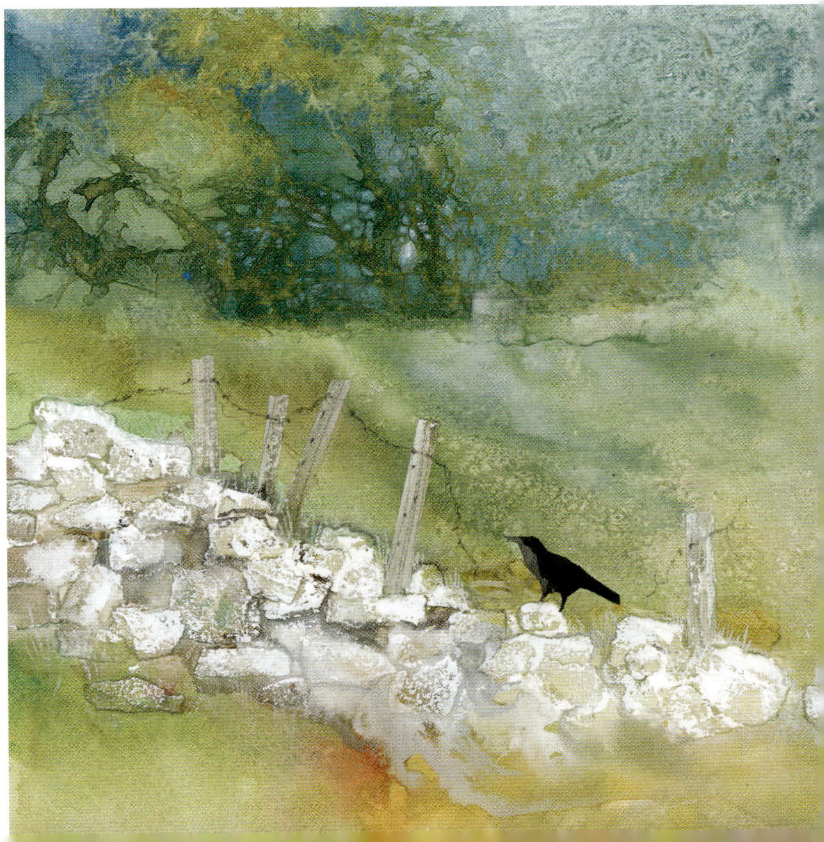

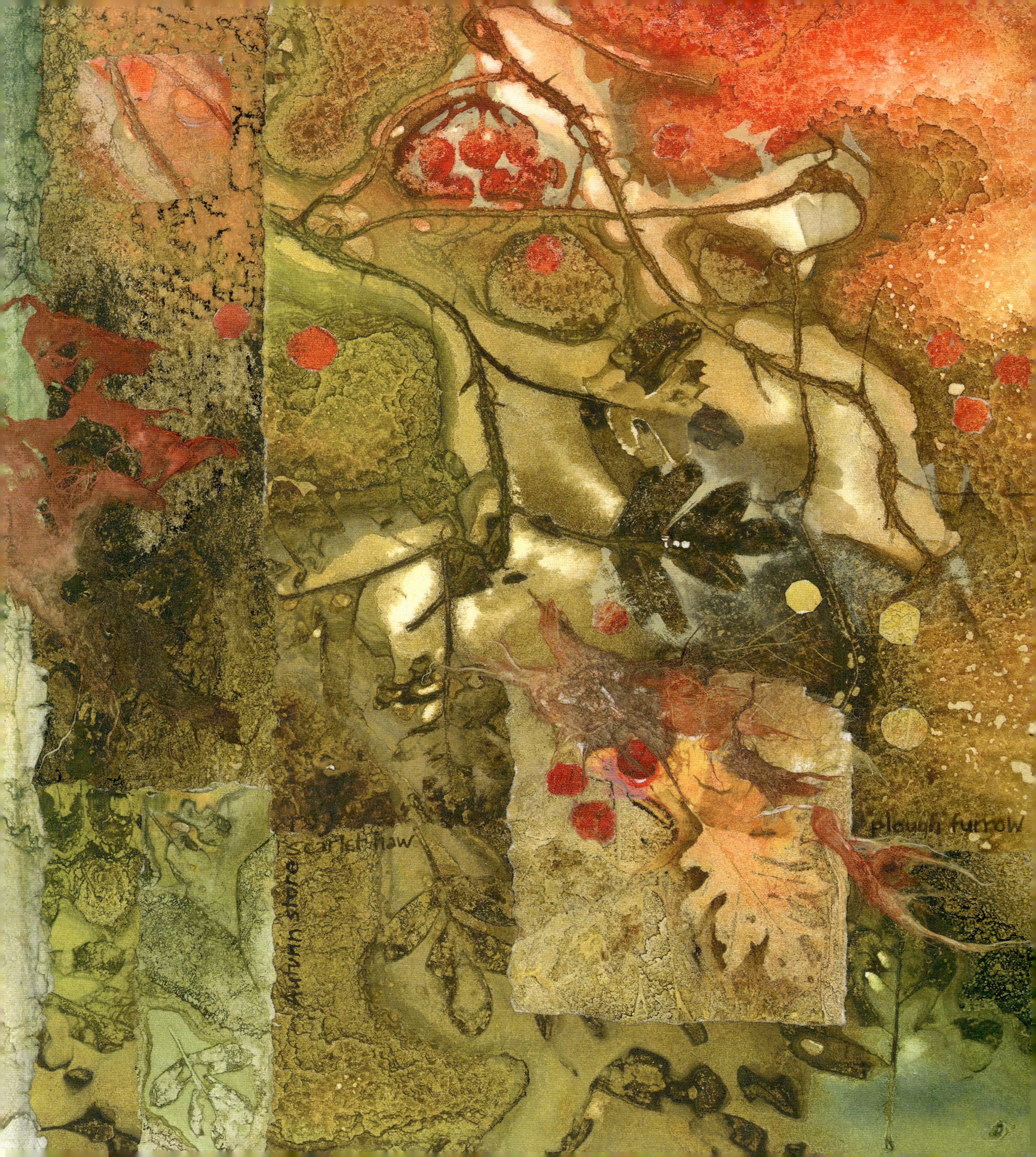

Autumn sunfire
scarlet haw
plough furrow

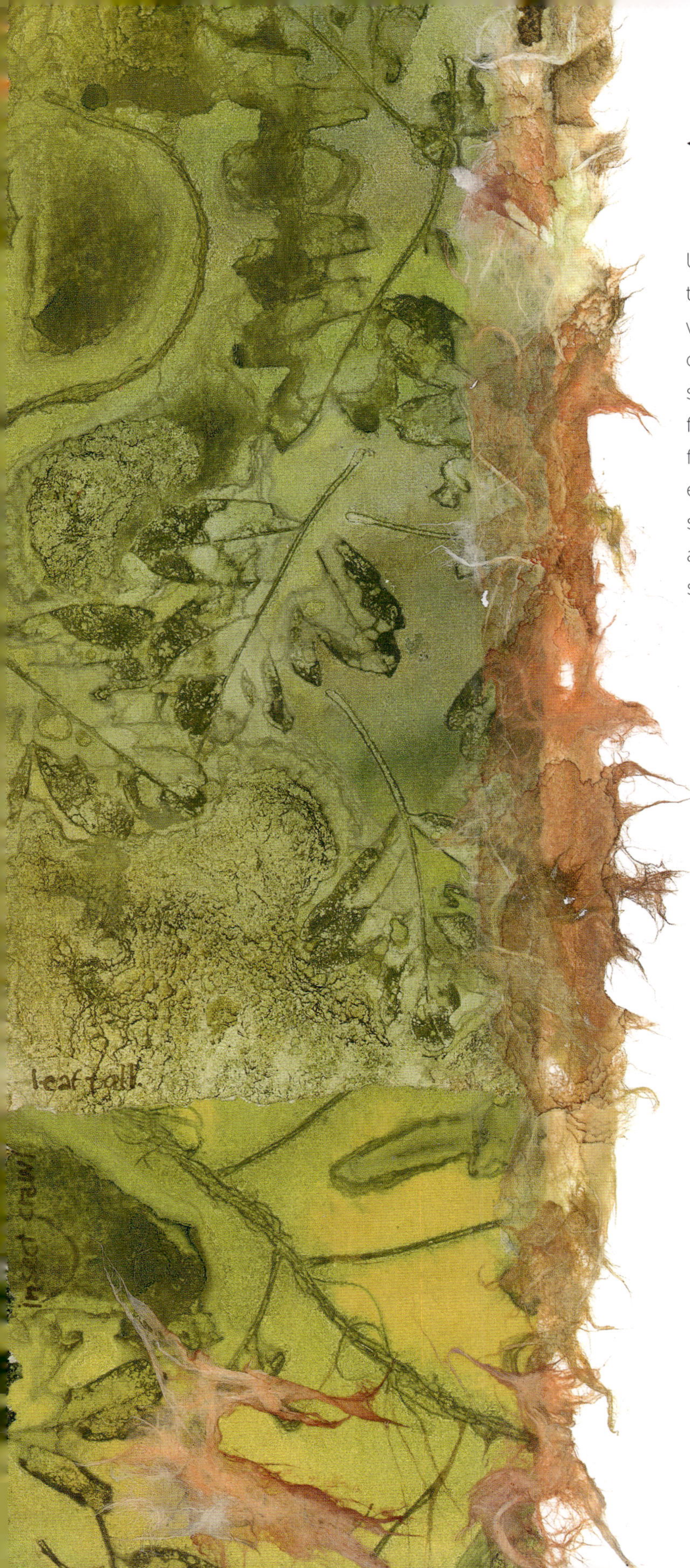

Towards abstraction

Use nature and its abstract patterns as a source of inspiration to produce effects and interpretations that allude to subjects without rigidly imitating them. Observations based on reality can be selected, exaggerated and altered until they become something new. The degree of abstraction depends on how far you develop your interpretations beyond their original form. When you capture an impression of a subject using elements such as texture, colour and shape while still retaining something recognizable the style could be called 'towards abstraction'. The loose style used throughout the book is a start in that direction, but let's see how we can take it further.

"THE WORLD OF REALITY HAS ITS LIMITS;
THE WORLD OF IMAGINATION IS BOUNDLESS."

JEAN-JACQUES ROUSSEAU

◁ Autumn Poem

Project: ABSTRACT BEGINNINGS

The other projects have all begun with some kind of reference material. This time the initial aim is the sheer pleasure of mark-making. We shall see what we can develop from it later. It is a great way to produce fantastic effects without any pressure to perform. The following demonstration uses cling film to create textures but any loose technique could be substituted.

1 Begin by making wet-into-wet washes. You can choose colours with something in mind or just be random and experimental. Make sure the watercolour is wet enough for each area to flow into the next. Remember that you are simply following your instinct with no other agenda. You can repeat this exercise later with more planned colour but do read my tips on page 109 first about lateral thinking.

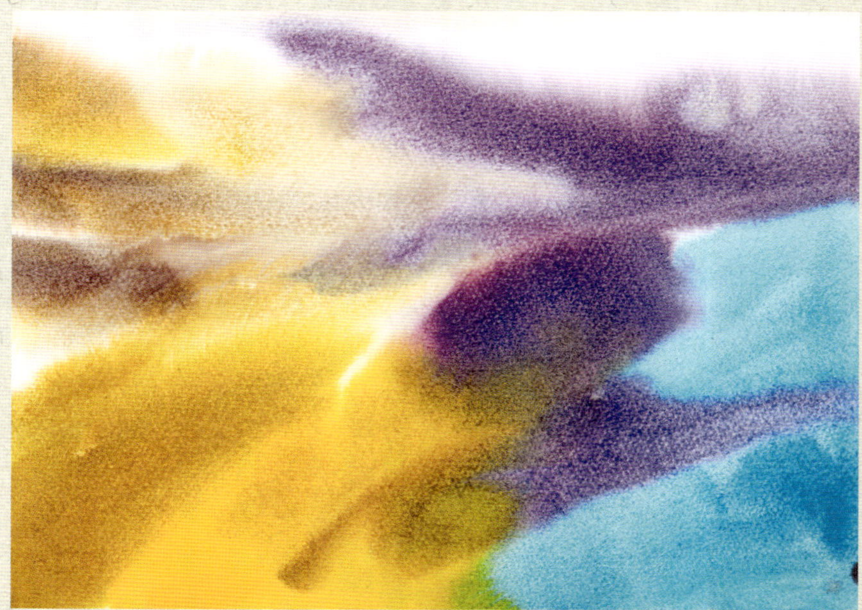

2 Immediately place pieces of cling film over the paint. You can make tight or loose crumples or pull the cling film into a linear effect. Darker shapes or lines form where the plastic touches the surface. If you want to play further, lift the edge of the plastic away from the paper a little and squirt ink or more watercolour underneath. If you are lucky the ink will find pathways through the maze of crushed plastic and make more interesting textures – but there are no guarantees!

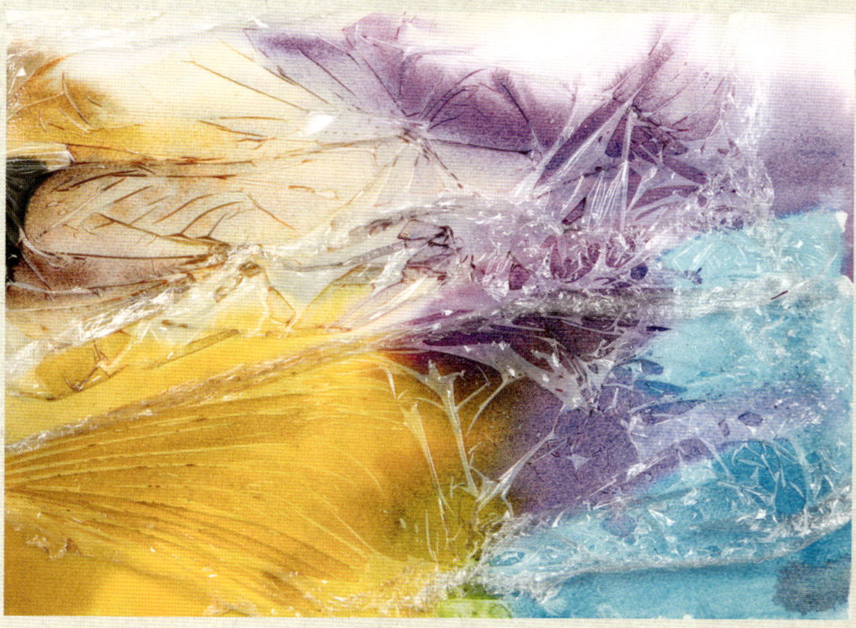

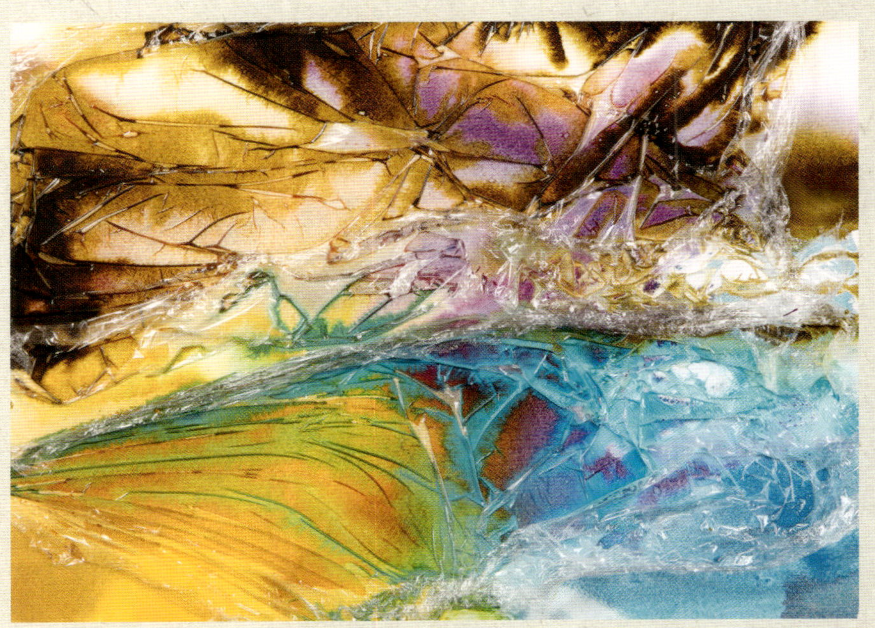

3 Carry on playing. You can manipulate the cling film, lift it up or rub it down in places to change its appearance, but try to limit how much you do this. The initial effect is often the freshest. If you work on rough paper the thin cling film will settle into the pitted surface to make further kinds of mottled texture. I used CP (Not) paper. Now you have to let this dry completely, which may mean leaving it overnight, depending on how wet the paint is. Speeding it up with a hairdryer will just blow the cling film away.

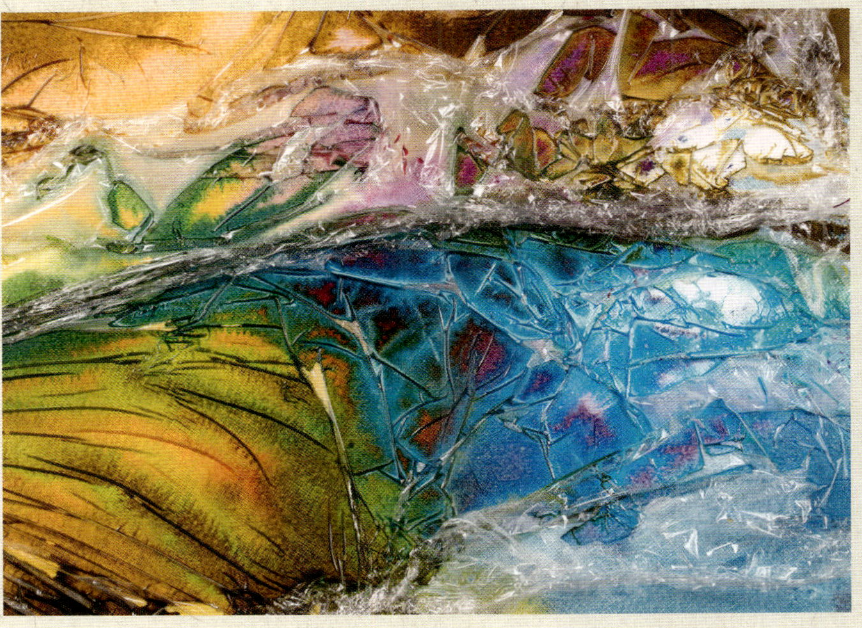

4 The cling film continues changing the textures in the paint until it starts to dry. It is quite fascinating to watch the kaleidoscope effect of the colours and tonal patterns alter as the plastic stays lifted or sinks onto the paper in accordance with the shifting wet paint. When the paint is dry you can peel the plastic away and look at your abstract patterns with an open mind.

5 Prop up the work and stand back from
   it, looking at it from all angles. Leave
   it somewhere prominent so that you
   see it as you move around. Look for
   elements that remind you of a subject,
   maybe something you have sketched
   or photographed. Do not be in a rush
   to make your decisions; be prepared
   to take days or even weeks as it is not
   always easy to see the way forward.
   When I turned mine upside down I
   eventually began to see an abstract
   landscape with a dark sky and the
   shape of a bird flying off the side.

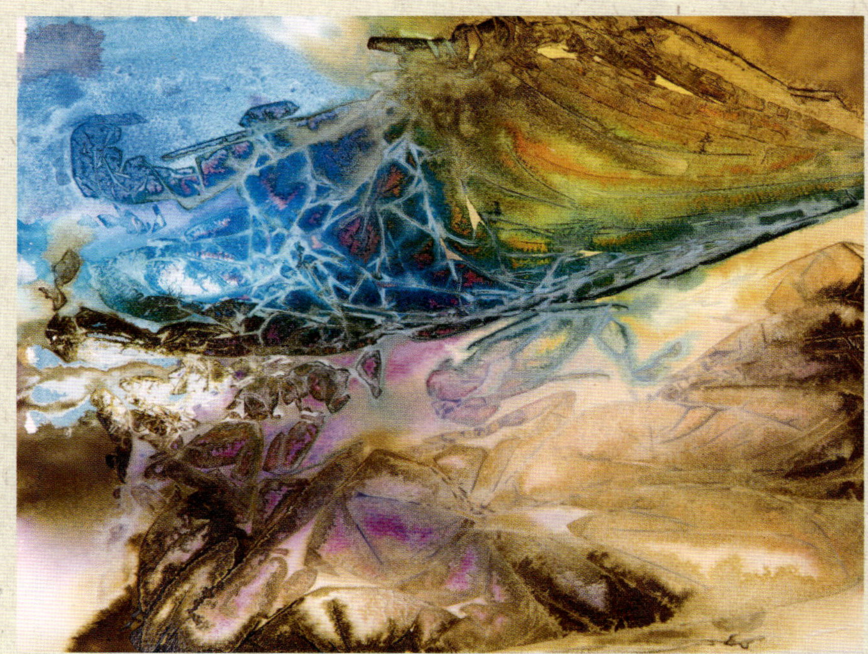

6 Cut a mount into two pieces so that you
   can play with cropping your picture to
   a smaller section or a different shape.
   Before you cut off unwanted sections,
   remember that complex patterns can be
   toned down using opaque mediums or
   covered with collage. If you do decide
   to crop, keep the scraps as they might
   come in useful for collage work in this
   or another picture.

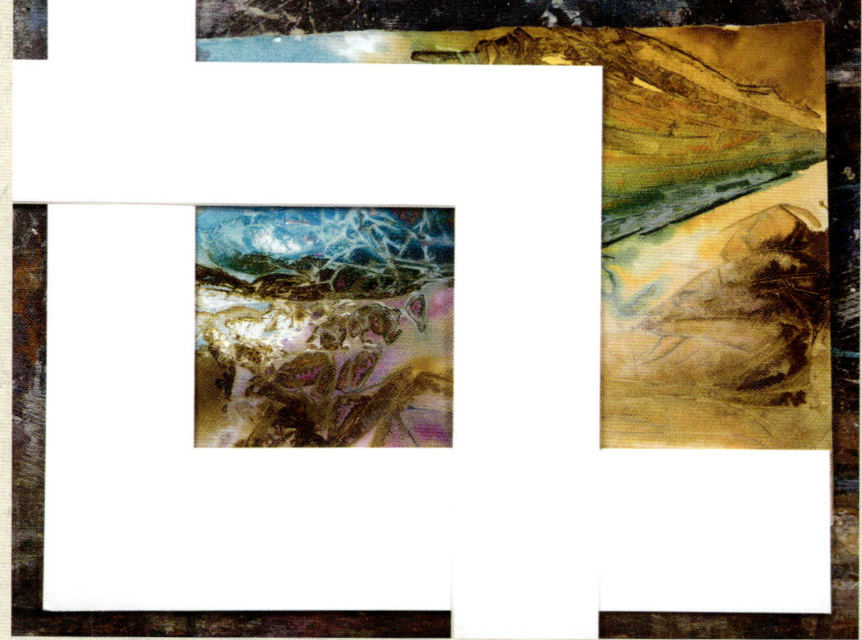

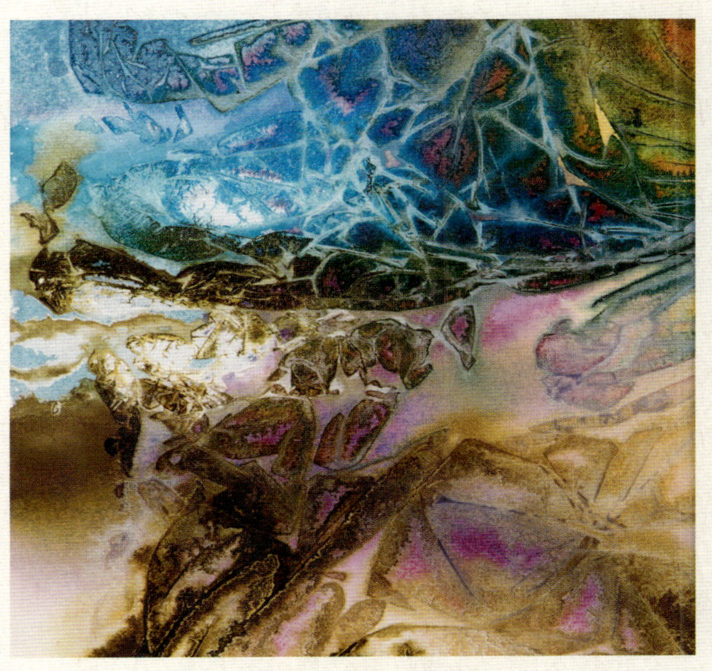

7 I cropped my rectangle to a smaller area. I preferred the blue, purple and brown colour scheme of this square with only a hint of the contrasting yellow and golds to the right. Although I could have adapted the whole picture, the selected area contained all the most promising patterns. The potential landscape with bird now looked a little clearer. The sky could perhaps be darkened and the textures in the foreground could be softened with a thin glaze of opaque paint, also adding more definition to the 'bird' shape.

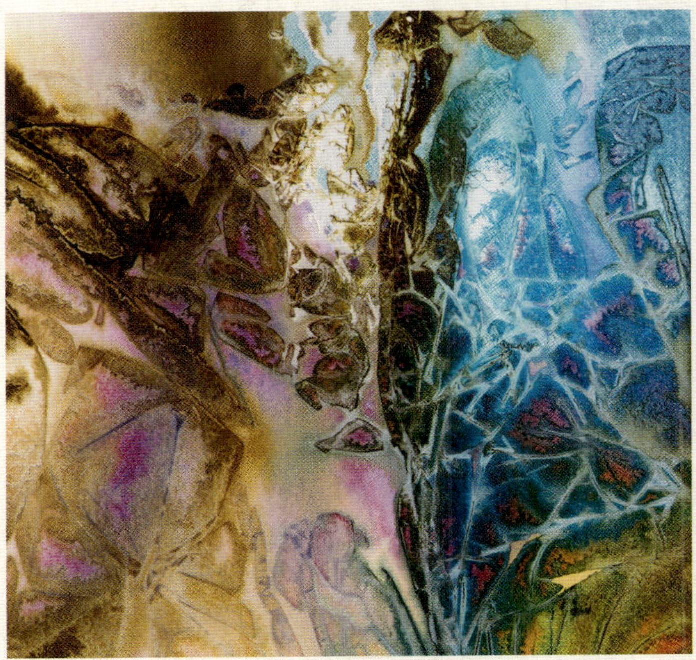

8 Before proceeding with the abstract landscape idea I happened to rotate the picture clockwise. As if by magic a potential tree emerged. The cling film markings had metamorphosed into branch textures and I became aware of a moonlit effect. I decided to go with this new plan. Was it the right or wrong choice? I do not know if there is such a thing. What's important is to make your decision, however long it takes, then go for it.

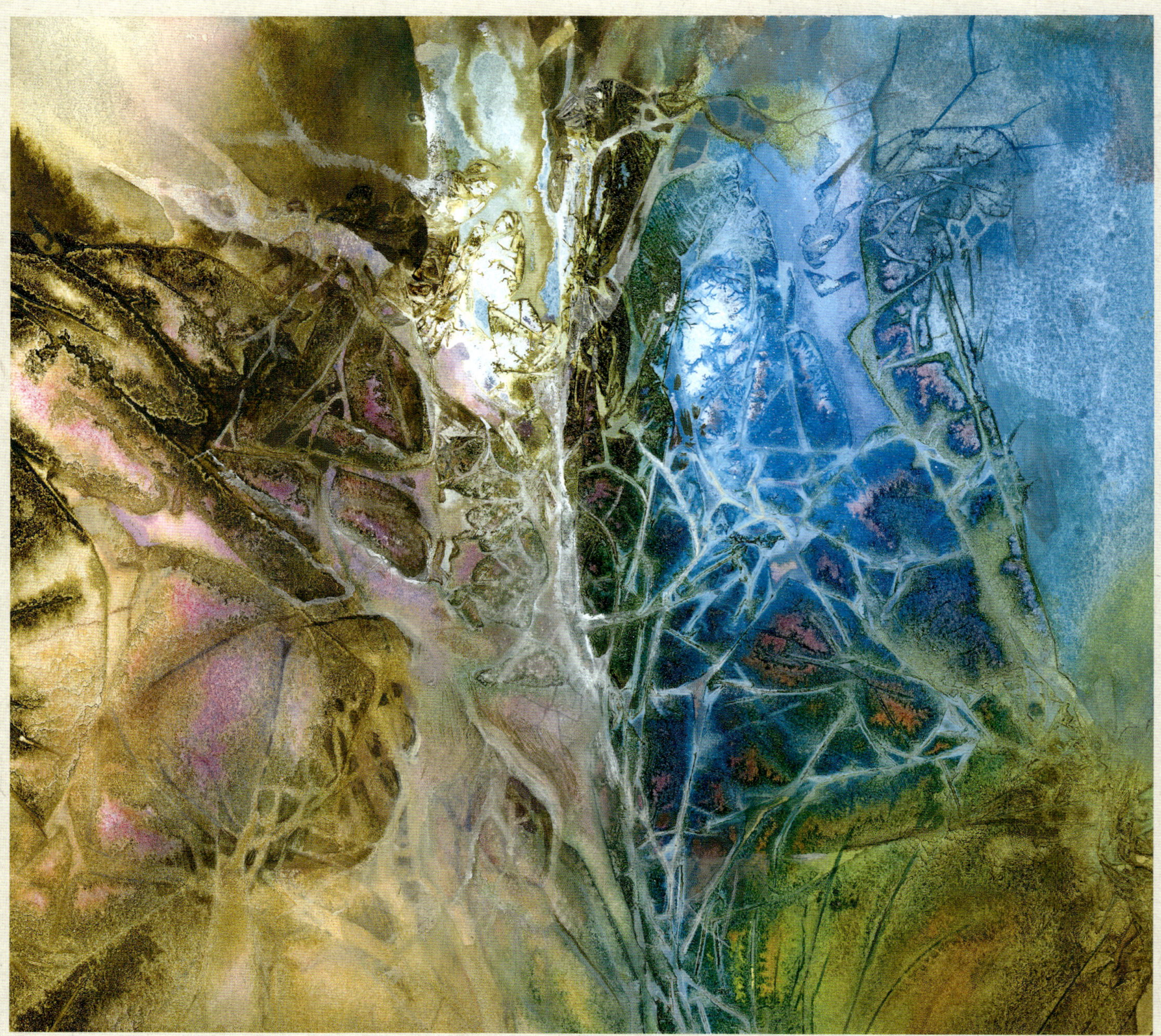

9 Once the decision had been made it did not take much work to coax the tree into life out of
its abstract beginning. I left a lot of the patterns untouched but used dark negative painting to
affirm the shape of the trunk and branches. I also reshaped a few details with gouache. You do
not need to explain and tidy everything up to force it to look real. This project is about being
semi-abstract in your approach. You can make a whole finished picture in this way, restrict the
effects to only part of a background or just treat the process as a studio exercise.

Taking it further:
LATERAL THINKING

The demonstration looked at ways to make sense of an abstract beginning and take it towards reality. The message is not about a particular technique. It is to do with lateral thinking – exploring paint in a spontaneous manner first and deciding how to develop the compositions later. The idea of naming the subject afterwards is a great way to help you loosen up. You can, of course, use the process to coax reality out of marks that have been deliberately chosen to suit a more considered subject. Working in this conventional direction has the advantage that you can choose suitable colours and techniques that are pertinent to your plan. The downside is that you may not gain the magical moments of surprise that come from unexpected juxtapositions of colour and texture. In other words, what you pick as being 'suitable' may also be rather 'predictable'. Using lateral thinking will help you to avoid being too literal.

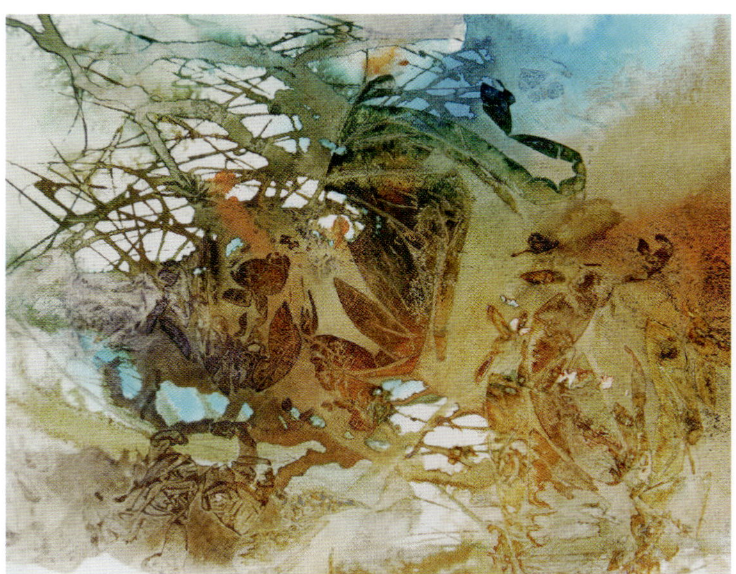

△ *Tree of Dreams* (stage one)
Make another abstract beginning using any method but this time use colours and marks to loosely fit a subject. In this version I dragged paint into lines which might have potential for representing dark branches.

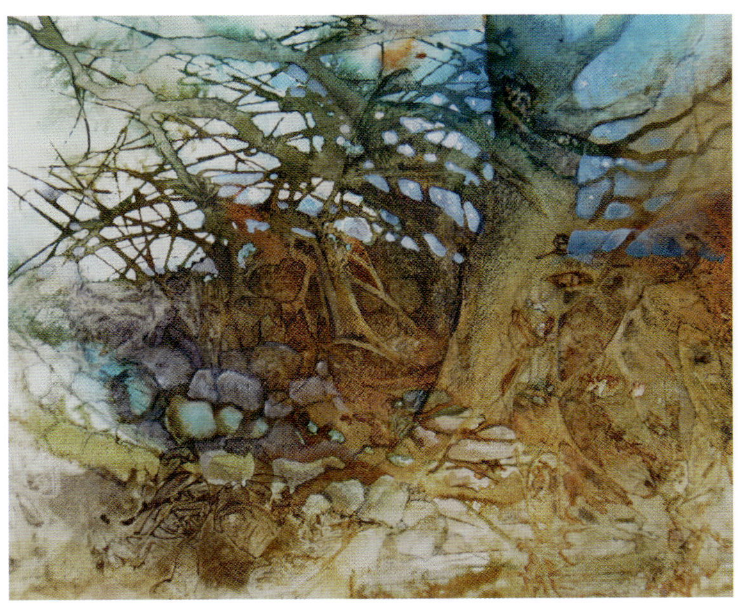

△ *Tree of Dreams* (stage two)
Look at your marks and be prepared to depart from your roughly planned theme. I did pursue my branch idea but in a different context to my initial subconscious thoughts. It is all about seeing things in a different way.

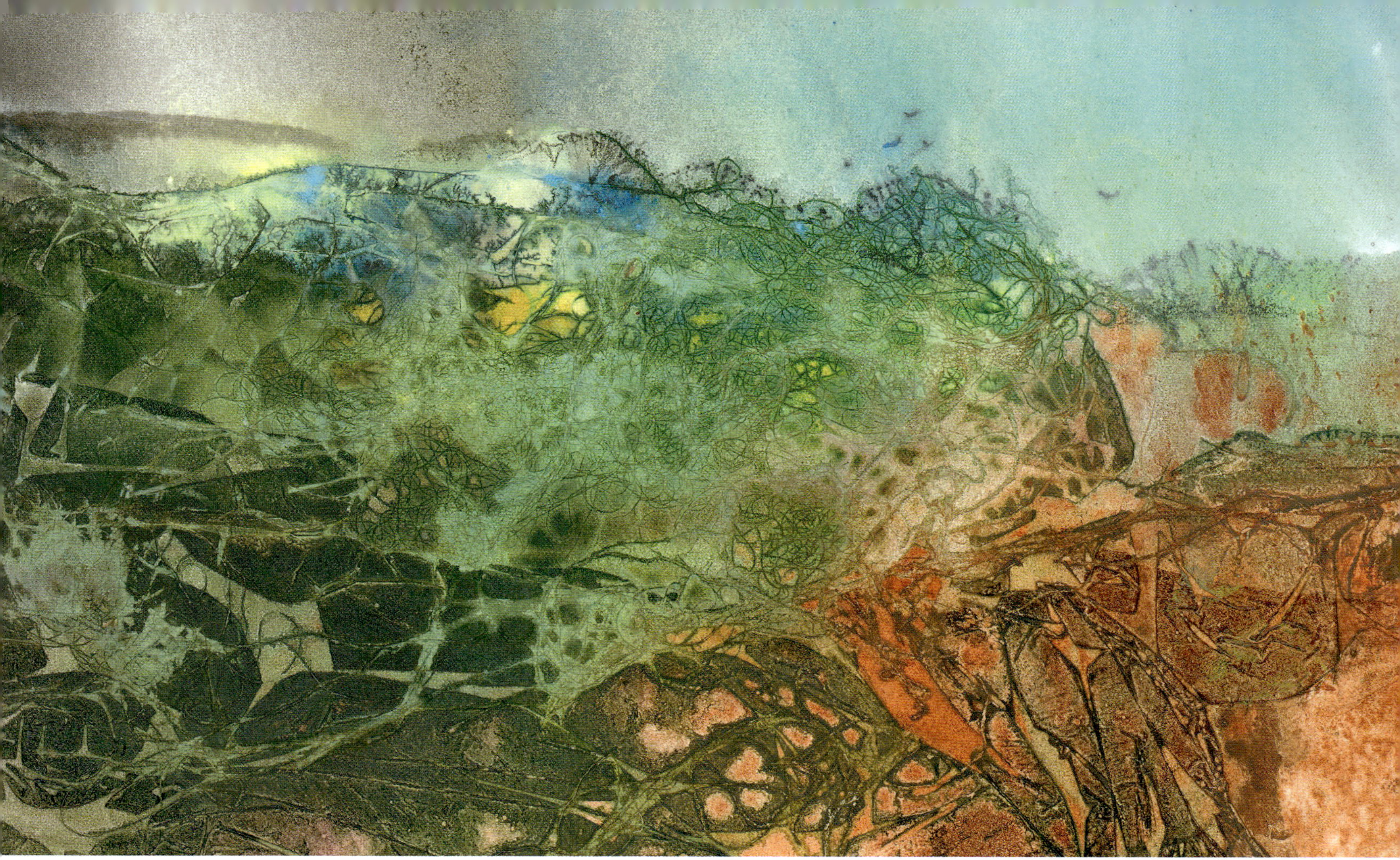

Adding focal points

In the demonstration an abstract beginning was analysed from all angles in order to make decisions about how to proceed. This process is like searching for clues to a puzzle, except there is no right or wrong answer. I saw two possible solutions within the patterns and chose the tree option, but a landscape would have been equally valid. The interpretations here were also developed out of random textures but this time focal points were added to evoke unusual atmospheric landscapes. What you include depends on the scene. This is where your collection of sketches, explorations and photographs are useful because you can search through them for ideas that are relevant to your own world. My favourite features include the distant trees and flying rooks that I see on daily rambles. This is usually at certain times of day when the sun is setting or the moon rising and these are useful and romantic elements to include. Populating landscapes with creatures, birds and whatever else you want to focus on brings the scene to life whether your style is abstract or representational.

△ **Landscape Textures**

The textures within this landscape are totally non-representational, but once a focal point was added the same marks gained context and were transformed into something more real. The lack of explained detail means that the landscape marks remain open to personal interpretation. I see ploughed fields, rocks and scrubby moorland. The distant hedge and flock of birds are more specific, but they were painted in a loose style that complemented the rest of the image.

This landscape also started with patterns and textures but these were chosen specifically to lend the idea of a gorse-tangled foreground. The blur of distant trees and speckles of rooks were initially intended to be the focal point.

On reflection I decided that this landscape needed more to focus on, so I added a closer, more detailed bird. Make conscious choices about how realistic your additions should be when completing an abstract background. In this interpretation there is a dialogue between the 'real' and 'unreal' elements and the bird is representational. If you want to keep to the more abstract approach choose looser mark-making methods or collage instead.

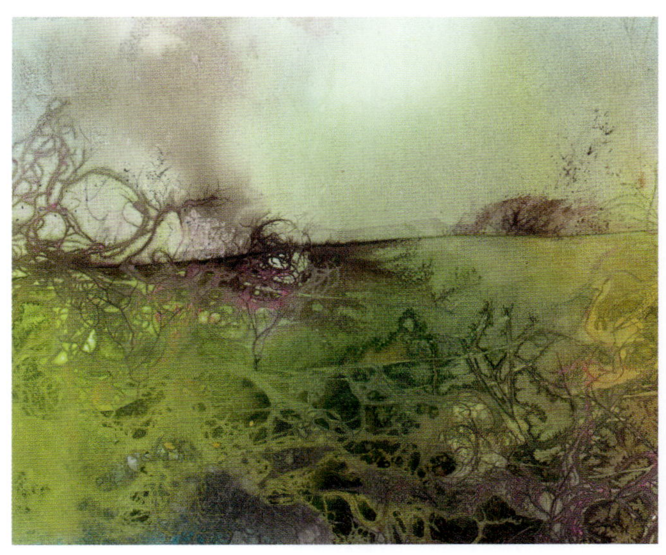

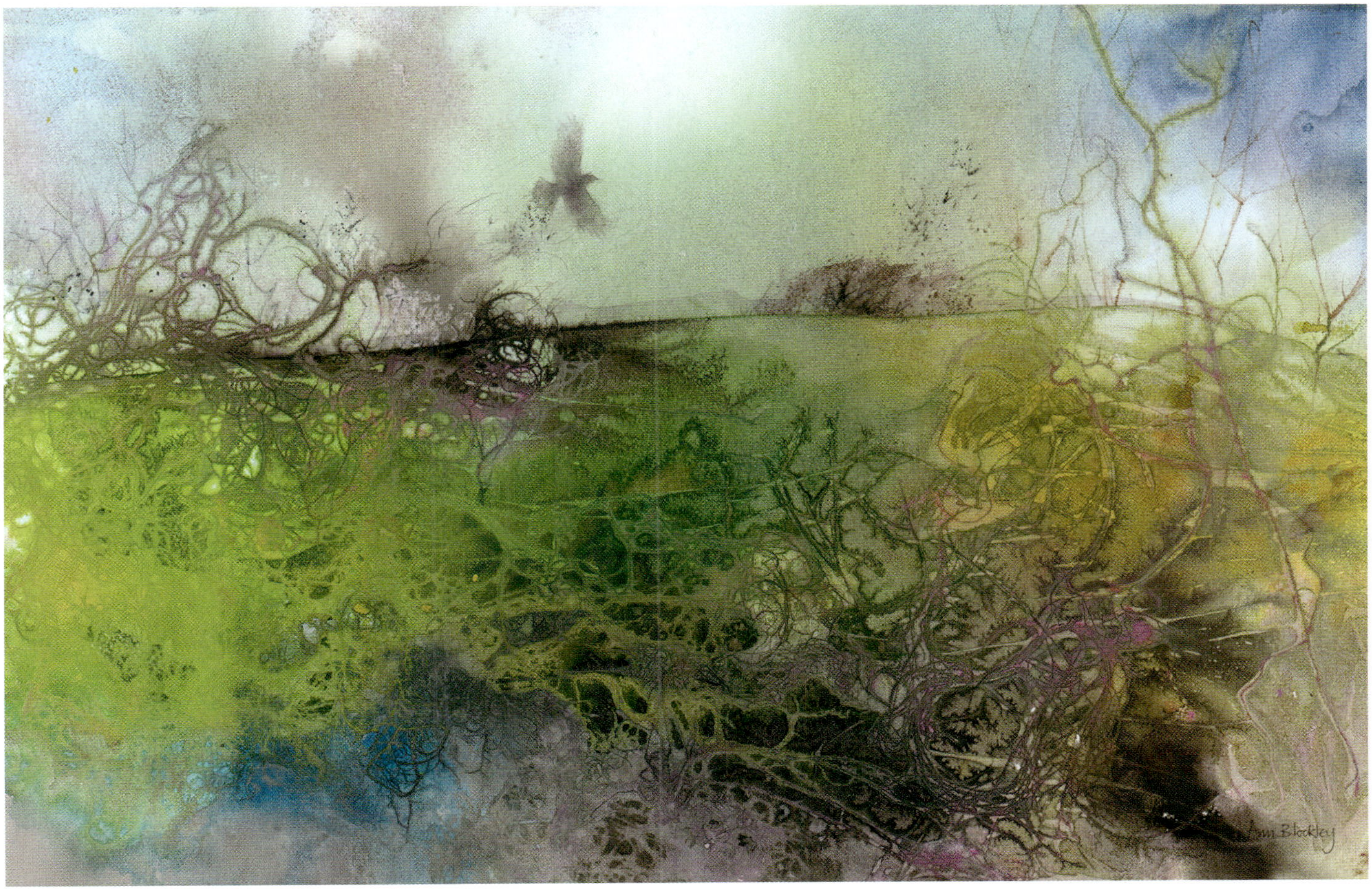

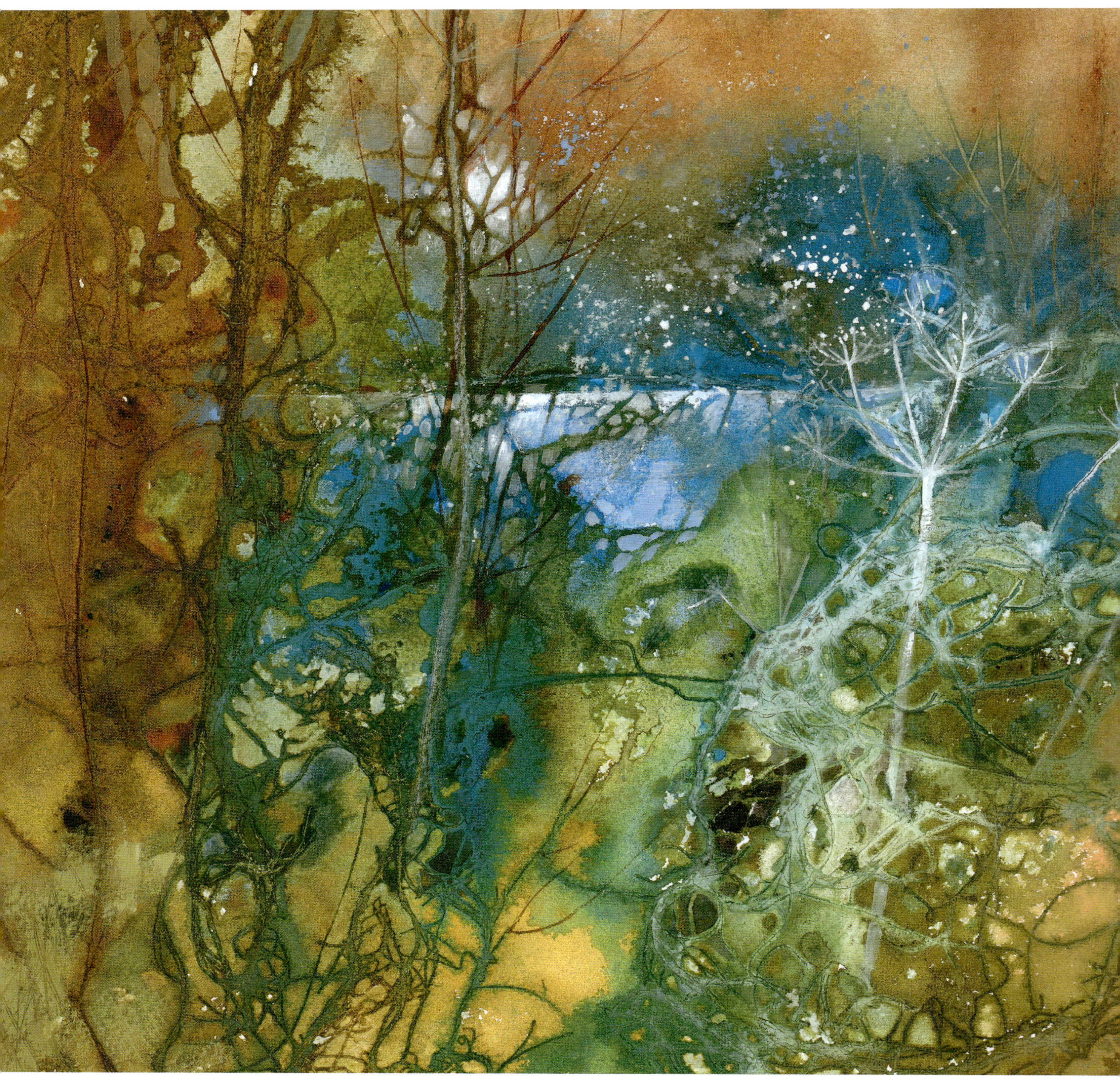

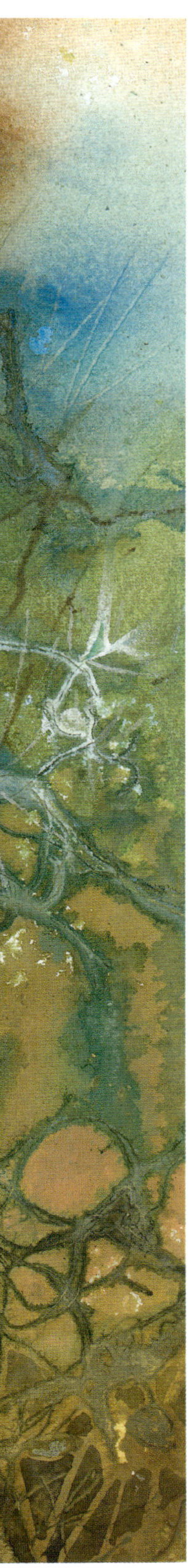

Echoing nature

My pursuit of the spirit of nature rather than a photographic imitation led me to what I call a more abstract approach, but I discovered in the process that often, after painting what I thought was a departure from reality, I would find similar shapes in nature. I have learned from viewing my reference material how abstract the landscape really is. I might paint for the enjoyment of the marks but then realize afterwards that I have a photograph or sketch that looks rather like it. Is this coincidence or the mind working in mysterious ways? Whatever the reason it is very satisfying and useful when that happens, so look through your sketches and photographs after you have been experimenting and you may find some surprises. You may feel this is a gimmicky approach and not for you, but it can be useful to rule things out as part of finding your own voice. Try to keep an open mind so that new kinds of thinking can still filter through.

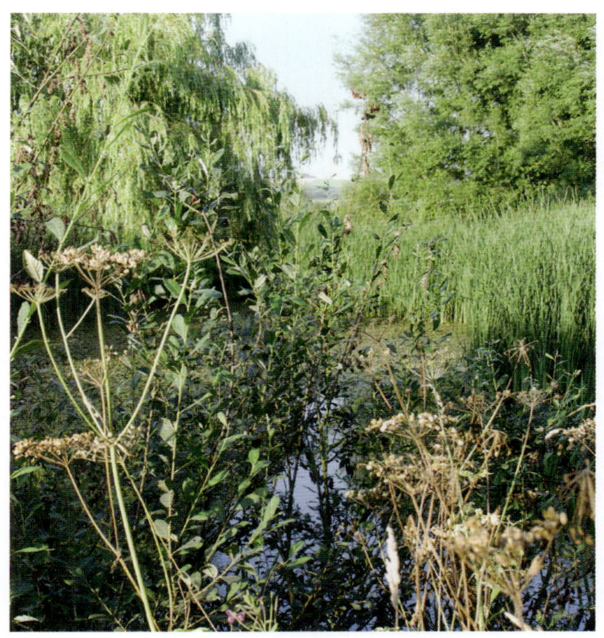

△ This photograph was discovered after completing the painting of the wild and natural pool (shown left).

◁ Moonlit Pool

This is another example of a painting that began life with mark- and texture-making for its own sake before planning a subject. By adding a few details and the shimmer of water through the tangles it became a moonlit pool, based on a country pond that I see on my local walks.

Techniques: ABSTRACTING SHAPES WITH MONOPRINTS

A different way to begin paintings is to make unusual monoprints with found materials. These unique results can be developed for different purposes. One route is to print from something in order to produce a distressed and abstracted version of itself. Another direction is to create prints as pure pattern so that the original form is almost lost, then you can refine it using lateral thinking as described on page 109. In the exercises here I have applied leaves which are ideal as they are flat. You could try all sorts of plant parts, bits of textured paper or fabrics. Anything very three-dimensional is unsuitable as only the areas in contact with the surface will leave an impression. The nature of this printing is hit or miss, so do not be disappointed if it is not what you hope for first time. Make many different versions and do some creative cropping in order to arrive at an original and exciting piece.

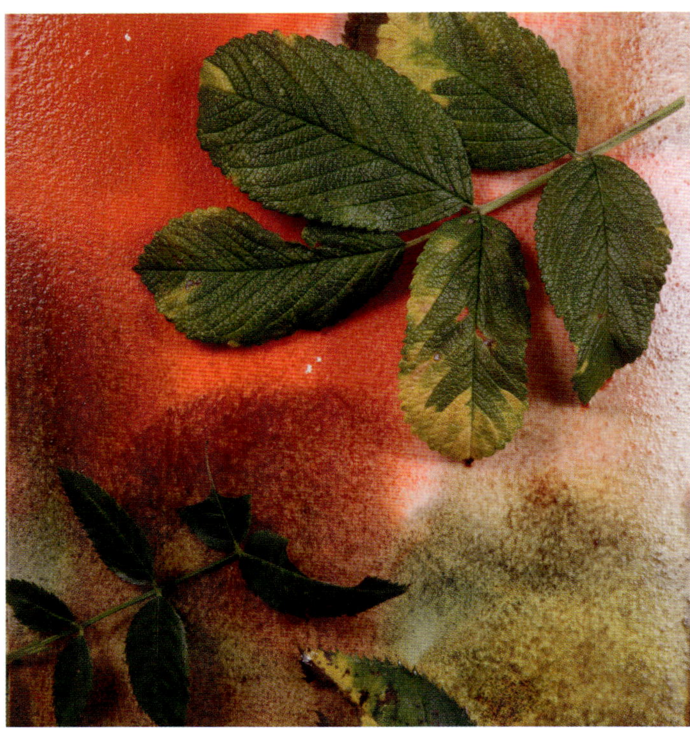

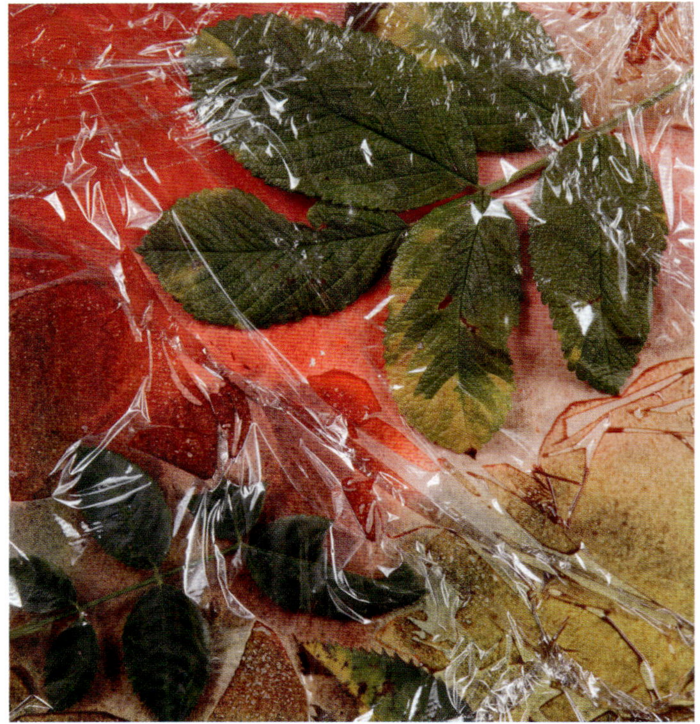

1 Mix colours based on reality or imagination as you prefer. I used Winsor Red based on the colour of rosehips and mixed French Ultramarine and Quinacridone Gold to match the rose leaves. Cover the paper with plenty of rich wet paint or ink. Lay your found objects on the wash, leaving gaps so that the cling film will have space to hug the paper.

2 Place cling film over the whole area. Your objects may not lie flat, so pin them down by placing a board on top. I suggest sandwiching it with a layer of paper to mop up spills. It may take a while to dry as the air cannot reach it, so do not even peep for at least a day. When it has dried everything can be peeled off to reveal its mysteries.

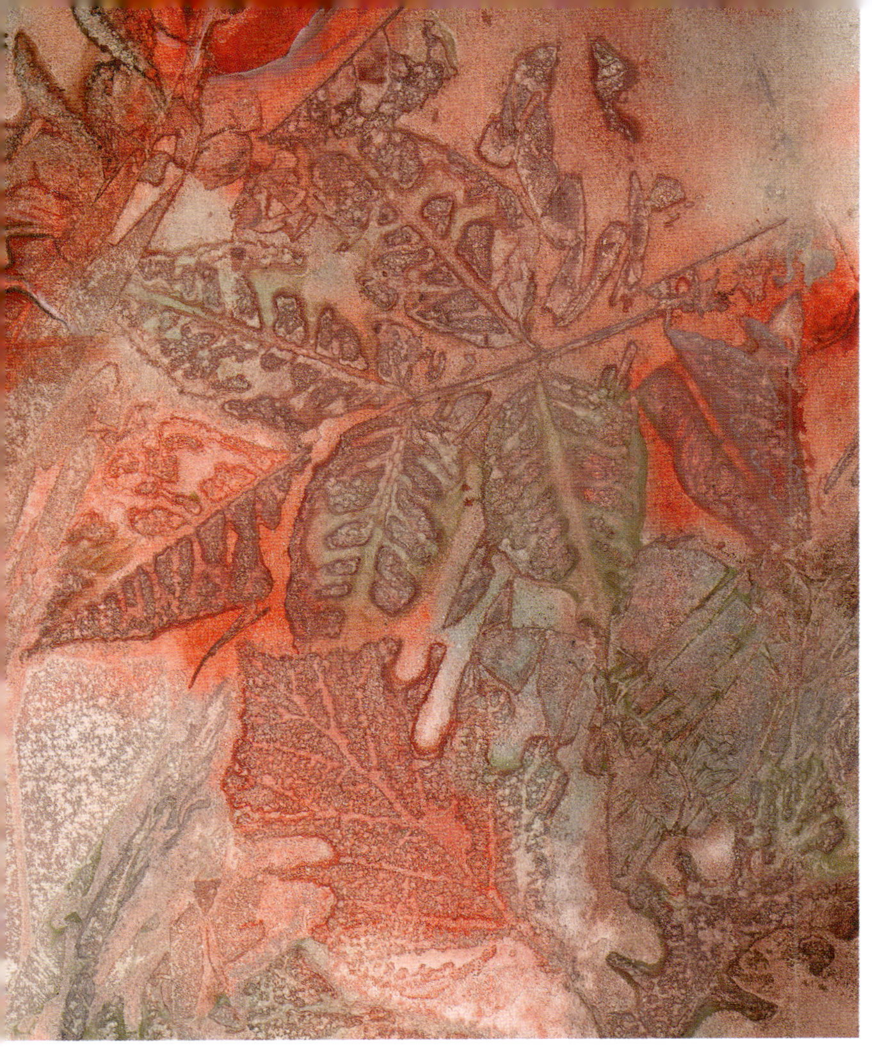

◁ I made several monoprints from rose leaves using the method shown opposite. Because this process is unpredictable it is a good idea to make a few prints to choose from. This version began with gentle washes of soft reds on watercolour paper. The process has abstracted the shapes into expressive patterns where impressions have either been printed or not registered. Enough information has been retained to be recognizable as leaves.

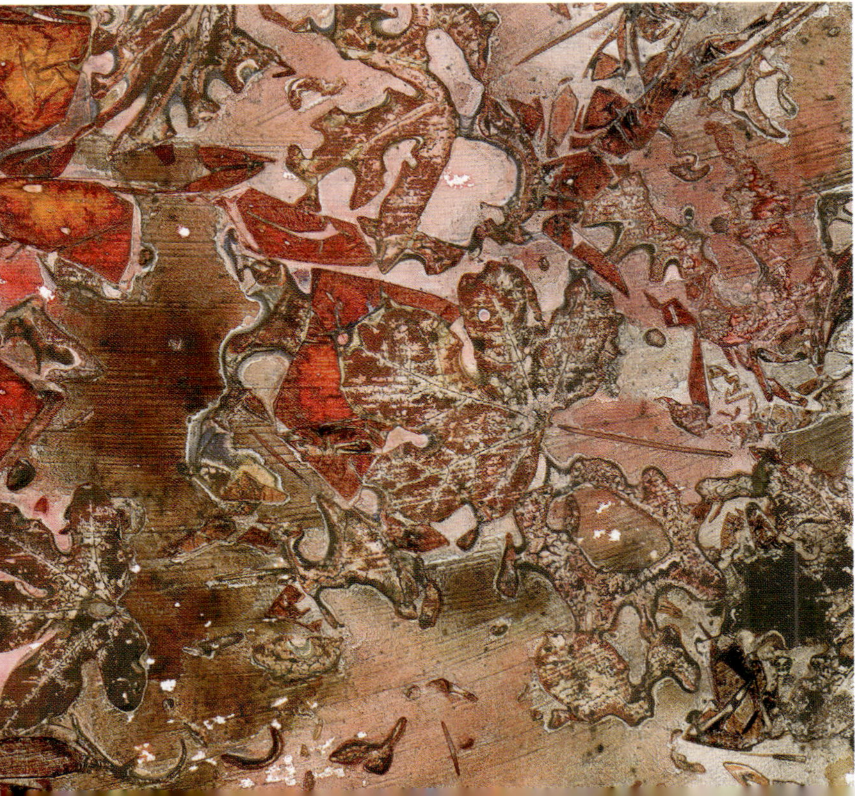

◁ This maple leaf monoprint was made on a smooth gesso-coated board. The shapes are much crisper on this hard surface than on the softer paper. It also has a more geometric and abstracted quality.

Developing your monoprints

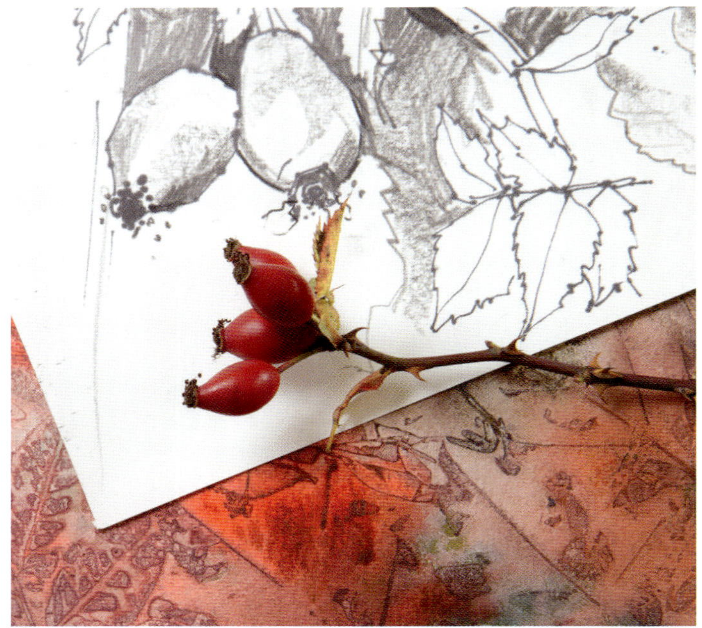

◁ Gather sketches, photographs and still-life pieces together to use as reference. However abstract or real you decide to go with your monoprint, it will always hold greater authority if based on observed forms and information.

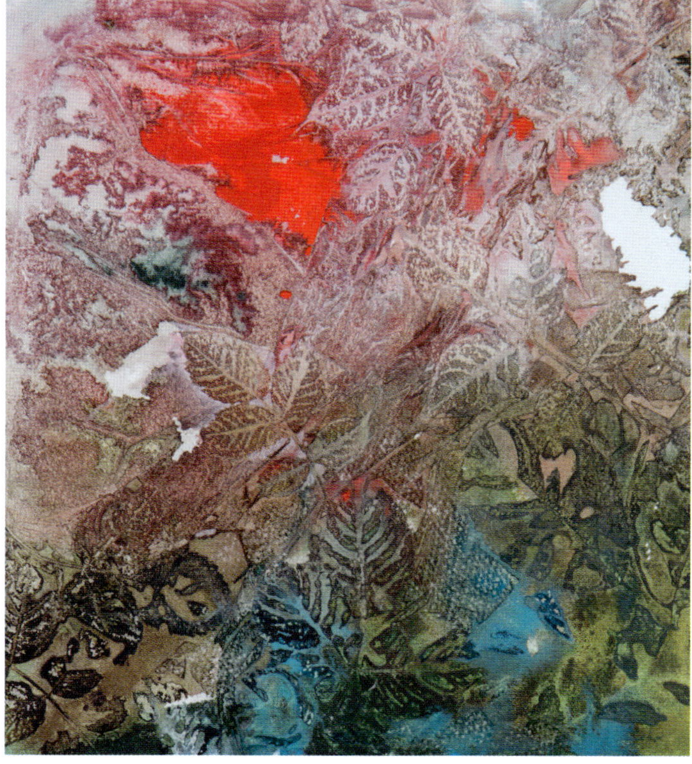

◁ The first stage of this print was made using rose leaves as shown on pages 114–115. I included a solid area of red ink as a base for some rosehips. It looks brash in its unfinished state because the ink is bright against the subtle mix that the watercolour made as it seeped under the leaves.

▷ **Through the Rosehip Hedge**
Most of the printmaking has been left untouched but I established the shapes of rosehips using reference material and a little imagination around the splodge of red. A few of the leaves were also given more definition. Use an opaque medium such as gouache to cover and develop your first layer but leave alone any marks that are beautiful in their original state.

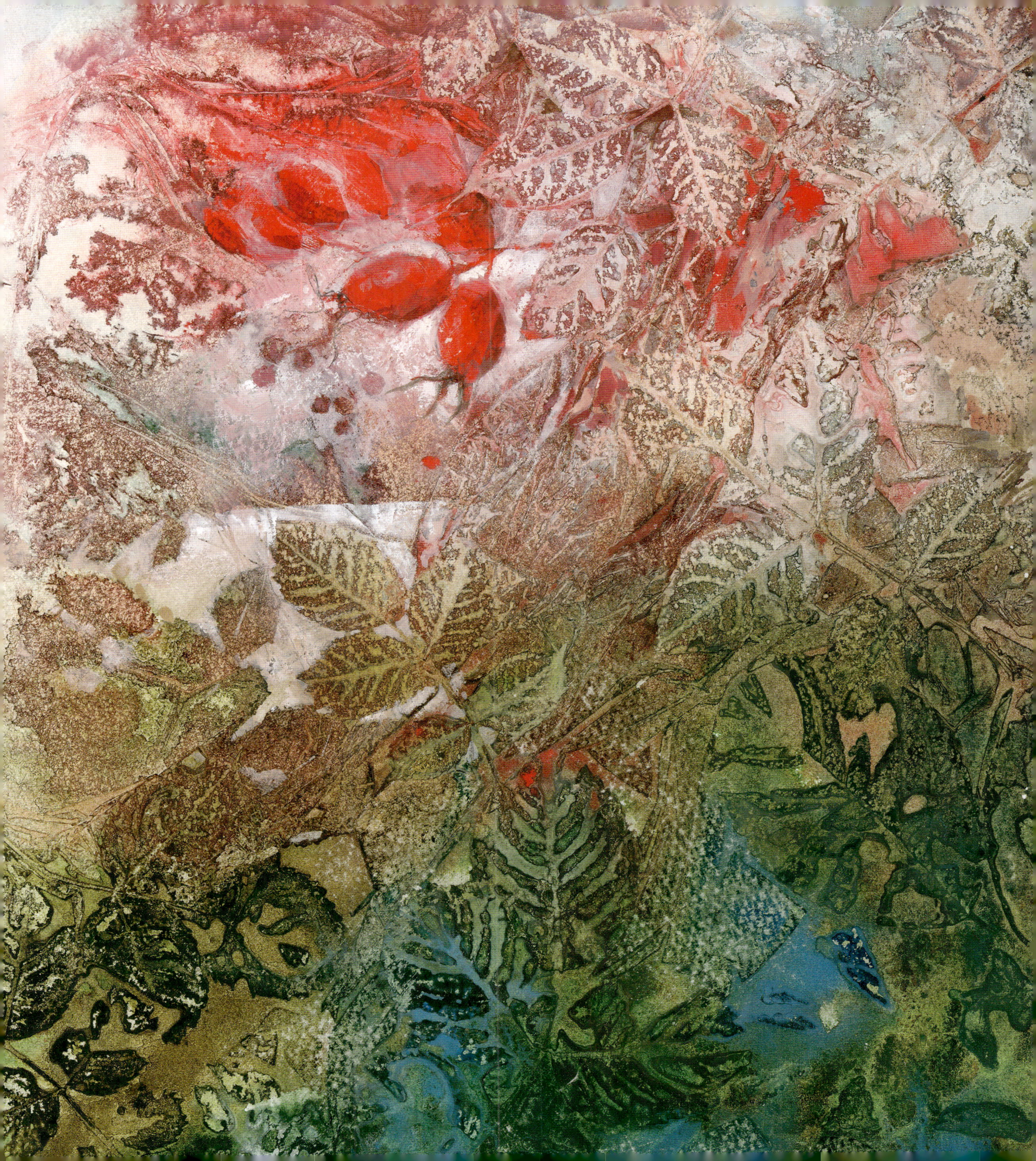

Project: FERN AND FLIGHT

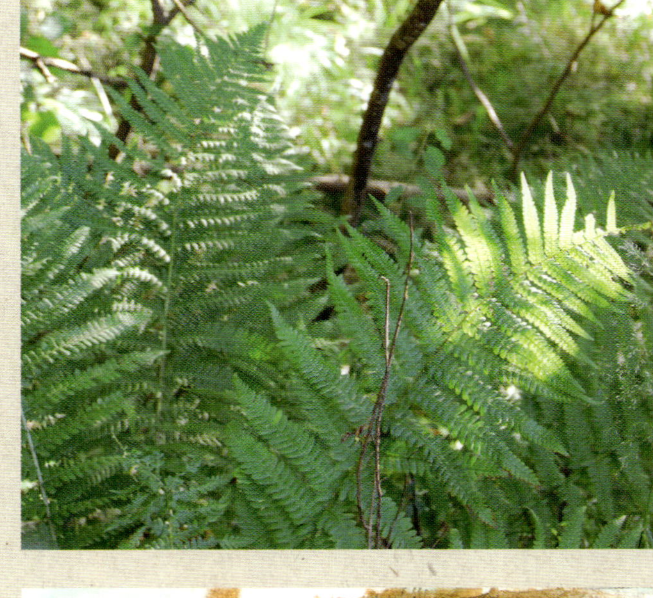

1 I found this photograph of a sunlit fern after completing this monoprint. It was interesting to have my ideas backed up. Whether your reference material is used to plan or affirm the content of your picture it adds to its provenance.

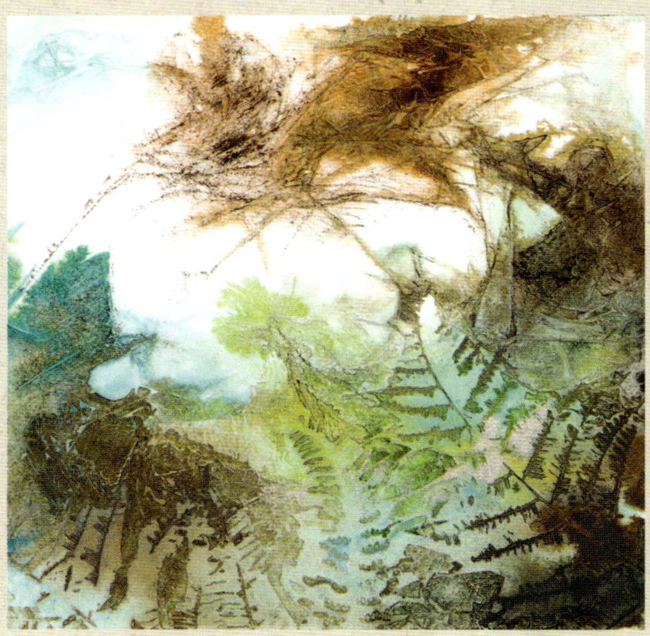

2 Use a plant or its parts to make a semi-abstract monoprint as described on page 114 and develop it into an unusual interpretation of itself in its natural environment. I used ferns and arranged them at the bottom so that they would appear to be growing there. A woodland habitat was suggested using Green Gold and Perylene Green watercolour with sepia ink.

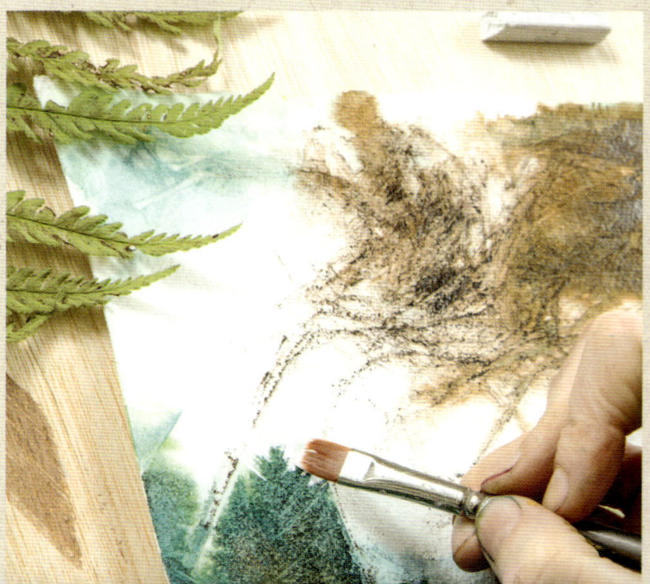

3 Have your reference material close by when deciding how and where to paint into your print. You will also need to adapt and use your imagination. I kept some ferns that I had used to print with next to my board and referred to them for details about their intricate shapes.

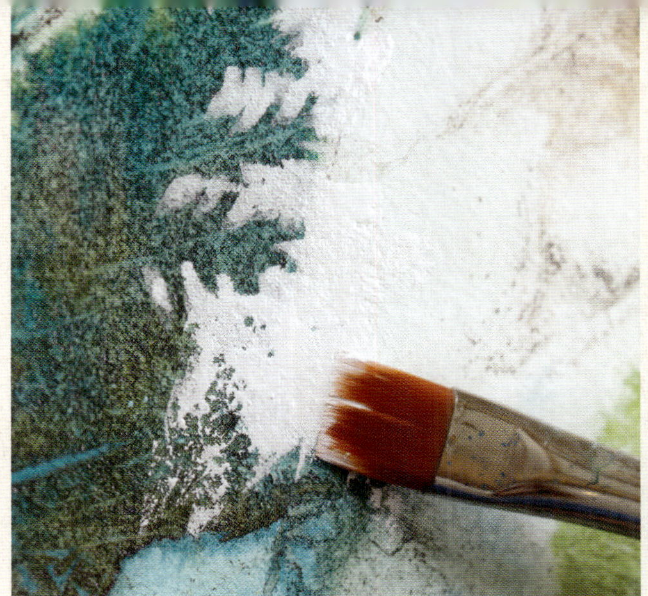

4   Pull shapes like this fern out of dark backgrounds using thick opaque paint. The background must be dry before you can do this. Applying the negative painting loosely helps to retain the impressionist effect of a semi-abstract beginning. I also created a bird silhouette in this way out of an area of brown paint.

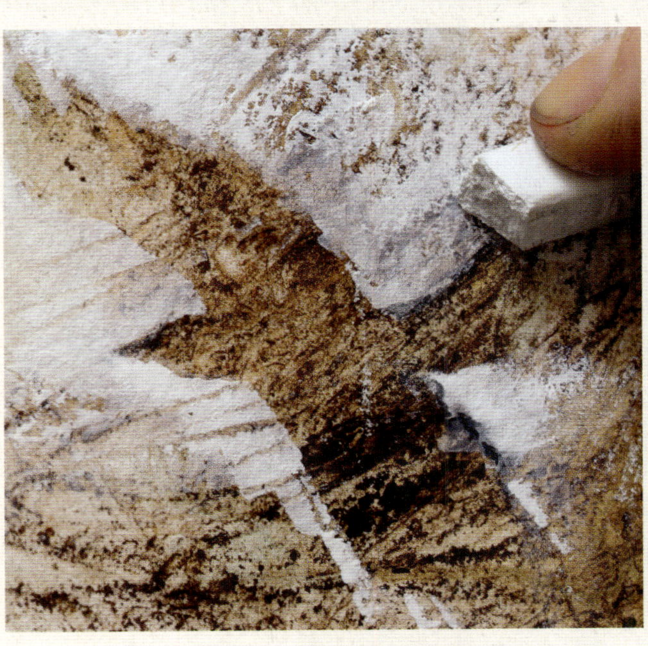

5   When you have painted around shapes you may like to break them up by scraping through the fresh pigment to reveal lines or marks of the background colour. This will help to integrate the different areas and create movement. You could also try adding crayon for a change to add broken texture around your newly discovered shapes. I used a white Inktense block.

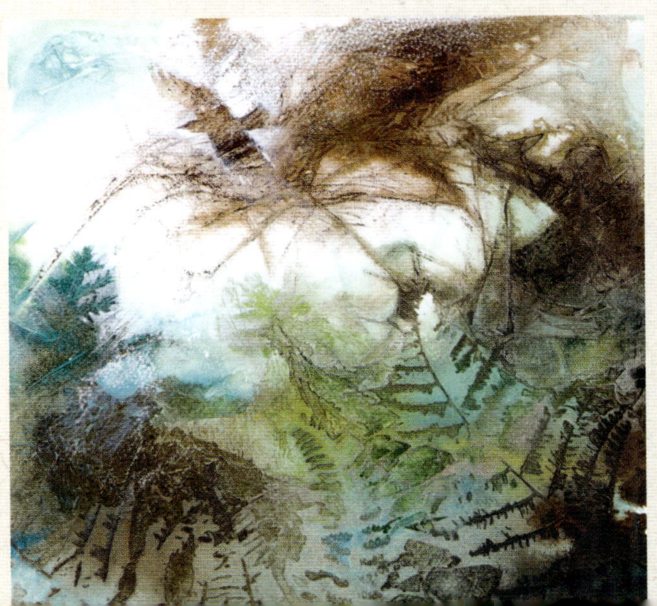

6   At each stage you will need time to review your picture before you can decide how to proceed. After some thought, I had painted around the amorphous green shapes, turning them into ferns. A dark area became a bird flying through the woodland undergrowth. You may feel that these developments are moving too far from the abstract approach. If so, you can choose to leave the mysterious shapes and marks unexplained. These are personal decisions. My choice is to try to achieve a balance between being obvious and enigmatic.

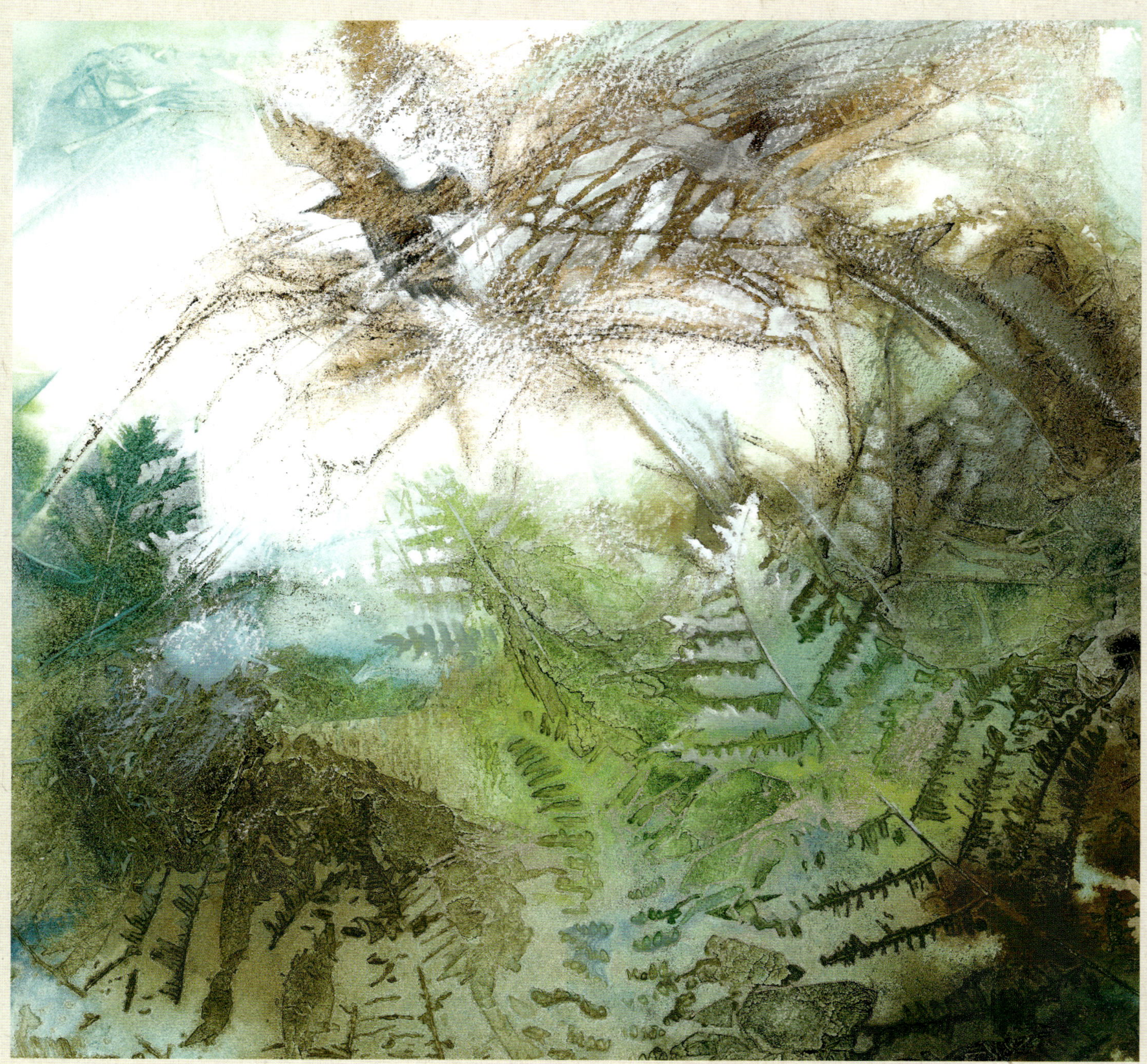

7 A patch of brown still dominated the softer greens, so I covered most of it with gouache but scraped through again using a scalpel to create movement and branch-like shapes. I also skated over the surface lightly with more crayon to break up this heavy area. Your picture will not be the same as mine, even if you use similar ferns and colours, because working this way is unpredictable. Therefore I am challenging you to deliberately aim for something different, making personal decisions about how to move forwards with your version but using some of the ideas described as a guideline.

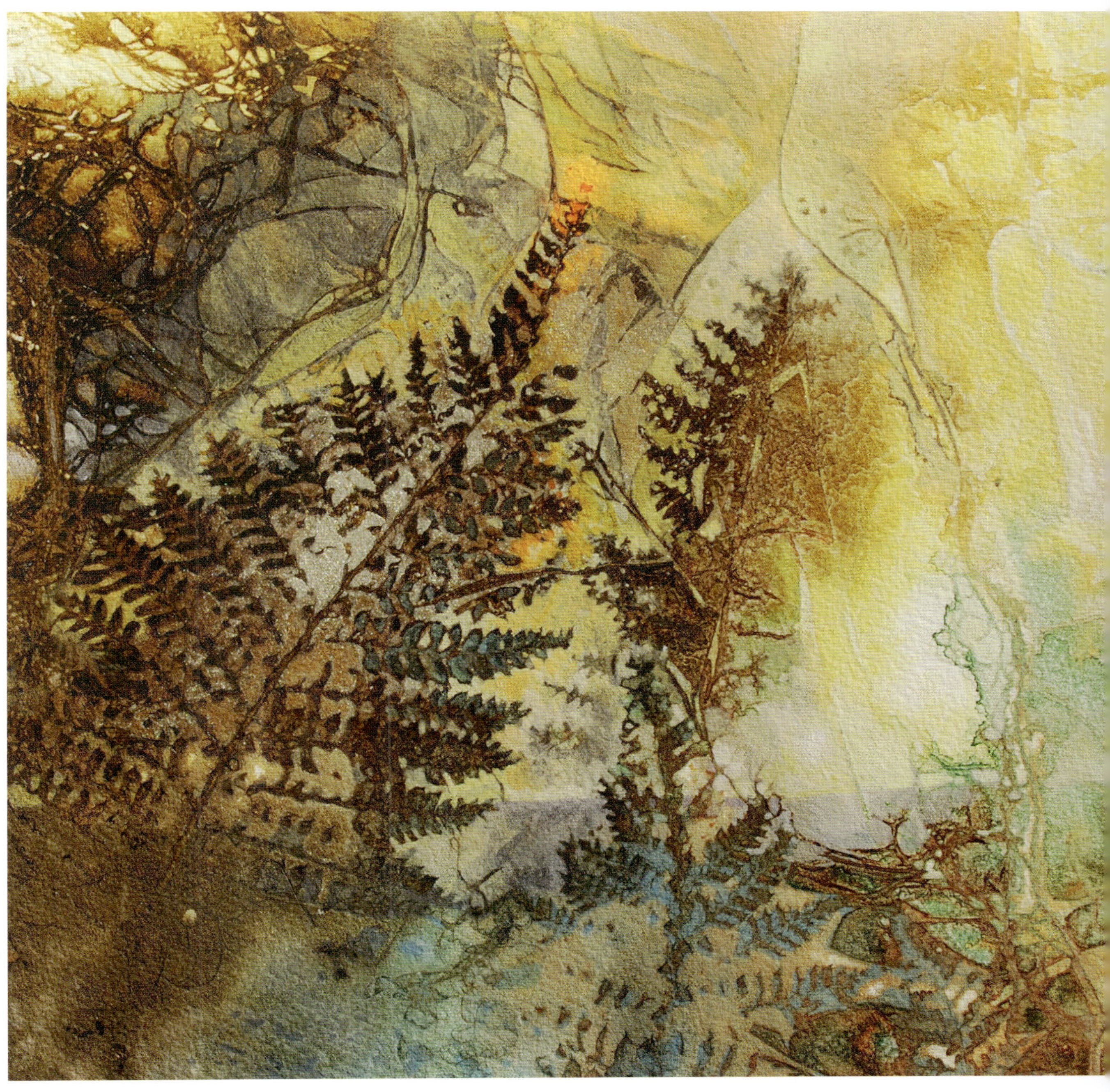

△ *Woodland Fern*

In another interpretation, I sprinkled some Schmincke Aqua Bronze powder
into the wet paint, using the fern as a stencil. This is a shimmery powder that
mixes with watercolour and I felt it suggested a mystical woodland light.

Taking it further:
FOUND MATERIAL

With the monoprint method you can take things a
step further by using relevant found materials to create
a textured or patterned background. What you choose
to build this with could be related to the subject that
you are planning to conjure out of this abstract
mark-making. The material used does not have to
actually represent itself like the fern in the project on
page 118–120 but simply to create appropriate abstract
texture. When you play with this idea remember that
what you print with does not have to be plant-based – it
can be anything at all that will make a mark. However, it
needs to be fine-textured and relatively flat to work best.

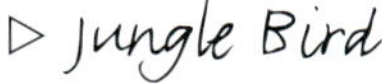

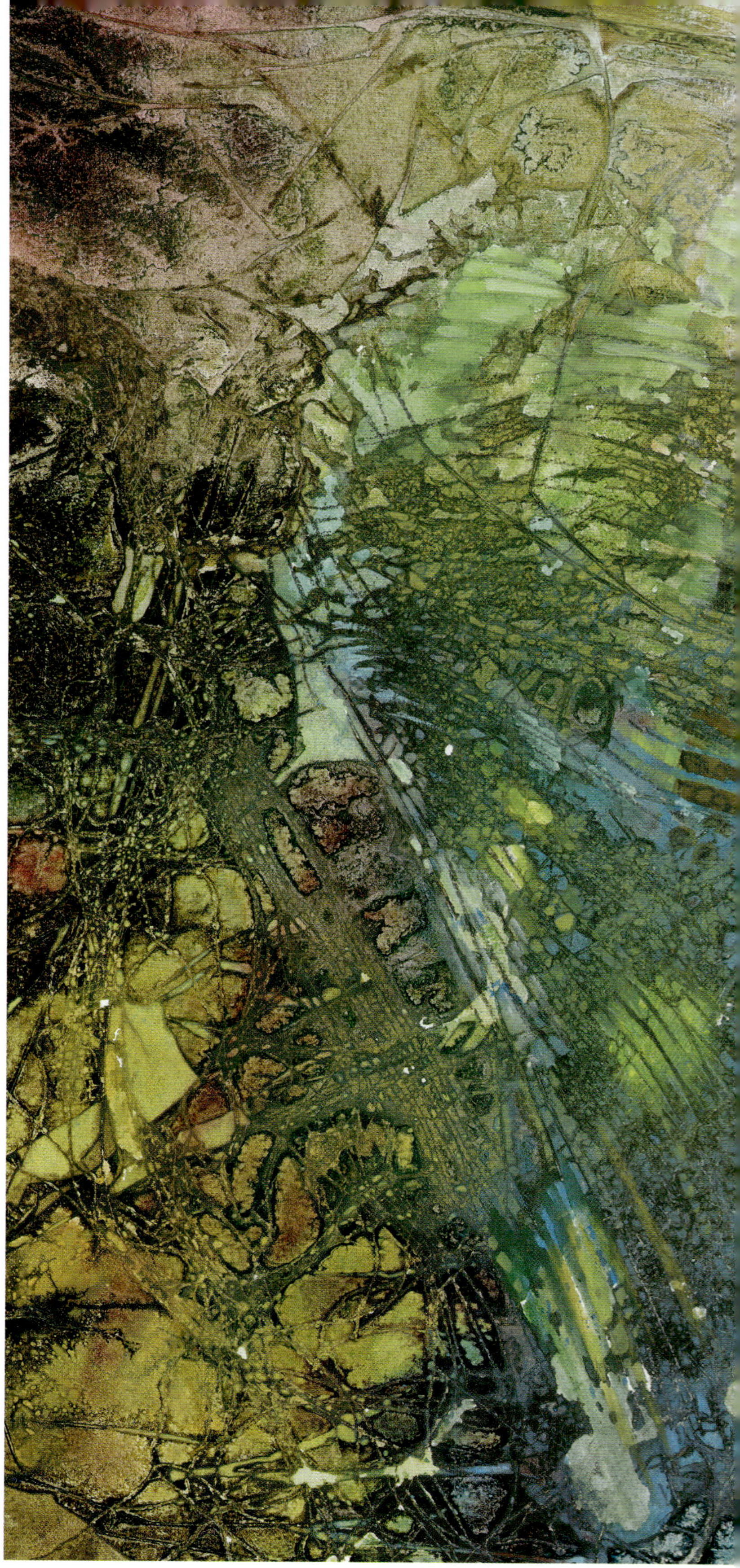

▷ Jungle Bird

On a trip to a tropical jungle, I saw dazzling birds called fairy
terns flitting through the interlocking fronds of the palm trees.
Their wings blurred into white shadows as they flew by. I
decided to capture this magical moment by collecting some
of the woven plant material that had already peeled away from
the trunk of a palm tree. This was used to print a rich woven
texture in jungle shades of green. I pulled the pale bird out of
this abstract beginning using white gouache. The diagonal
patterns made by the plant materials helped create a feeling
of movement. The painting has a strong presence that really
takes me back to that honeymoon rainforest. I believe this is
because I used part of that very jungle to create the painting.

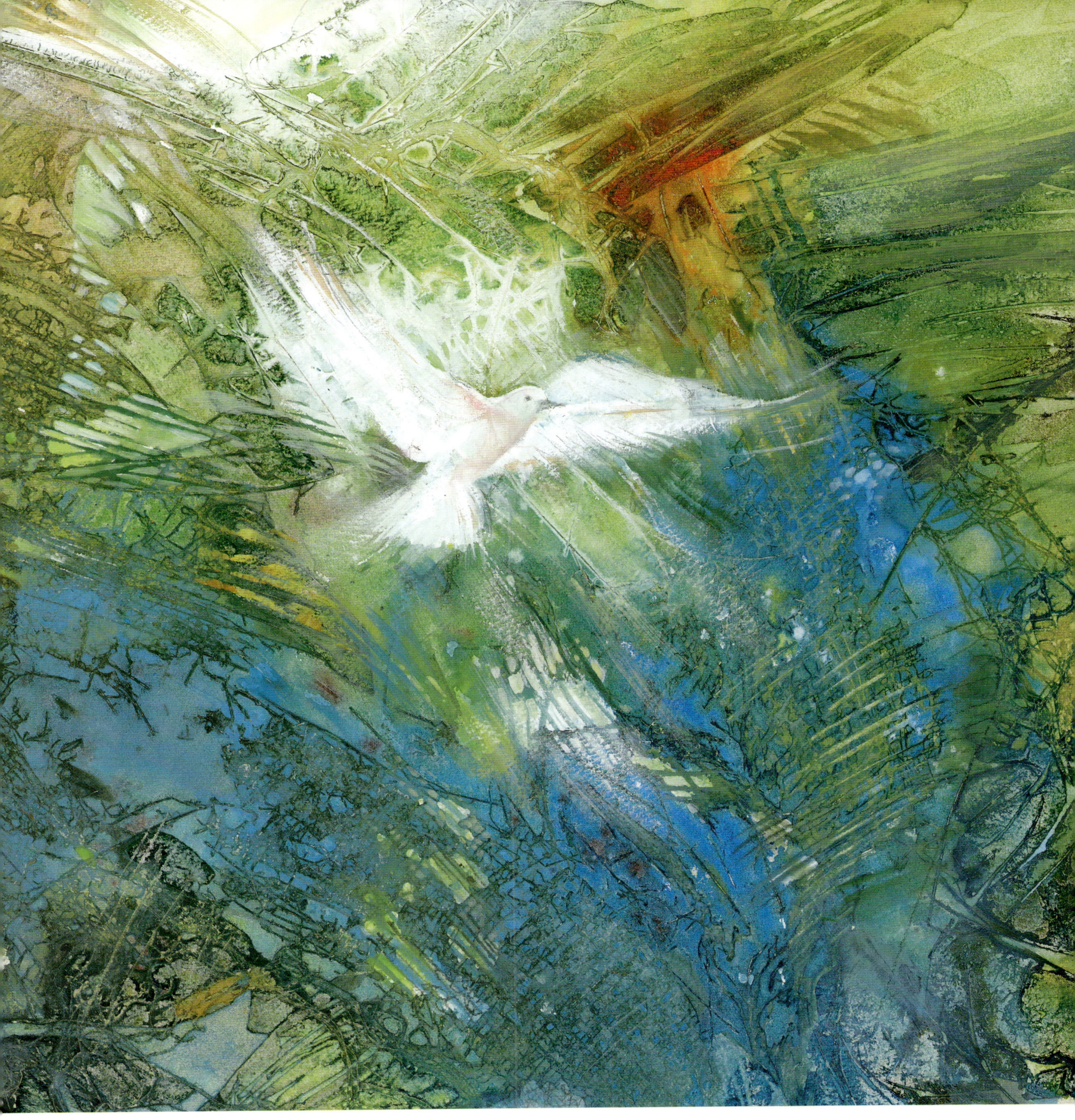

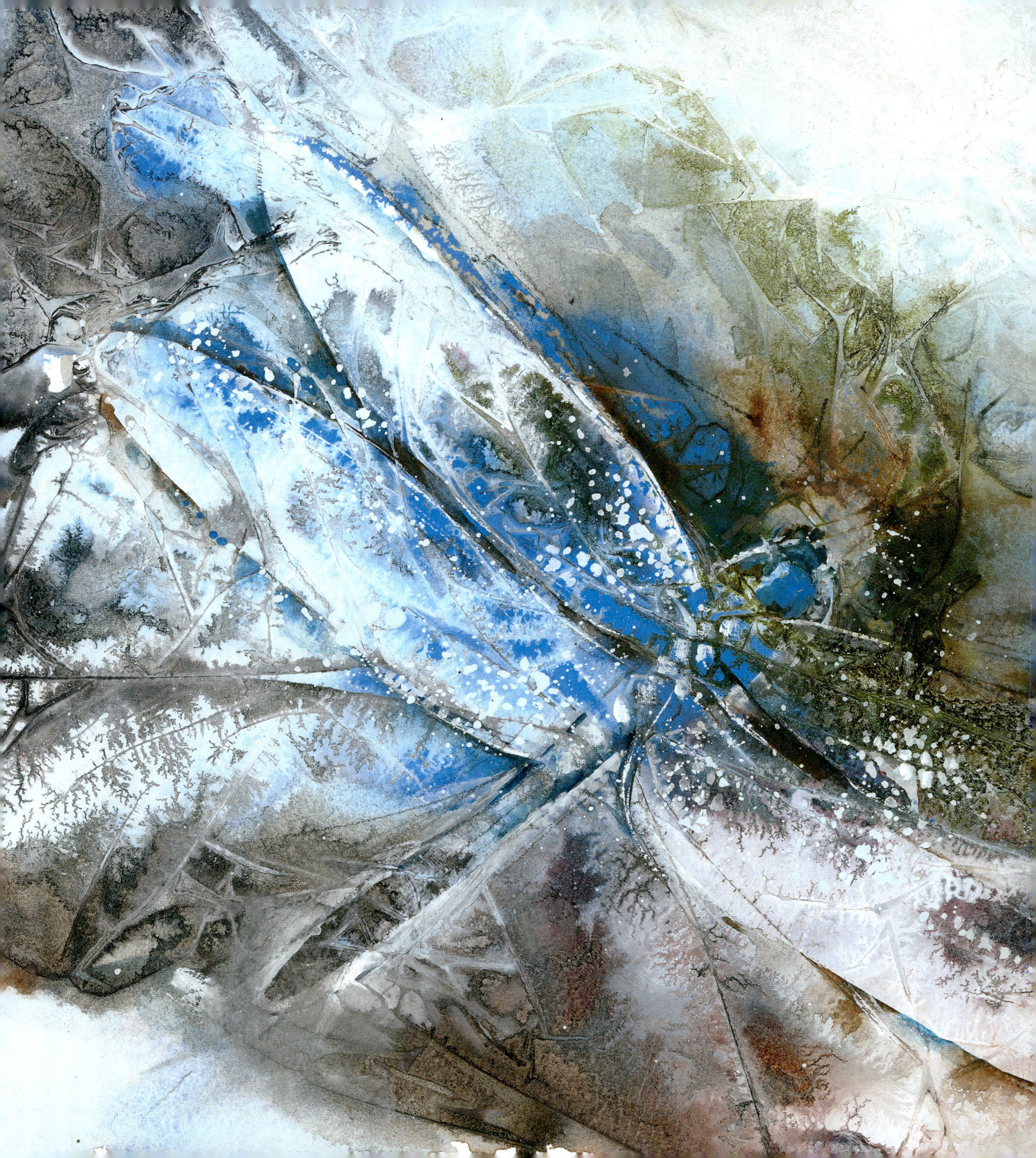

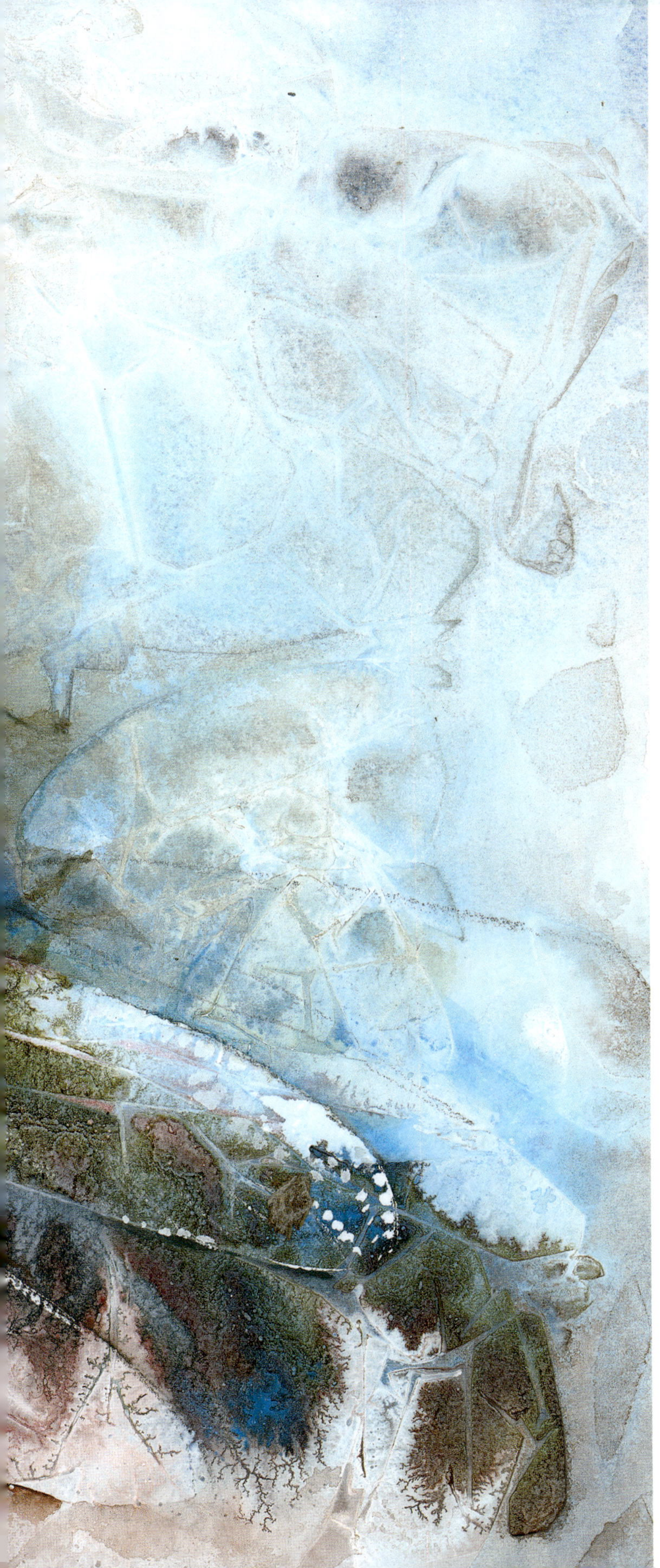

Moving forwards

We have reached the last pages of this book, but it is not the end of the watercolour workshop. Take the information you have gained from the different projects, ideas and interpretations and now revisit the earlier pages and start all over again! Enjoy the techniques but remember that these are only part of the story. See how you can reinterpret the paintings and exercises that you have already done in a slightly or radically different way. You may look at them with a fresh perspective after reading the later sections.

I had always thought of painting as being a journey to reach an elusive creative utopia where everything falls into place. I have recently realized that the important part is to paint in a mindful way, concentrating on the pleasures of activity and discovery rather than the end product. The important bit is the process of doing it and casting aside negative thoughts or self-doubt. The learning process includes the discovery of new ideas but also involves discarding some of them or even revisiting old ones. Try to be motivated by the intrinsic pleasure of being creative rather than your external reasons for painting, whatever form they may take. If you paint to feed your soul the chances are that the other stuff will follow. In this book I have tried to act as facilitator as well as teacher because when you put the book aside all the decisions and judgements will be yours alone to make. Just follow your instincts and be true to yourself. Now, over to you!

◁ *Dragonfly By*

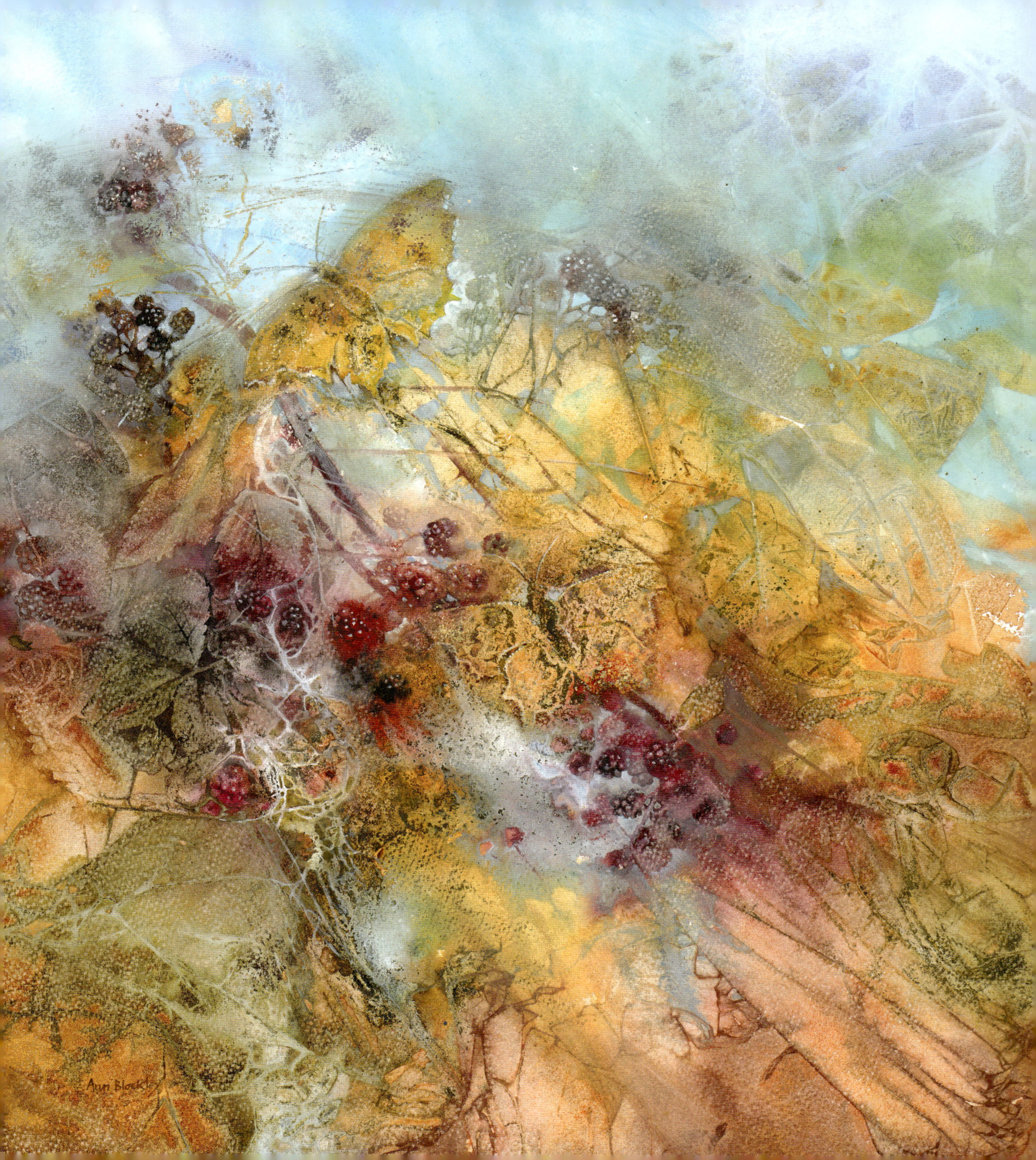
Ann Blockley

Finding Me

I thought I was the butterfly
fluttering against the pane
to seek an opening through
and hide deckle-edged wings
among spotted ragged leaves
in a tangled land of bramble.

I thought I was the bee
in a shape-shifting swarm,
searching for the next place
where I would feel at home
and fill it with the golden hum
of sweetness and activity.

I thought I was the tree
with bare and broken bough
but where the wind tore
parts of me away I saw
tiny buds of hopeful leaves
and a different story grow.

I thought I was a metaphor,
that I could metamorphose
into something ... more,
and with morse code marks
create a kind of allegory.
But I turned fresh leaves
and realised after all
that I was simply – me.

Ann Blockley 2017

Index